Resting on the Future

Resting on the Future

Catholic Theology for an Unfinished Universe

John F. Haught

Bloomsbury Academic
An imprint of Bloomsbury Publishing Plc

B L O O M S B U R Y
LONDON • OXFORD • NEW YORK • NEW DELHI • SYDNEY

2015

Bloomsbury Academic

An imprint of Bloomsbury Publishing Inc

1385 Broadway	50 Bedford Square
New York	London
NY 10018	WC1B 3DP
USA	UK

www.bloomsbury.com

BLOOMSBURY and the Diana logo are trademarks of Bloomsbury Publishing Plc

First published 2015
Reprinted by Bloomsbury Academic 2015, 2016

Library of Congress Cataloging-in-Publication Data
Haught, John F.
Resting on the future: Catholic theology for an unfinished universe/John F. Haught. – 1st [edition].
pages cm
Includes bibliographical references and index.
ISBN 978-1-5013-0622-8 (hardback: alk. paper) – ISBN 978-1-5013-0621-1 (pbk.: alk. paper) 1. Religion and science. 2. Cosmology. 3. Catholic Church–Doctrines. I. Title.
BL240.3.H385 2015
261.5'5–dc23
2015000841

ISBN: HB: 978-1-5013-0622-8
PB: 978-1-5013-0621-1
ePub: 978-1-5013-0623-5
ePDF: 978-1-5013-0624-2

Typeset by Deanta Global Publishing Services, Chennai, India
Printed and bound in the United States of America

To Evelyn

Contents

Preface and Acknowledgments

The theological vision expressed here has been developing for many years, and it is far from finished. I offer it now only with the expectation that it will require further scrutiny and revision in the future, a process that I welcome. The present book considers in a fresh way, this time in the context of Roman Catholic theological inquiry, issues in science and theology that I have been working on for many years. Several chapters adapt and modify ideas presented in more rudimentary form earlier, and so I wish to acknowledge the following: Chapters 1 and 2 borrow from my chapter "Teilhard de Chardin: Theology for an Unfinished Universe," in Ilia Delio (ed.), *From Teilhard to Omega: Co-creating an Unfinished Universe* (Maryknoll, NY: Orbis Books, 2014), 7–23. Chapter 4 uses material from my chapter "To Women and Men of Science: Science, Spirituality and Vatican II," in Anthony J. Ciorra and Michael W. Higgins, (eds), *Vatican II: A Universal Call to Holiness* (New York: Paulist Press, 2012), 150–65. Chapter 5 modifies and expands on a lecture I delivered to the American Teilhard Association, "Darwin, Teilhard, and the Drama of Life." And Chapter 13 draws in part on my essay "Transhumanism and the Anticipatory Universe," in John Haughey and Ilia Delio (eds), *Humanity on the Threshold: Religious Perspectives on Transhumanism* (Washington, DC: The Council for Research in Values and Philosophy, 2014).

I want to thank Haaris Naqvi and the editorial staff at Bloomsbury Press for the cordial and careful way in which they have received and shepherded this work toward publication. And in a special way I want to express my gratitude to Ursula King and Charles O'Connor, III for their helpful comments and advice.

Introduction

Science has now demonstrated beyond all doubt that our universe is unfinished. It is still coming into being. Discoveries in geology, biology, cosmology, and other fields of science have shown that nature is on a journey far from over. Knowledge that the world is a work in progress, I believe, provides a fertile new framework for thinking about the meaning of Catholic faith and life. If we take seriously the fact that the universe is a drama still unfolding, we may think new thoughts about God and other perennial themes of theology, and we may do so without losing any of the tradition's great treasures. Above all, hope will gain an expansive new horizon, one that can renew our spiritual lives and widen our sense of the coming kingdom of God.

News that the universe is dramatic, however, has yet to penetrate deeply into Catholic sensibilities. Our devotional life still presupposes an essentially static cosmos. The Church continues to nurture nostalgia for a lost original perfection and longs for union with an eternal present untouched by time and history. Its ageless inclination to restore an idyllic past or take flight into eternity has bridled the spirit of Abrahamic adventure and dampened the sense of a new future for the whole of creation. Meanwhile, intellectual culture at large remains stuck in a stagnant materialist pessimism that also suppresses our native need for a future in which to hope.

This book asks what Catholic faith might mean if we take fully into account the fact that our universe is still on the move. What would it imply theologically if we looked forward to the future transformation of the whole universe instead of trying to restore Eden, or yearning for a Platonic realm of perfection hovering eternally above the flow of time? What if Catholic theologians and teachers began to take more seriously the evolutionary understanding of life and the ongoing pilgrimage of the whole natural world? What if we realized that the cosmos, the earth, and humanity, rather than having wandered away from an original plenitude, are now and always invited toward the horizon of fuller being up ahead?

The new scientific setting is one in which our universe must be pictured as still coming to birth. We live in the age of evolutionary biology and Big Bang cosmology. These fields of research, along with many others, have demonstrated that cosmic and biological origins were relatively rudimentary and that enormous spans of time were required to bring about the wondrous outcomes we call life, consciousness, and culture. The universe has always had a future and has always had to wait. We know this better than ever now that the new sciences have lengthened our sense of cosmic time beyond all previous imagining. Until recently, we had no idea of the almost fourteen billion years during which the universe has labored to reach its present state of being. Creation, we must now acknowledge, has not been instantaneous, and it has a future stretching toward we know not where.

This new sense of a cosmic journey, I believe, is much more momentous spiritually than most Catholics seem to have noticed. Since Christianity is a forward-looking faith and feeds off the future, Catholics cannot be content with seductive dreams of an initially perfect creation or with contemplation of an eternal now. In our age, it is more appropriate instead to picture the fulfillment and healing we look for, in a more biblical way, as a state that has never yet been fully actualized but that we hope will come into being in the future by God's grace and creaturely cooperation. The Bible's sense of time and history arouses hope for an unprecedented future even as it deflects nostalgia for a paradisal past or a state of perfection cut off from the world of becoming. The ancient narratives of a promising God, one who always opens up a new future whenever dead ends appear, encourage us now to move beyond preoccupation with a lost Eden and an eternal present. Abrahamic faith directs us outward and forward into an open future. It instructs us to look for fulfillment up ahead, in the direction of new creation and a fulfillment of the cosmic process yet to appear. It encourages us to wait for the advent of a God who draws the world toward new being from out of the future.

Evolution and the cosmic process, I argue in these pages, sit comfortably in a religious setting grounded in wayfaring hope. Instead of diminishing our sense of divine transcendence, science now allows us to experience and cherish the all-surpassing love and power of God in a vitalizing new way. A science-conscious theology, therefore, can remain entirely continuous with the long history of our religious searching even as it widens the quest for fulfillment. Evolution and cosmology do not require the termination but the transformation of our search for meaning and redemption.

Without intending to do so, scientists over the last two centuries have raised the curtain to a new future for the universe and, along with it, spiritual space for a fresh throb of hope. Theologians may still draw upon Catholic tradition's affirmation of divine transcendence, incarnation, and sacramental presence. However, science now gives these classic themes an unprecedented dramatic twist that tilts all of creation—and spiritual seeking—in the direction of a new future. Science's fresh picture of nature-as-narrative invites theology to transplant the central biblical motif of divine promise onto a cosmological terrain that can give new breadth, nourishment, and vitality to our spiritual and ethical lives. It makes room for a theology that frames our unfinished universe with Abrahamic hope. So, when I refer in these pages to an "unfinished universe," I am pointing to a world that may have future outcomes unimaginable at the present. In any case, if there were ever an occasion for the renewal of hope, it lies in our new sense of a still-emerging cosmos.

This book, however, is not an invitation to lessen our sense of indebtedness to the great traditions of Catholic thought and spirituality, but instead to think new thoughts about them in the context of our current scientific awareness of a universe that is clearly far from being completed. The following chapters apply and extend ideas of scientists, philosophers, and theologians who have awakened in me an appreciation of our newly enlarged cosmic horizons and who have nourished my own intellectual and spiritual life. However, I take liberties with their ideas and carry them in directions their authors may not always have intended. Several such companions in this exploration are notable twentieth-century Catholic thinkers, above all, Pierre Teilhard de Chardin and to a lesser extent Bernard Lonergan and Karl Rahner. What follows, however, is not a slavish exposition of their thought but my own synthesis based on four decades of reflecting with them (and many others too) on the relationship between theology and the natural sciences. Accordingly, I do not rely on direct quotations from their writings, except occasionally from Teilhard. The fact that Teilhard, Lonergan, and Rahner were all Jesuit priests, and the author a Catholic layperson who has taught for many years at Georgetown, a Jesuit university, is purely coincidental. It is not a coincidence, however, that I share with these adventurous thinkers an awareness of the need for Catholic thought to take evolutionary science and cosmology more seriously than ever.

What follows is not a systematic theology, a project that would hardly accord with the unfinished and, hence, unsystematic state of our universe. Rather, the objective is simply to acclimatize Catholic theological and spiritual concern to the new environment of a dramatic cosmos. I attempt, with the inspiration of the aforementioned Catholic thinkers and many others, a change of tone that preserves the substance of Catholic faith, but that does so with a constant awareness of the new cosmological setting of all educated thought today. My purpose, then, is not to develop separate new tracts on Christology, the Trinity, the Church, sacraments, grace, sin, creation, redemption, and eschatology. Instead, I set forth a series of transitions toward renewal in Catholic thought that have already had uncertain beginnings but which I now want to carry further. These are transitions *from* a prescientific *to* a more futurist—or anticipatory—understanding of Catholic thought than was conceivable throughout most of our theological history. I do not intend to abandon the sacramental or analogical character of Catholic thought but to rethink it all in terms of the biblical theme of promise, and to do so in conjunction with our new scientific sense of an unfinished universe whose being and meaning are not yet settled. I propose to situate Catholic tradition in a context that deliberately combines the Bible's openness to the future with contemporary science's discovery of deep time. Just as post-Einsteinian physics does not discard Newtonian science as irrelevant but instead transposes it into a richer composition of time, space, and gravity, my objective here is not to forsake, but to reflect consistently on, the meaning of Catholic Christianity in the context of a universe still emerging. Exactly what this transformation implies for each area of theological specialization has yet to be worked out. Here I can only point in a general way to what seems to me to be the need for a seismic shift in cosmological and metaphysical assumptions without which Catholic thought is likely to become increasingly irrelevant to scientifically schooled inquirers.

A word about science and theology

This book contributes specifically to Catholic theology, but in a more general way, it is also part of ongoing conversations in science and theology. Readers may be interested, therefore, in how I came to be involved in this field of interest and how I approach questions related to it. I recall now that it all began in my early twenties when I first started reading Teilhard. Ever since then, his vast writings, in spite of their incompleteness, have kindled my interest in relating science to Catholic faith. I am not unaware of contemporary objections to some aspects of Teilhard's thought, but what I cannot ignore is his longing to familiarize his Church with the fact of an unfinished universe. What I most appreciate is Teilhard's making new space for hope in our age of science. This aspect of his thought is more important than ever at a time when most Catholics still lack a sense of the cosmos and when many scientifically educated thinkers have settled for a debilitating pessimism regarding the world's and humanity's destiny.

After studies at The Catholic University of America, I began my teaching career in 1969 in the Department of Theology at Georgetown University. As early as 1971, I felt the need to develop a course on science and religion for undergraduates, and I taught it almost every year until my recent retirement. I have always loved science, even though as an undergraduate I majored in philosophy and did my graduate work in systematic theology. While I was teaching science and religion at Georgetown and writing books on the topic, I had to read and study a large amount of scientific literature, especially in the areas of cosmology and biology. Although I had cut my undergraduate philosophical teeth on Thomistic metaphysics, I came to the conclusion early on that in spite of its brilliance, Thomism cannot adequately contextualize the discoveries of evolutionary biology, cosmology, and astrophysics.

As the intellectual backbone of my teaching, therefore, I began to rely more heavily on science-friendly twentieth-century religious thinkers such as Alfred North Whitehead, Michael Polanyi, Bernard Lonergan, and Hans Jonas. My books *Science and Religion: From Conflict to Conversation* (1995) and, more recently, *Science and Faith: A New Introduction* (2012) reflect an approach developed in dialogue and sometimes disagreement with these authors over many years in the classroom. During the 1990s, I became especially interested in issues related to evolution, not only because of the growing importance of Darwin in the intellectual world but also because of my frustration that creationists and prominent scientists alike were needlessly declaring that evolutionary biology is irreconcilable with Christian faith and theology. The assumed hostility between evolution and theology eventually led me to write *God After Darwin, Deeper than Darwin,* and *Making Sense of Evolution.*[1] These and other works have led to my lecturing on theology and evolution both nationally and internationally. One of my more interesting experiences in dealing with evolution and faith was that of being a witness for the plaintiffs at the famous Harrisburg PA trial that led to a ruling in 2005 against the teaching of Intelligent Design (ID) in public schools. This testimony must have had something to do with my being honored as a "Friend of Darwin" by the National Center for Science Education, an award I was pleased to accept as a token of public recognition of the compatibility of Catholic theology with evolutionary biology.

My underlying concern in teaching, speaking, and writing during the last four decades has been that of making room in the age of science for faith, and of fortifying faith's sincerity by exposing it continually to science. In the United States, unfortunately, a major obstacle to their reconciliation is the persistence of biblical literalism. As far as reading the Bible is concerned, literalism can mean different things in different periods of history, but in the age of science, it has typically come to mean the expectation that our holy books, to prove that they are truly "inspired," should yield a quality grade of *scientific* information. This assumption, ironically, ties contemporary New Atheists closely to their creationist opponents. Sam Harris, for example, insists that "the same evidentiary demands" that science follows must also be used to measure the truth-status of religious writings and creeds. Consequently, he wonders why Christians are not as puzzled as he that the Bible, "a book written by an omniscient being," would fail to be "the richest source of mathematical insight humanity has ever known," or why the Bible has nothing to say "about electricity, or about DNA, or about the actual age and size of the universe."[2] Harris is not alone. Daniel Dennett, Christopher Hitchens, and Richard Dawkins also apply the same literalist standard to their own reading of the Scriptures. Since the Bible is supposed to be "inspired," they demand that it be scientifically accurate if enlightened readers are to take it seriously.[3]

Approaching ancient texts with modern scientific expectations, of course, is an anachronism that ends up making the Bible and the faith traditions based on it appear altogether incompatible with modern science. Theology, as I understand it, however, reads the Scriptures in search of levels of meaning and truth that scientific method is not wired to receive. Literalism is a way of avoiding a serious encounter with classic religious texts. It protects the religious fundamentalist from hearing the word of God while giving the New Atheist a pretext for mocking ancient religious literature for its scientific naïveté.

I am assuming in the following chapters that theology and science are distinct but related ways of experiencing, understanding, and knowing. Both theology and science are rooted, each in its own way, in the human desire to understand and know, but they seek understanding and truth from within formally distinct *horizons* of inquiry. These horizons do not overlap, compete, or conflict with each other, and what constitutes data, evidence, and confirmation in one is not the same as in the other. Here, of course, I am using the idea of horizon metaphorically. Visually, a horizon is the field of all the things that can be seen from a specific vantage point. Following Bernard Lonergan, what I mean by a "horizon of inquiry" is the whole field of data, insights, and propositions that can be seen, understood, and known from a determinate point of view.[4] The horizon of science is distinct from that of theology, so there is no necessary competition or conflict between them.

Why then do so many prominent scientists and philosophers still claim that science and theology stand in opposition to each other? In keeping with the metaphor just introduced, I would answer that it is usually because of a *horizon-fixation*. In the case of the New Atheists and other scientific skeptics, the impression of conflict stems from the unverifiable belief that the horizon of scientific inquiry is expansive enough to embrace the totality of being. In addition to and alongside of science, however, there are other horizons, such as those of ethics and theology, that do not compete or conflict meaningfully with science. Science, ethics, and theology belong to noncompeting horizons of inquiry. They give the appearance of competition and conflict only when one edges out or devours the others.

This can happen, for example, when a devotee of *scientism*—the belief that science is the only reliable method of arriving at right understanding—declares that ethical values are verifiable scientific "facts," as Sam Harris does in *The Moral Landscape*.[5] It happens even more stunningly when Richard Dawkins claims that the question of God's existence can be settled only from within the horizon of scientific inquiry. In *The God Delusion*, he refers to the "God hypothesis" as though it were a scientific idea in competition with evolutionary biology. Since scientific method, in Dawkins's belief system, is the only reliable way to arrive at a true understanding of anything, no other horizon is available to him within which to locate human thoughts about ultimate reality. So it is within the territory proper to science that discourse about "God" has to present and prove itself. Belief in God, Dawkins then concludes, has now been rendered obsolete by modern science, and particularly by Darwinian biology.[6]

It is not a redeemable part of science, however, to decree as Dawkins does that there exists one and only one reliable horizon of inquiry. This declaration is an unwarranted totalistic belief, not the outcome of scientific research. In other words, Dawkins's defense of atheism is not the result of the application of scientific method but of his unverifiable belief that the modern scientific horizon of inquiry leaves room for no others. Dawkins, I must add, has a lot of company.[7] Instances of an identical intellectual imperialism show up these days among scientists and philosophers who consider cosmology encompassing enough to answer questions formerly assigned to theology and metaphysics. The physicist Sean Carroll, for example, writes that "if and when cosmologists develop a successful scientific understanding of the origin of the universe, we will be left with a picture in which there is no place for God to act."[8] I am thinking here also of how the words "nothing" and "nothingness" get tossed around by some metaphysically ambitious physicists today. Fusing the horizon of scientific cosmology with that of creation theology, they exclaim that the universe came from the "nothingness" of a quantum vacuum *rather than* from a beneficent divine creator.[9]

Science, however, by definition, strives to understand physical transformations taking place *within* the natural world—which after all is something and not "nothing." Empirical science itself can make contact neither with the supernatural nor with an abyss of nothingness. Referring to a universe-generating quantum vacuum as "nothing," therefore, has absolutely nothing to do with "nothing" as the term is used in the theological doctrine of divine creation of the world *ex nihilo*.

Such confusion can be avoided only by tolerating a plurality of explanatory levels and distinct horizons of inquiry. Any truly open conversation of theology with science requires that the various sides acknowledge the differences between scientific method on the one hand and theology—and other ideological interests—on the other. This means that the conflation of science with materialist philosophy by the New Atheists and countless other scientific skeptics is no less a defilement of intellectual integrity than the creationist's treating biblical creation stories as though they are trafficking in scientific information. Such corruption is an obstacle both to the prospering of science and to a fair and honest interpretation of religious literature.

Theology's horizon of inquiry, meanwhile, corresponds to questions that are markedly distinct from those of science. Yet, in struggling to answer its own proper questions, theology may lend support to the tacit assumptions every good scientist has to embrace in order to do science at all. For example, the scientist has to trust that the universe is intelligible, for otherwise science cannot get off the ground. Theology, for its part, seeks to justify this trust by pursuing the question: Why is the universe intelligible? Any good scientist has to assume also that truth is worth seeking. Theology seeks to support this assumption by relentlessly asking why truth is worth seeking. The scientist, moreover, must believe that honesty is essential to being a good researcher. Theology asks: What makes the commitment to honesty (and other virtues essential to being a good scientist) unconditionally right?

In addressing these "limit-questions," theology is not looking for the kind of information that falls within the horizon explored by science, so there can be no meaningful competition or conflict.[10] And yet, by working from within its own horizon, theology may be able to discover a vision of reality that justifies—rather than conflicting with—the whole scientific enterprise. In view of the unfinished state of the cosmic process, however, I believe that Catholic theology must now adopt—more deliberately than ever before—an *anticipatory* metaphysical vision wherein the search for meaning and truth coincides with hopeful concern for the future and final destiny of an entire universe.

Nature: From Sacrament to Promise

"Nothing is so beautiful as spring," exclaims Gerard Manley Hopkins in the opening line of one of his loveliest sonnets. The Jesuit poet (1844–89) rejoices at "weeds in wheels," thrush's eggs like "little low heavens," "birds' echoes that rinse and ring the ears," and pear tree leaves and blooms that brush "the descending blue."

Hopkins asks: "What is all this juice and all this joy?" The vernal excess, he answers, is "a strain of the earth's sweet being in the beginning/in Eden Garden." Sin has clouded over the world's original innocence, but the flush of springtime brings sacramental reminders of paradise and, as the poet observes elsewhere, the "dearest freshness deep down things." Springtime glory recaptures imperfectly and fleetingly the creation that had been made perfect by God in the beginning. We should hold fast, then, to seasonal reminders of the primordial plenitude: "Have, get, before it cloy . . . and sour with sinning."[1]

Like generations of other Catholics, Hopkins exhibits here a spiritual sensibility nourished more by sacramental piety than prophetic expectation, more by nature's transparency to eternity than its promise of something yet to come. His fellow Jesuit, Pierre Teilhard de Chardin (1881–1955), on the other hand, regards the passing glories of nature in a different light. The flowering of life need not turn us nostalgically back to "the earth's sweet being in the beginning." Evolutionary science, after all, rules out any epoch of paradise in early terrestrial history. The earth, and with it the entire universe, is still coming into bloom. Nature has yet to be fully actualized. Indeed, the true being of the universe lies up ahead, in the future. Teilhard would agree with Hopkins that earth is "bleared, smeared with toil and wears man's smudge" and that the juice has indeed soured. To the Christian evolutionist, however, God's creation still needs time to ripen.

For Teilhard, autumn rather than spring was the happiest time of the year. Fall opened his soul to the limitless space of the up-ahead and the not-yet, freeing him from the seductive charms of warmer seasons. The divergent spiritual sensitivities of Hopkins and Teilhard, both Jesuit priests, reflect a tension that persists in the contemporary Catholic spiritual world. Bent toward melancholy by birth, both visionaries scanned the natural world for hints of a perfection that would lift up their hearts, but the satisfaction they found there came to expression in different ways. Hopkins found spiritual comfort in seasonal reminders of a primordial innocence. He felt in the depths of nature an inexhaustible freshness now largely lost but ready to break out on occasion to remind us of the fullness of God's creation "in the beginning." Teilhard, more thoroughly schooled in the natural sciences as they have taken shape since Darwin, looked toward the future of a still-unfinished universe. He found an opening for hope in his realization that "creation has never stopped," that it is "one huge continual gesture, drawn out over the totality of time." Creation, he noticed, "is still going on; and incessantly even if imperceptibly, the world is constantly emerging a little farther above nothingness."[2] It is toward the world's future pilgrimage into the infinite that the soul may now strain to find what it longs for.

Hopkins, though conversant with the science of his day, did not live long enough to ponder the religious meaning of the new story of nature that was emerging in the geology and biology of the nineteenth century. Teilhard's scientific training, by contrast, taught him that nature could never literally have played host to Eden. It could not have come into full flower in an opening instant of divine creativity to be lost later because of sin. Teilhard agreed that the universe needs redemption, and he shared Hopkins's sense of the brokenness of our world. However, it matters to Christian life, he thought, that creation was not completed at once long ago and that the world is still aborning. It makes a difference theologically that something significant is now taking shape up ahead, in the cosmic future.[3] Hopkins's spirituality, informed as it was by Ignatian principles, was by no means otherworldly, and it continues to have ecological significance.[4] My point, however, is that even the most spiritually healing instances of traditional Catholic sacramentalism cannot capture the full relevance to faith and theology of the new sense of a universe open to *more being* in the future.

Teilhard, as it happens, was one of the first scientists during the last century to realize that the cosmos is a story and not a state, that it has never fully implemented an eternal design, and that the drama of its creation still goes on. Early in the twenty-first century, however, Catholic theology has so far failed to reflect much on what it means that we live in a still-becoming universe. With rare exceptions, Catholic thinkers have yet to draw out the devotional and moral implications of evolutionary biology and Big Bang cosmology. Ecclesiastical institutions and religious educators still cling, at least implicitly, to ancient and medieval images of a fixed universe, an original human innocence, a historical Fall, and a God who exists "above" the natural world.[5]

Most Catholic theologians, it is true, allow vaguely for biological evolution and Big Bang cosmology, but our theology so far indicates only a soft awareness of natural history as science sees it. For that matter, the wider intellectual world, including the majority of scientists and philosophers, has also failed to explore in depth what the new evolutionary sciences imply about life, humankind, and the universe, let alone about God. Staled by a purely physicalist understanding of life, the reigning cult of scientific naturalism—the belief that the totality of being is reducible to what scientific method can find out—has closed off contemporary intellectual life to the most important implications of science. Secular philosophers have yet to make much of the fact that the world is new every day, that the cosmos may still be only at the dawn of its creation, and that a vast and indeterminate future of new being lies open before it.

As far as Catholic theology is concerned, our understanding of the meaning of God, human nature, Jesus, sin, redemption, and morality still sags under the weight of prescientific and early modern cosmological baggage. Scientific discovery has demonstrated on multiple fronts that the cosmic process is far from being over and done with, but earthlings, including most Catholics, have yet to explore carefully what an unfinished universe really implies for our spiritual and ethical lives. The universe meanwhile is still coming into being. This, Teilhard insisted, "is the basic truth which must be grasped at the outset and assimilated so thoroughly that it becomes part of the very habit and nature of our thought."[6] Science's great new discovery of a still-emerging universe, however, is far from having become habitual to Catholic thought and spirituality. During his lifetime Teilhard often lamented the prevalent theological and ecclesiastical indifference to scientific discovery. Were he with us today, he would surely deplore our persistent unresponsiveness to the new understanding of the universe as a work in progress.

It is time, I think, for Catholic theology to carry forward with renewed enthusiasm Teilhard's pioneering work of revision. Given the Church's increasing irrelevance to the lives and aspirations of countless thoughtful people, the task is more pressing than ever. Catholicism is facing serious challenges. Among these are the flourishing of secularism in Western cultures and the uncritical dominance of scientific naturalism in the intellectual world. Within the Church, efforts toward renewal are encountering powerful restorative trends in liturgy and in moral and doctrinal theology that are now seeking to reinstate spiritualities originally tied to prescientific pictures of the natural world. What is needed now, especially in view of developments in science, is not "no God," as several highly visible atheists are shouting, but a "new God," a revolution in our understanding of the divine mystery in the age of science.[7]

Internally as well as outwardly, Catholicism is in crisis. Pope Francis might make a difference, but an increasing number of honest seekers now want nothing to do with the Church. Weary of its condescending treatment of women, its sexual naïveté, clericalism, financial corruption, and cover-ups of priest predators, many are looking elsewhere for a religious home—that is, if they have not given up the spiritual search altogether. Disillusioned Catholics lament the lethargy of a Church still weighed down by a deadening traditionalism and doctrinal immobility. They are appalled by their Church's unwillingness to practice internally the justice it preaches externally. Above all, they are weary of the unacknowledged fear and hopelessness implied in its reluctance to look at new developments in human thought, especially in the sciences.

And yet we stick with the Church. It carries the Gospel, the sacraments, and liturgical splendor. It has the resources for its own renewal. Countless of its members have devoted their lives to good works, often heroically. Its biblical and traditional writings still offer reasons for faith and hope. The Church hosts local eucharistic communities with whom to worship. It still proclaims the good news of the coming kingdom of God. Its call to love one another gives meaning and joy to our lives.

Still, things have to change—and radically so—since the roots of our ecclesial dysfunction run deep. At bottom, I am convinced, the problem is both cosmological and metaphysical. The Church still harbors a worldview that lacks sufficient hope for the world's future, and it clings to a sense of being that has yet to face the fact of the world's becoming. For many educated people, the Church's preaching and teaching no longer ring true. Its teachers and theologians have failed to stay in touch with science and other developments in the world of thought. We Catholics have become too comfortable with a spirituality out of step with evolutionary biology and contemporary cosmology, not to mention the social sciences. We feel only faintly the massive cosmic current carrying life along. To enlarge our faith and widen our hope today, we need to link our spiritual lives more closely than ever to the unfinished universe now stretching out ahead of us. Our expectation of the kingdom of God needs to join up with hope for the universe.

Human existence, science tells us, is tied to a fourteen-billion-year-old Big Bang cosmos still struggling to be born. A faith that fails to acknowledge this cosmic passage seems too unadventurous, both intellectually and spiritually, to attract the dedicated following of educated people. And our sense of God is too small. What we need, as Teilhard wrote in 1919, is a God "as *vast* and mysterious as the Cosmos." Any God who seems smaller than the world revealed by science is unworthy of our worship.[8] Early Christian apocalyptic writings, along with the Pauline letters to the Romans, Colossians, and Ephesians, sought to enlarge the scope of faith by extending the redemptive influence of Christ over the entire cosmos. Today, this means that Catholic theology and teaching need to be clothed in the raiment of deep time, cosmic immensity, and a sense of nature's emerging complexity.

Unfortunately, prescientific cosmic sensibilities still imprison our souls. Many scientifically educated people now breathe more deeply within the expansive universe of scientific discovery than they do in church. It is a scandal that Catholic preaching and teaching have failed to address the sense of suffocation that scientifically and religiously adventurous people often feel in ecclesiastical environments. Today the intellectual, spiritual, and ethical lives of countless thoughtful people are sparked more by scientific discovery than religious instruction. Their true spiritual masters are Darwin, Einstein, Hubble, and Hawking. To the pure naturalist, God is not a name that brings joy, peace, and a sense of adventure. Often it evokes instead only a feeling of indifference or, as we witnessed recently in the New Atheism, even hatred. Instead of a free and open space, God-talk too often signifies enclosure. Even though the idea of God is supposed to expand our souls toward infinity, it often evokes feelings of confinement rather than freedom, of attachment to the past rather than openness to the future.

Only seldom do Catholic preachers and teachers proportion their portraits of God to the new cosmic horizons. Yet, until Catholicism arouses a sense of God that infinitely outstrips the universe of contemporary science, it cannot meet the religious needs of enlightened people. Recently, at the margins of contemporary Catholic thought, the wider universe has been coming into view, but the Church at large is paying little attention. It is now time, I argue in the following chapters, to return the cosmos to the center of Catholic thought. My intention is to explore what science could mean for our faith today if we were to take its findings seriously.

In principle, Catholics should never have lost touch with the universe. The Church's sacramentalism has always implied that the good and beautiful things of nature reveal the infinite goodness and beauty of God. Hopkins's poetry is a splendid witness to this sacramental vision. Natural phenomena such as light, air, water, trees, oil, fertility, and seasonal changes have been indispensable symbols opening us to the mystery of God. Why would this not be true all the more of the new picture of an expanding universe so lavishly laid out by contemporary science? Sustained theological reflection on the fact that we live in a still-emerging universe could enlarge our vision of God and the world and still remain consonant with biblical hope. Traditional appreciation of nature's sacramentality, I propose, must now be linked to a cosmos that still has a future.

This book offers an alternative to both scientific secularism and the Church's lingering prescientific cult of immobility. It looks at the scientific picture of an unfolding cosmic drama with a mood of expectation, regarding the fourteen billion years of natural history and the four billion years of life's evolution as pregnant with a promise yet to be revealed. In spite of the contemporary academic preference for cosmic pessimism, the following chapters argue that the most open-minded and morally motivating stance we can take toward our unfinished universe is one of hope. We may still justifiably cherish the Catholic sense that God touches the world, but now we need to realize that this touch is simultaneously an invitation, a summons to look toward new creation. Catholic theology, in other words, needs to supplement its classic sacramentalism with an *anticipatory* vision of the universe.

Catholics traditionally have not worried much about the long-term cosmic future. We have sought vertical attachment to eternity at the expense of concern about what is going on in the universe. A static sacramentalism has existed in tension with the Bible's wayfaring hope, and a cult of the "eternal now" has charmed us away from concern for the future of creation. It still does. Our sacramental spirituality, I suggest, must now meet up again with the spirit of the Bible. Every sacrament needs to be seen as a promise, an opening not so much to what once was, or to what is vertically above, or even to what is deep within, as to what is coming from up ahead.

Catholic spirituality in the age of science, in other words, needs to embrace more emphatically than ever the promissory substance of biblical faith. God is infinite being, infinite goodness, and infinite beauty, but God is also the inexhaustible future calling creation to become new. To the so-called transcendentals of traditional Catholic metaphysics—being, goodness, truth, unity, and beauty—we need to add *futurity*, at least if we sincerely believe we are children of Abraham. Understood in a fully biblical context, a sacrament is not just an epiphany of the eternal now, but also an anticipation of the not-yet. The *parousia* for which we long is not so much a perfect presence as a transforming *adventus*.

Today, as a result of science, we can see that creation is still happening. For all we know, the universe is presently only at the outset of its journey in time and space. Because of science, faith now has a new horizon—the future of creation. In the age of science, a wholesome Christian devotional life can host a sacramental spirituality only if it nurtures simultaneously a sincere concern for the world's future. Since the universe is still on the way, a sacramentalism divorced from expectation blocks out the sense of an open future for all of creation. Attachment to an unworldly timeless absolute, moreover, fosters an unrealistic moral and spiritual perfectionism. An obsolete hierarchical cosmology still shores up the clericalist strains of Catholicism. It nurtures, in addition, an unreasonable demand for presently perfect "design," an obsession that shows up in contemporary Christian distaste for Darwin whose science demonstrates that life is an ongoing story full of flaws and imperfect adaptations. Not only Christian anti-Darwinism but also the New Atheist hostility to faith in God, stems from a tacit demand that creation (along with our religions) should be instantaneously complete. The New Atheists, in other words, are no less perfectionist—and unrealistic—than the scientifically uninformed creationists and ID devotees they love to hate. It is the good luck of contemporary theology, therefore, that science has revealed an unfinished and still unperfected cosmos. It gives us a world picture that requires patience even as it opens up the future for hope. A Catholic theology attentive to science will understand that an unfinished creation cannot now be perfect by definition. The world's imperfections, moreover, are not the consequence only of human sin but emblems of a universe still coming into being.

Consequently, we may now experience the good things of the world not only as analogies of an eternal present but also as installments of a future still to come. In pondering the question of what ails Catholicism today, I have come to suspect that our problems are traceable, in part at least, to an unrealistic sacramental perfectionism that over the course of centuries has supplanted the cultivation of a fully prophetic hope. There has always been something anticipatory in Catholic spirituality, of course, but the biblical straining toward the age to come has too often been translated into a vertical pietism that reaches only toward an eternal present. Biblical hope has surrendered too much and too often to a stationary Parmenidean oneness, a Platonic idealism, and an Aristotelian formalism. The Second Vatican Council seemed at times aware of the Hellenistic metaphysical drag on traditional Christianity, but its encouraging Catholics, especially in *Gaudium et Spes* and *Dei Verbum*, to become more evolutionary in their understanding of the world and more biblical in their spirituality still requires close attention. I hope in this book, therefore, to contribute to the new "analysis and synthesis" that, according to the Council, an evolutionary worldview now requires of Catholic thought.[9]

Theologians in the Catholic tradition have usually reflected on the meaning of God's incarnation by first developing a generic idea of divine transcendence (*de Deo Uno*), usually with the help of ancient and medieval metaphysics. Ignoring the God of Abraham, and bypassing the biblical understanding of God as one who makes and keeps promises, they have cultivated a nonbiblical understanding of ultimate reality as an eternal present or as being-itself. In this conceptual setting, the doctrine of the incarnation refers to a paradoxical metaphysical union of the infinite with the finite instead of the breaking in of a new future for the world.[10] If, however, creation is an unfinished drama, as science has shown it to be, God's incarnate presence must now be understood as a disturbing but also enlivening arrival of the future. Catholics may now declare openly that our main interest is not the survival of the Church but the thriving of creation. Our concern is not just for human life but for the whole of nature and history. What matters most now is the world's future and not the Church's honor.

No doubt the Bible has influenced Catholic ideas of God even when Platonic and Aristotelian influences have been dominant, but it seems undeniable to me that the God of classical Catholic thought is not in full harmony with the responsive God of Israel's hopes. "Being-itself" is not exactly the same as the promising God who raised Jesus from the dead. We still need to ask what the timeless God of Neoplatonism or the *Ipsum Esse Subsistens* of Aquinas has to do with the Yahweh of the prophets or the *Abba* invoked by Jesus. Granted, the idea of an eternal present appeals to our longing for permanence in the face of perishing and responds to faith's need for a truly transcendent God distinct from nature. Yet, all too often classical theology encourages a premature human flight from temporal existence instead of a fresh hope for the future of creation.

The readjustment I have in mind—and one that began to take place at Vatican II—requires not the forsaking but the transforming of traditional Catholic sacramentality and medieval metaphysics in the direction of an anticipatory spiritual vision. It wagers that the universe, life, and human history are leaning toward something momentous up ahead. It wants to avoid the implicitly hopeless conviction that the passage of time is destined to be nullified in the presence of eternity. As I argue in the chapters ahead, Catholic thought needs to adopt a more biblical trust that what goes on in nature and history as well as in our personal lives makes a permanent difference to the inner life and identity of God. The idea of an apathetic absolute unaffected by time and history—an understanding of deity that still lurks, sometimes tacitly, in the background of Catholic theological metaphysics—cannot adequately address the infinite longings of the human heart, heal our anxieties, or motivate us to productive moral action.

In summary, what I propose as a conceptual setting for Catholic theology in the age of science is a deliberate shift from a still implicitly Platonic and medieval metaphysics of participation to a more biblically inspired and scientifically up-to-date metaphysics of anticipation. I offer in these pages a theological reading that finds beneath the narrative face of nature reasons for a transformative religious hope that coalesces with the promissory themes in biblical literature. Finally, while my primary focus is on the need for Catholics to appropriate such a perspective, I hope that non-Catholic readers also will find my arguments applicable to their own reflections as we struggle together to find out what it really means to be Christians in an unfinished universe.

God: From Governor to Goal

How may we think about God in the context of an unfinished universe? The question needs to be asked not with the intention of moving outside of Catholic tradition, but to facilitate the tradition's thriving far into the future. Unfortunately, the relatively few Catholic thinkers who are interpreting Christian faith in a way that takes advantage of science's new story of the universe are seldom taken seriously by the faithful at large, by seminary instructors, or by official teachers and parochial preachers. And, of course, they are almost completely ignored by the secularist academic elite.

The reworking of Catholic thought to fit an unfinished universe had a promising beginning with Teilhard de Chardin, but the innovative Jesuit scientist had too little opportunity to develop his ideas with the systematic rigor his creative insights demand. Even though Teilhard's ideas were circulating during the Second Vatican Council, subsequently his synthetic efforts have had little effect on Catholic life and thought.[1] What Teilhard brings to Catholic theology today as in his own lifetime, however, is a sense of the universe that supports the revival of hope. This may turn out eventually to be his greatest contribution to the history of Christian thought. Hope, as the Protestant theologian Jürgen Moltmann puts it, "has the chance of a meaningful existence only when reality itself is in a state of historic flux and when historic reality has room for open possibilities ahead."[2] Moreover, only hope can provide an appropriate setting for effective love. Love can become real, in other words, only if what we love has a future in spite of all apparent dead ends. So it is a great gift to Christian faith, as Teilhard noticed, that science now provides irrefutable evidence that the whole universe is in flux, and hence open to realizing new possibilities in the future. Cosmology— exploration of the nature of the universe—is not irrelevant to our search for the meaning of faith, hope, and love.

If the word "love" appears only occasionally in the text below, it is not because I consider it less important than the other theological virtues. It is because I think theology must first ask what the world must be like if love is to make any real difference. Before love can be actualized, it needs a world open to yet unrealized possibilities. It is not enough for theology to talk about God and the Gospel mandate to love one another. It must also ask what kind of universe might open up to a future in which love can take on a body. The assumption of an initially finished and perfected universe does not allow for such openness. Instead, it "clips the wings of hope."[3] For if we harbor the impression that everything important has already been accomplished by God in creation before the "Fall," can anything really worthwhile still remain for humans to do "after the Fall"—as more than one modern philosopher has rightly asked?

The impression of a static universe hinders the full release of love because it fails to make sufficient room for hope. The traditional theological assumption of an initially completed creation, often based on a literal interpretation of Genesis and fortified by ancient and medieval metaphysics, not only diminishes the space for hope, but in doing so, also shrinks the field of love's impact. A "fixist" view of the universe limits ethical life to the acquiring of virtuous habits that enhance our moral character and our worthiness to inherit eternal life, but it allows little room for "building the world," a motivation that Vatican II made essential to Catholic moral life.[4] If we assume, along with most classical Christian theology, an initial human Fall from a primordial integrity, then pursuit of the ethical life would perhaps be motivated by a sense of shame at our rebellion against God, by the need to restore through expiation the primordial perfection that had been defiled, or, more nobly, by a commitment to do good simply for the sake of the good. Heroic though it may be, however, the practice of virtue in that case has little to do with contributing cooperatively with God to the creation of something new.

The traditional Catholic understanding of innocence, evil, and redemption has been tied more often than not to an understanding of the world that assumes an initially complete creation.[5] The myth of an integral original creation and of a primal innocence followed by a sense of defilement has deeply influenced our sense of sin, conversion, virtue, and God. Today it still lays out the spiritual and ethical itinerary of countless Catholics. Admittedly, the ancient narratives about the origins of evil assume a view of the universe that allows for exemplary human lives and a kind of spiritual adventure fraught with perils and adorned with momentary triumphs. An understanding of nature as essentially immobile does allow humans to experience personal meaning as they struggle from exile toward paradise, detaching themselves along the way from the lures of a material world. Yet, returning to Eden can no longer be the aspiration of scientifically informed believers. The ideal of an initially fixed and finished universe has subtly channeled our spiritual energies into the nurturing of nostalgia rather than the full liberation of hope. Certainly Hopkins's "Spring" is a moving expression of the universal religious sense that the world at present is not what it is intended to be, and this is why we may still profit spiritually from his lyrics. Indeed, this great poet's literary labors are themselves a miracle of new creation. Nevertheless, the evolutionary sciences have revealed a strain of souring that was part of nature long before the sinning. Can a prescientific theology make sense of this fault before the Fall? Furthermore, if the universe had been essentially complete in the beginning, would not our lives in time consist at best of participating in an enterprise of recovery or restoration of what had formerly been perfect but is now in pieces? Our longing for fuller being, or for the infinite, might then exhaust itself in premature mystical flights *from* the universe rather than in long-suffering hope *for* its ongoing creation and fulfillment.

Not only the sense of an initially completed creation, but also the habit of thinking about God as an "eternal now" fails to provide sufficiently hopeful space for the realization of love. It ignores in effect the primary matrix of Christian faith, namely, the ancient Abrahamic expectation and prophetic thrust into the future. In contrast to classical and medieval forms of Catholic metaphysics, a religious worldview reflective of the Abrahamic turn to the future can make religious space for recent scientific discovery. It can accommodate our new awareness that the whole universe, and not just the people of God, is on a long journey into an indeterminate future. Catholic spirituality, however, remains shackled to a vertical, hierarchical picture of the universe in which nothing much other than decay is going on across the reaches of time. The classical metaphysics of the eternal present is inclined to interpret the beauties of nature as reminders of a lost innocence rather than anticipatory signs of a cosmic future still coming to birth. Once we absorb the scientifically incontestable fact that the earth was not host to Eden in the beginning, however, we may come to realize that the cosmos and, along with it, our personal lives and communities, can still become *more* than they are now.

The universe as portrayed by contemporary science is a work in progress, still undergoing a creative transformation that began around fourteen billion years ago and that winds its way toward we know not where. Each of us is part of an immense cosmic drama, a fact that may give new significance to our lives and moral efforts. Prescientific cosmology and metaphysics cannot support the full liberation of human hope, love, and action. Without a horizon of expectation that links our present efforts to the universe's future and its final destiny, we can easily underestimate the importance of our lives. The new scientific sense of an emerging universe, as I argue throughout this book, can help us connect our hopes meaningfully to the anticipatory outlook of Abraham, the prophets, and Jesus.

A static cosmology, on the other hand, orients our ethical and religious aspirations toward retirement in a timeless spiritual heaven above and beyond the physical universe. A universe that seems to undergo no significant transformation itself can only be "left behind" in the ecstasy of the soul's final release from this "vale of tears." An exclusively otherworldly expectation may be excusable given the impossible political and economic conditions in which so many human beings have lived, but an excessive preoccupation with the "next world," as Vatican II's *Gaudium et Spes* acknowledges, can wither our hopes and divert the ethical passion necessary to build *this* world.[6]

A predominantly otherworldly optimism, moreover, provides no substantive resistance to contemporary scientific naturalism and its dogma that the universe is pointless and doomed in the end to the nothingness of being forgotten forever. A pure supernaturalism, in fact, is intellectually powerless against the current academic cult of cosmic pessimism. By cosmic pessimism I mean the belief that nature has no purpose, that it is the product of blind deterministic causes arising out of a mindless physical past, and that whatever meaning or value the world seems to have is really only a fleeting and illusory human concoction. As long as Catholics think of human destiny as an escape from the messiness of earthly existence, it matters little to them if the physical universe has no meaning other than being a temporary stage for our own moral efforts and achievements. Excessive otherworldliness is a compromise with rather than an opponent of cosmic pessimism.

If the universe is still coming into being, however, none of us is in a secure position at present to declare, as cosmic pessimists do, that the universe makes no sense in the long run. After all, geology, evolutionary biology, and cosmology now situate the earth, life, and human existence within the framework of an immense cosmic drama that is still going on and that may turn out to have a kind of meaning or purpose that presently remains out of sight. Natural history includes reversals, calamities, and long periods in which not much happens, and in which what happens often seems to make no sense. Yet, temporary shadows and even whole epochs of darkness are completely consistent with a dramatic understanding of the universe. Since the cosmic performance may still be far from its final act, there is room left for the meaning of things to emerge gradually and in a manner that will remain obscure to human understanding at any present moment. Even if one is temperamentally skeptical about such a possibility, it is not unreasonable to be open to it in principle, especially since not all the evidence is in yet. And even if the laws of physics predict a final cosmic collapse, this is not enough, as I argue later on, to prove that the cosmos is pointless. For all we know, the cosmic drama may be the carrier of meanings that can be registered only in the compassionate life of God and that now remain inaccessible to scientific investigation and prediction.

It is undeniable by any standard of measurement that the cosmic drama so far has drifted over the course of deep time from simplicity toward relatively more physical complexity. And corresponding to this general directionality, the universe has trended from less toward more consciousness.[7] Once we realize that the universe *can* become more, therefore, we have no compelling reason to take the road that leads to cosmic pessimism. Nor is it required that Catholics and other Christians today have exactly the same thoughts about the Creator, sin, virtue, the meaning of life, or human destiny as before. If the world is still emerging, we need no longer think of Christ and his mission in as narrow a way, cosmically speaking, as previous ages have. As far as the life of the Church is concerned, its worship, sacraments, and spirituality may need to undergo a cosmological transfiguration that our religious ancestors could never have envisaged on the basis of a static and hierarchical understanding of the natural world. Above all, our sense of God and the effectiveness of the Holy Spirit may now be framed in a more biblical way than ever by an awareness that creation is still going on. God, as Teilhard rightly sensed, is not so much the governor as the goal of an ongoing cosmic process. Put otherwise, God creates and governs the world not so much by dictatorial management from above, or by pushing it from behind, as by drawing it toward a future of new being—and new meaning—up ahead.

Fidelity to traditional theology and spirituality will, of course, be theologically essential to the reshaping of Catholic religious identity in the new setting of an unfinished universe. Still we need not imprison our souls and minds in depictions of the cosmos that are too small for scientifically learned people. Other theologians have made these points before, I realize, but in view of the current identity crisis of Catholicism, I think we need to examine more carefully than ever the metaphysical and cosmological assumptions at the root of the Church's stubbornly pre-evolutionary understanding of nature, God, and personal existence. Certainly the lamenting of sin's souring, to use Hopkins's term, will always be relevant, but in the context of an unfinished universe, an awareness that things are not what they were intended to be may arouse a new surge of hope for the human and cosmic future rather than shame—or flight—at the impression of being exiled from Eden.

Catholic teaching and theology will seem increasingly irrelevant to thoughtful people unless we reflect more deliberately on the meaning of the vast and still-emerging universe exposed by contemporary science. Christians who profess to love God and to have been saved by Christ will lose nothing and gain everything by transplanting their sacramental spirituality into the new cosmological setting. Our sense of the Creator, the work of the Holy Spirit, and the redemptive significance of Christ can now grow wider and deeper by immense orders of magnitude. The love that rules the stars will now have to be thought of as awakening and embracing over two hundred billion galaxies, a cosmic epic of fourteen billion years' duration—and, as we shall see later, perhaps even a multiverse.

Thinking about human life, ethics, and worship without also attending to science's picture of an unfinished universe has two negative consequences. First, it perpetuates the unfortunate impression that Catholic faith is intellectually irrelevant, and, second, it saps the "zest for living" that a theological vision must sponsor if it is to make a difference in the world.[8] If hope is to have wings, and life zest, nothing less is needed than a theological vision that opens up a new future, not just for the faithful but also for the cosmos. I call this indispensable new worldview a "metaphysics of the future."[9] The term "metaphysics" refers to a person's or community's understanding of what is really real or what underlies and gives being and intelligibility to everything else. So by a metaphysics of the future, I mean a way of understanding the world that locates what is really real in the arena of the future. A metaphysics of the future gives primacy to what is yet to come, to what corresponds to hope rather than present intellectual curiosity or sacramental piety.

No doubt, philosophers and theologians who have been conditioned to thinking of the world and God in the context of ancient and medieval notions of being will object to the whole idea of a metaphysics of the future. They will assume that since the future is "not-yet," it cannot be ontologically foundational. However, those who take seriously both the fact of an unfinished universe and a biblical understanding of time based on the ancient Hebrew discovery of the future will understand what I am talking about. Hope, if we are to take it seriously, requires a whole new understanding of being. Those who dwell within a worldview rooted in the motifs of promise and hope will rightly suspect that Platonic, Aristotelian, Thomistic, and most other philosophical syntheses, convincing as they may have been in a prescientific period, can have the effect of blunting the futuristic edge of biblical faith and of making the created universe seem smaller than it really is.[10] Indeed, most of the metaphysical systems that Catholic theologians have tried out for 2,000 years are not ready-made to frame adequately either contemporary science or, for that matter, the kind of expectation that animated the lives of our biblical ancestors. Consequently, I employ the intellectually unsettling expression "metaphysics of the future" to designate an anticipatory worldview that can accommodate in one wide vision both biblical hope and contemporary science's unfinished universe.

The idea of a metaphysics of the future may be conceptually unclear, but there is a reason for its opacity. A sense of darkness, a realization that the intelligibility we seek lies up ahead and is now partly out of range, is inevitable in any universe that is still *in via*. As long as the universe is not yet fully actualized, it cannot possibly be fully intelligible presently to those who are traveling along with it.[11] Intelligibility, in any kind of human inquiry, is something that human minds can only anticipate, not possess. The fullness of meaning is something for which we must always wait. If a horizon of meaning or intelligibility is to be a continuous source of nourishment, we can only draw toward it, never pretend to master or control it. The more we reach for it, the more it recedes. Consequently, the sense of a now incomprehensible future is an appropriate—even if cloudy—philosophical setting for contemporary theology as it reflects on a universe that is still coming to birth. Such a worldview is needed to counter the two dominant metaphysical alternatives that have persistently "clipped the wings of hope." I refer to these rivals, respectively, as the *archaeological vision*, which espouses a metaphysics of the past, and the *analogical vision*, which relies on a metaphysics of the eternal present. Let us examine them briefly here and postpone more extended discussion and criticism until Chapter 5.

Alternatives to hope

The archaeological vision tries to understand nature by digging back into earlier chapters of terrestrial, biological, and cosmological history in search of solid ground on which to erect an understanding of the world. Adopting unconsciously a *metaphysics of the past*, it expects to explain all present realities completely by going far back temporally, and deep down analytically, to retrieve the subatomic units that over the course of cosmic history have led successively to atoms, molecules, cells, organisms, and, eventually, human brains and their cultural products. A metaphysics of the past assumes that human inquiry can arrive at a full understanding of the universe only through the reductive methods of contemporary science. Pure analysis is enough to uncover the "really real" world consisting of lifeless and mindless elements that made up the earliest stages of the cosmic process.

Recently a few scientific naturalists have become aware that the organizing principles operative in successive emergent stages of the cosmic process cannot be reduced simply to material and efficient causes arising from the past. Something previously unknown (though purely natural), they now suspect, steals quietly onto the cosmic scene with each new chapter in cosmic history.[12] Yet, instead of acknowledging that these emergent developments require a whole new metaphysics, the same scientific thinkers try desperately to fit every new scientific discovery onto the grid of an obsolete atomistic materialism.[13] Contemporary adherents to materialist metaphysics generally believe that only by going back into the physical past will they place human thought on a firm foundation. The problem is that this archaeological vision, as I will be calling it, forbids the arrival in the cosmic process of anything truly new. For contemporary materialists, nonlife, which dominates past cosmic history, is the ground state of being and (because it submits to measurement) "the intelligible par excellence," as the philosopher Hans Jonas has critically commented. A materialist metaphysics of the past, then, is in effect an "ontology of death" in which lifelessness is primary, and life secondary, epiphenomenal, and, hence, not "really real."[14] This deadening, past-oriented, and pessimistic view of the universe is still the most imposing intellectual challenge to a theology of hope. Its simplistic physicalism has found an increasingly comfortable home in academic settings all over the planet. So, by understanding the universe almost exclusively in materialist terms, many of today's most celebrated intellectuals turn out to be no less impervious to the future than religious traditionalists who seek to restore prescientific pietism.

Scientific analysis by itself leads our minds downward reductively, and backward temporally, toward a region of natural history inhabited only by scattered units of matter—and thus toward a region of physical incoherence.[15] Analysis as such is unobjectionable, since this is what science does best, but what is questionable is the atomistic belief that breaking everything down into elemental physical particles alone can place human thought and life on a reliable metaphysical foundation. The Duke University philosophy professor Alex Rosenberg, to give only one of many available examples of contemporary materialist atomism, puts it bluntly: "Everything in the universe is made up of the stuff that physics tells us fills up space." Physics, he continues, "can tell us how everything in the universe works, in principle and in practice, better than anything else." "All the processes in the universe from atomic to bodily to mental, are purely physical processes involving fermions and bosons interacting with one another." Why, though, should we base everything on what particle physics has to say? "Well, it's simple, really," Rosenberg answers, "We trust science as the only way to acquire knowledge," and that, he concludes, "is why we are so confident about atheism."[16]

Bringing human inquiry to rest in a field of scattered bits of matter and units of energy, however, fails to yield an ultimate explanation of anything. Analysis can provide a scientifically essential map of the universe's elemental constituents, and it can help us piece together, chapter by chapter, the long cosmic story of the universe's journey up to the present. So physical analysis is an important contribution to human understanding, and those of us who view the universe in narrative terms are indebted to it for giving us a general sense of the cosmic itinerary to date. What is objectionable, then, is not analytical science as such but the atomistic philosophical mentality—exemplified by Rosenberg—that reduces all of nature to protons, quarks, leptons, fermion, bosons, and so on. This reductionist worldview is what I mean by a metaphysics of the past. It is an all-encompassing vision of reality that professes to make the world intelligible but that, in fact, succeeds only in leading our minds downward and backward into an atomic mist that becomes increasingly diffuse the further back we travel in time.

Whether this kind of reductive physicalism can lay any plausible claim to being intellectually coherent I shall examine later, especially in Chapter 10. Here, though, I want to look at another unsatisfactory alternative to the metaphysics of the future I am endorsing. This second way of looking at the world also clips the wings of hope, though not to the extent that the analytical illusion does. I will be calling it a *metaphysics of the eternal present.*[17] It locates the fullness of being and intelligibility in a domain of timelessness immune to all becoming. It is rooted in Platonic, Aristotelian, and Neoplatonic philosophies that, to one degree or another, tend to extract us from the flow of time and hence deliver us of any serious concern for the cosmic future. It may also be called the *analogical vision* since it assumes that all created beings participate imperfectly, or by analogy, in the uncreated, eternal being of God.

The metaphysics of the eternal present has provided the main intellectual setting for traditional Roman Catholic theology. Attaching itself principally to this analogical vision of the world, Catholic theology has assumed the overwhelming realness of an immaterial world located "above" the transient sphere of terrestrial and cosmic becoming. Catholic sacramental spirituality, represented nowhere more beautifully than in the poetry of Hopkins, is a product of the analogical, participatory metaphysics of the eternal present. The analogical vision offers solace to individual souls, but it holds out little hope for a universe that is still coming to birth. Today its most ardent defenders—and they are many—fail to reflect deeply on the scientific evidence that weaves each species of life and each human person intricately into the story of a universe still being born. Moreover, the classical Catholic understanding of the self, world, and God, as Teilhard rightly complained and as Vatican II seemed to agree, provides insufficient incentive for robust moral action in the world.[18]

Again, there is something of timeless religious value to be rescued from a metaphysics of the eternal present. It expresses our legitimate longing for transcendence, perfection, and ultimate fulfillment. However, if a metaphysics of the past prohibits anything truly new from ever occurring in the universe, is this not also true, at least to some extent, of a metaphysics of the eternal present? The latter's insistence on the radical transcendence of God and the ontological dependence of the world on divine creation is indispensable religiously, of course, but the idea of an eternal *now* can make us indifferent to the passage of time in which cosmic creativity, human hope, and moral action find their appropriate place.[19] It allows too little room for the created world's becoming more, and this impression is fortified whenever Catholic thought takes literally the biblical narrative of a primordial souring of nature's "sweet being in the beginning." The idea of a "Fall" from primordial innocence has sometimes had the effect of turning the history of human life, religious existence, and the practice of virtue into a project of restoration rather than renewal.

Consequently, the myth of the world's initial perfection, in combination with a cult of the eternal present, can easily detach our moral lives from the joy of cooperating with the Creator in bringing about something truly unprecedented. In spite of Vatican II's acknowledgment in *Gaudium et spes* that humanity's understanding of the world is now changing from a static to an evolutionary one,[20] a metaphysics of the eternal present continues to undergird much, if not most of, contemporary Catholic theology, ethics, and spirituality. Apart from a few notable exceptions, Catholic thought remains relatively indifferent to the scientifically demonstrable notion of a universe still coming into being. And because of this cosmological indifference, it fails to link up fully with the promissory core of biblical faith.

The world rests on the future

Teilhard himself professed to being weary of metaphysics, but his reserve is due mostly to the fact that the term "metaphysics" has generally been used in reference to the two future-suppressing worldviews I have just sketched. Nevertheless, Teilhard turned out to be thoroughly metaphysical in the sense that he too sought a firm foundation upon which to ground the emerging universe that the evolutionary sciences have uncovered. His lifelong intellectual and spiritual journey, like that of other profound thinkers, was one of looking for a bedrock solidity upon which to rest a coherent vision of reality. After much anguish and intellectual searching, he finally discovered the foundational firmness he hungered for only by looking steadily in the direction of the future. He arrived, in other words, at an *anticipatory vision* of the universe, or at what I am calling a metaphysics of the future.

It was not without a deep personal struggle, however, that he did so. Teilhard's search for foundations on which to erect a scientifically informed worldview led him at first to consider the apparent durability of "matter." Yet he soon realized that materiality cannot be foundational since it dissolves into separate individual bits when subjected to ever more refined scientific analysis. A purely physicalist philosophy of nature leads our minds downward in space and backward in time toward an ultimate incoherence.[21] A metaphysics of the past is a dead end, literally. Contemporary scientific naturalism, nevertheless, continues to dig back "archaeologically" into natural history in search of timeless laws and deterministic causes on which it expects to rest its search for nature's intelligibility. Yet, the further back naturalist materialism and atomism look in search of what is intelligible and "really real," the more the world they find there falls to pieces.

The analytical illusion on which contemporary materialist metaphysics still builds its crumbled sense of reality has, because of its apparent simplicity, seduced countless educated people into embracing the fantastic belief that breaking physical complexity down into its most indivisible atomic or subatomic components will somehow make the present world fully intelligible.[22] Teilhard, on the contrary, came to realize that the remote granular cosmic past uncovered by analysis cannot realistically function as the ground of the world's being, as it seems to do for materialist scientists and philosophers such as Rosenberg. Instead of leaning on the past, or being suspended from on high, Teilhard gradually realized, the world leans on the *future* as its true foundation. The universe can become intelligible to us, in other words, only if we turn around after our long analytical journey into the past and look forward, toward the horizon of what is yet to come.[23] What gives coherence, unity, and intelligibility to our still-unfinished universe is not the atomized and diffused cosmic past—incoherence in other words—but the world's being drawn toward the horizon of a constantly receding and still indeterminate unity up ahead. It is in the direction of the future, therefore, that we need to look for what is ultimately real.

Teilhard's discovery of the future, more than any other aspect of his thought, can help us fashion an appropriate metaphysical setting for Catholic theology in an emerging universe. Such a worldview will be more Abrahamic than Platonic or Aristotelian, more anticipatory than analogical. A metaphysics of the future can link the scientific discovery of an unfinished universe to a biblical theology in which only the love emanating from a God of promise, a God who creates the universe from out of the future, can make the world one, intelligible, good, and real. By thinking of God as the universe's ultimate future and goal, therefore, we may also understand how the world comes into being. To create is to unite, and true union (as distinct from uniformity and homogeneity) belongs to God's future more than to the physical past. So we need to challenge not only scientific naturalism's metaphysics of the past, with its exclusive reliance on explanation in terms of material and efficient causation, but also classical Catholic theology's assumption that an unchanging and timeless perfection alone can render the world fully intelligible. It is the world's being drawn toward deeper union and communion up ahead—that is, its *anticipation* of future coherence in God—and not an atomistic past or a vertical sacramental participation in a timeless and finished perfection above, that gives the world its consistency and presently opens it toward more being.

In summary, neither the materialist metaphysics of the past nor the classical theological metaphysics of the eternal present can account adequately for the world insofar as that world is becoming *more*. A futurist metaphysics in which God is conceived of as the ultimate term of cosmic process, then, is a worthy alternative. As the ultimate goal of cosmic emergence and convergence, God may be thought of as creating the world by drawing it toward more intense ontological unity from up ahead (*ab ante*) rather than by "pushing" it into being from out of the past (*a retro*). God, of course, was in the beginning, is now, and ever shall be. And, yes, God is both Alpha and Omega. However, God is more Omega than Alpha.[24] In an unfinished universe, the metaphysical search for what is "really real" leads forward in the direction of the "not-yet" rather than backward toward the "has-been" or upward toward the "is-now." The currently indubitable fact of a universe still in process invites Catholic theology to think in new ways about God as the creator of all things visible and invisible.[25] The invisible side of creation now includes not only worlds spatially out of sight but also a future beyond all past or present frames of reference. In subsequent chapters, I draw out more specifically what a metaphysics of the future might imply for contemporary Catholic reflection on other theological themes.

Doctrine: From Deposit to Development

The Second Vatican Council called for a new "analysis and synthesis" of what Catholic faith means in the age of evolution. This book is a response to that invitation. It takes for granted that the Church too is part of an unfinished universe and that, like other living systems, it needs to adapt in order to survive and thrive. The deposit of Catholic faith is not a smoothly rounded rock rolling down the corridors of time cushioned from changing cultures and fluctuating intellectual environments. Doctrine can, and must, develop if it is to be the basis of an enlivening spirituality for different periods of time. In fact, theology has always been one of the ways in which living religious traditions have struggled to survive. The main argument of this book, then, is that Catholic thought needs to adapt deliberately and critically to the new scientific picture of an unfinished universe, beginning with evolutionary biology. Before going any further in our inquiry into the theological significance of evolution, however, let us pause and look first at the struggle Catholic thought and teaching have already undergone in reacting to Darwin's science.

From the last third of the nineteenth century until the middle of the twentieth, Catholic officials and theologians expressed various degrees of hostility to Darwin's theory of evolution. "Darwinism" seemed inseparable from "naturalism," "materialism," "rationalism," "socialism," and other creeds taken to be atheistic. During the papacy of Pius IX (1846–78), who promulgated "The Syllabus of Errors" (1864), Church officials suspected that evolutionary ideas are an expression of godless materialism, the belief that mindless matter is the ground and destiny of all being. Suspicions about evolutionary science may have seemed theologically justifiable during Pius IX's papacy since atheists such as Karl Marx and Ernst Haeckel publicly embraced Darwin's *Origin of Species* in support of their own versions of materialist philosophy. Even Darwin suspected that evolution entails materialism, although he modestly refrained from trumpeting his own doubts about the existence of a providential God. By the early twenty-first century, however, outspoken evolutionists such as E. O. Wilson, Richard Dawkins, and Daniel Dennett were noisily declaring what many previous thinkers had more circumspectly assumed, namely, that Darwinian biology is altogether inseparable from materialism.

Associating evolutionary biology with materialism, of course, renders it theologically unacceptable on any terms, so it is no surprise that scientifically unsophisticated popes and theologians in the late nineteenth and early twentieth century were appalled by Darwin's new ideas about life and human beings. Nevertheless, almost from the time of the *Origin's* first publication in 1859, several Catholic intellectuals accepted the theory of evolution as scientifically significant. Most prominent among them was the biologist St George Jackson Mivart (1827–1900), a convert to Catholicism and a close acquaintance of Darwin. Mivart initially embraced Darwin's theory without much difficulty. Later on, however, he came to doubt that the impersonal evolutionary mechanism of natural selection can account for consciousness and the human soul, and this dissent spelled the end of his friendship with Darwin. Mivart, incidentally, later on became estranged from the Church as well.

Before the mid-twentieth century, several other Catholics, notably John Zahm (1851–1921), an American priest and professor at The University of Notre Dame, and later Pierre Teilhard de Chardin (1881–1955), the French Jesuit priest and geologist introduced in the preceding chapters, defended nonmaterialist versions of evolution. Until the last half of the twentieth century, however, most Catholics were at best unenthusiastic about Darwin's ideas. G. K. Chesterton and Hilaire Belloc stood out as popular Catholic enemies of evolution. Catholic reluctance to embrace evolutionary science was nourished in great measure by the Irish Catholicism that significantly shaped the spirituality of Catholics in North America and elsewhere.[1] The Vatican's suppression of "Modernism" under Pope Pius X was motivated also by the impression during his papacy that secularist debunking of religion and morality could be accounted for partly by the propagation of Darwinian ideas. The Vatican chastised, and in several cases excommunicated, Catholic intellectuals who had employed vaguely evolutionary ideas in their attempts to update the faith for a new intellectual environment. Among the thinkers who incurred the Vatican's suspicion, though not to the point of excommunication, was Teilhard whose anticipatory vision of nature will help guide us in this book.

No official condemnation

In spite of its initial distrust of Darwin, the Church never officially condemned evolution. In 1950, Pope Pius XII, in his controversial encyclical *Humani Generis,* finally acknowledged that evolution is a theory that Catholics may explore. Pius and his successors, however, have uniformly insisted that the human soul is infused into each person directly by God. This qualification has seemed necessary to safeguard the Church's constant belief that human beings are created in the "image and likeness" of their Maker. This belief is one of the main topics in Chapter 8 where I consider the question of human dignity after Darwin. For now, though, it is enough to observe that ever since Pius XII's papacy, Catholic thinkers and educators have increasingly accepted Darwin's science while rejecting the materialism that more often than not still accompanies it. As I have mentioned already, *Gaudium et spes*, one of the most important documents promulgated by Vatican II (1962–65), indicated unmistakably that official Catholic teaching by the time of the Council had begun to assimilate evolutionary themes. And more recently (1996), Pope John Paul II issued an official statement maintaining that the evidence for evolution is strong and must be considered "more than a hypothesis."[2]

Several important events in modern Catholic history paved the way for the Church's eventual coming to terms, at least in principle, with evolutionary biology. The first was Pope Leo XIII's instruction in the encyclical *Providentissimus Deus* (1893) that Catholics should not look for scientific information when reading the Scriptures. Readers of the Bible will find there neither confirmation nor refutation of insights that scientific research can in principle discover on its own. Centuries ago, Augustine of Hippo (354–430) had already cautioned readers of Genesis not to take literally its cosmological assumptions since painting pictures of nature is not the Bible's concern.[3] If a Christian catechist were to demand that prospective converts interpret the biblical portraits of nature literally, Augustine advised, this would only lead them to ignore the Bible when it speaks of more important matters. So, by acknowledging officially that the text of Genesis does not provide a strictly scientific account of origins, Pope Leo XIII confirmed what many educated Catholics, including Galileo (1546–1642), had already held.

A second, and more substantive, reason for the Church's eventual warming up to evolution was a dramatic shift in the style and approach of nineteenth- and early twentieth-century biblical scholarship. The transition to a historically conscious interpretation of the Bible, unlike earlier readings, could now acknowledge the diverse cultural and social settings, oral traditions, and literary genres represented in the biblical text. The new historical-critical approach concluded that ancient biblical writings could never have intended to make modern scientific claims and should not be evaluated or interpreted in terms of narrowly modern scientific notions of "evidence." Accounts of cosmic and human origins in the book of Genesis, for example, obviously predated the birth of modern science, and so their intention is certainly not one of satisfying our present-day craving for scientific information. Distinguishing biblical writings from the horizon of scientific inquiry has freed theologians to look for levels of meaning in inspired texts that science by definition does not even ask about.

Popes, bishops, and Catholic theologians had initially been suspicious of the modern critical approach to the Scriptures, but in 1943 Pope Pius XII issued the important encyclical *Divino Afflante Spiritu*, officially allowing Catholic scholars to take advantage of new literary, archaeological, philological, and historical research in their reading of ancient sacred texts. No longer required to place biblical writings in competition with Darwinian biology, Catholic biblical scholars could now focus more deliberately on retrieving the theological intent of the Scriptures. By contrast, even into the early twenty-first century, nearly half of non-Catholic American Christians, along with some prominent atheistic evolutionists, continue to read the Bible as though its authors intended it to be a font of scientific truth. Biblical literalism today not only fuels creationist hostility to evolutionary biology, but it also shapes the New Atheist debunking of biblical religion. Sam Harris, Richard Dawkins, Christopher Hitchens, and Daniel Dennett all base their rejection of theism partly on their assumption that the biblical authors, if they are truly "inspired," should not have been ignorant of evolutionary biology and Big Bang physics![4] Meanwhile, ever since the middle of the twentieth century, Catholic scientists and theologians have made peace with nonliteralist biblical criticism. As a result, they have felt increasingly free to accept evolutionary biology, geology, and paleontology as compatible with biblical faith.

A third factor facilitating the reception of evolution by Roman Catholics has been the traditional Catholic emphasis on the importance of the sacramental dimension of faith as distinct from the Protestant emphasis on the "word" of God. Roman Catholicism has characteristically looked for divine inspiration and religious guidance not only in the written word of Scripture but also in a more encompassing "deposit of faith" handed down by a long teaching tradition, a hierarchical Church, and a highly elaborate sacramental system centered in liturgical life. In many varieties of Protestantism, on the other hand, the main medium of revelation has been the biblical word of God. One result of the Protestant privileging of the text of Scripture, especially in the case of biblical literalists, has been the tendency at times to mistake "inerrant" scriptural propositions for impeccable scientific truth claims. Whenever this conflation of the Bible with science occurs, it is impossible to reconcile evolutionary and cosmological accounts of origins with Christian faith.[5]

After 1950, Catholic thought, by gradually detaching itself from biblical literalism, grew more comfortable with the view that God creates continuously by way of evolutionary and other secondary natural processes. The acceptance of evolution by Catholics, however, should not be mistaken for a mature appropriation of Darwinian discoveries. Doctrine requires development if it is to come alive in the new intellectual setting of an unfinished universe, and most Catholic thought in the early twenty-first century has yet to be influenced more than superficially by evolutionary interpretations of life or by contemporary cosmology. Very little Catholic systematic theology, for example, has dealt in depth with what it means that we find ourselves in a universe where Darwinian processes have shaped the journey of life on earth. This neglect is ironic since Catholicism has a strong tradition of "natural theology" that has always sought coherence between faith's trust in God on the one hand and patterns of nature on the other. But even today the meaning of evolution has yet to become a widely shared concern of Catholic theology.

Unfortunately, not only neglect but also outright distrust of evolution still persists in some high places ecclesiastically. Pope John Paul II's favorable comments on the discoveries of contemporary evolutionary biology at a meeting of the Pontifical Academy of Science in 1996 signaled a departure of ecclesiastical instruction from previously lukewarm concessions to evolutionary science. Disappointingly, however, on July 7, 2005, Cardinal Christoph Schönborn of Vienna, who had previously overseen the writing of the *New Catholic Catechism,* expressed misgivings about contemporary evolutionary biology in an essay for the *New York Times.* He allowed for evolutionary descent but complained that "neo-Darwinian" biology, since it makes considerable room for randomness in evolution, is irreconcilable with faith in divine providence. Schönborn's essay even belittled Pope John Paul II's important 1996 endorsement of evolutionary biology. His remarks immediately drew the criticism of American Catholic scientists and theologians who had embraced neo-Darwinian biology and who understandably considered Schönborn's column a step backward in Catholic efforts to interpret evolution. The Cardinal later softly qualified his views, claiming that what he really opposed was not evolutionary biology but materialist interpretations of it.[6] Still, the fact that this former student of Pope Benedict XVI failed to distinguish carefully between evolutionary science and materialist philosophy has only reinforced the widespread opinion in the intellectual world that Catholicism is inherently indifferent to science.

Bernard Lonergan and Pierre Teilhard de Chardin

During the twentieth century, on the other hand, several Catholic thinkers had begun to think appreciatively and in depth about evolution. I believe the

most intellectually astute understanding of evolutionary theory to date—by
any serious thinker—is that of the Jesuit philosopher and theologian Bernard
Lonergan (1904–84). Reflecting on modern science with his vast knowledge
of both medieval and modern thought, Lonergan's formidable work *Insight*
(first published in 1957) presents a sophisticated worldview that makes
evolution intelligible in a manner that avoids both the materialism of most
evolutionists and the narrowness of creationist and "Intelligent Design"
opposition to Darwin's science. Lonergan demonstrates that the seemingly
unintelligible "accidents" that occur in world process—the contingent
events that so troubled Cardinal Schönborn—become intelligible when
understood from the perspective of a universe of "emergent probability." For
Lonergan, the first step toward making theological sense of evolution is to
understand the basic structure and dynamics of the wider physical universe
in which Darwinian process has come into play. Once we understand the
basic "design" of the cosmos—what Lonergan calls "emergent probability"—
the evolutionary formula for life's development becomes intelligible both
scientifically and theologically.[7]

As I interpret Lonergan, our universe is one in which predictable laws are
combined with unpredictable probabilities so that nature takes the form of a
story still being told. What happens in the cosmic story is unpredictable but,
nonetheless, intelligible. What I have been calling an unfinished universe,
Lonergan refers to as an *open* universe. This means that what happens in the
cosmic story is not fully determined by physical laws, as modern mechanist
and materialist thinkers still maintain, but that it, nonetheless, has an
intelligibility that can be captured by a historical understanding of nature.
In other words, the universe may have what I will be calling a *narrative
coherence* whose possible meaning is still unfolding and hence is, at present,
not fully comprehensible. That is, the kind of intelligibility the universe has is
analogous to what one experiences when reading a story. For just as reading a
story requires that readers assume a posture of *waiting* for the story's meaning
to emerge gradually, so also patient waiting is essential to our awakening to
any possible meaning in the cosmic story, including, especially, the story of
life. The biblical emphasis on the need to wait in hopeful anticipation for the
self-revelation of God—or for God's will to be done—is consonant with the
intellectual stance a universe of emergent probability requires of us as we
look toward a narrative coherence still out of sight. In this sense, therefore,
a biblical vision of reality can easily accommodate the Darwinian portrait of
life, and it can do so without having to accept the materialist and atheistic
claims that many evolutionists espouse today.

Unfortunately, however, very few theologians, scientists, and philosophers
have bothered to become familiar with Lonergan's narrative reading of the

universe as emergent probability. What follows then is a brief summary of what I take from Lonergan as I explore the theological meaning of an unfinished universe in subsequent chapters.

1. Emergent probability is the fundamental "design" of the universe.[8] The sciences have now uncovered our universe's staggering spatial immensity and temporal duration, along with the incalculably large number of possible opportunities and events in which elemental components are arranged in ever more complex patterns. Given the enormity of time, spatial distribution, and the large numbers of events that can occur in the cosmos, sooner or later, here and there, the components converge and combine in cycles and series of cycles (schemes of recurrence) that may seem initially improbable. Over the course of deep time, some combinations and series of combinations will be more likely to arise and survive than in other times and places. In certain circumstances, in other words, what was once only possible can become increasingly probable.

2. Many combinations will emerge, but not all will have the stability to survive, so we need to distinguish between the probability of emergence and the probability of survival.[9] The probability of emergence and the prospect of survival will differ according to varying amounts of time and spatial distributions. Some emergent combinations will be selected for survival, others discarded. Once selected, however, the surviving combinations may allow for yet newer combinations and conditioned series of combinations.

3. Biological evolution, which involves random variation, natural selection, and development over time, is an instance of emergent probability. What evolutionary science calls "random variation" is a special instance of the more general probability of emergence; what evolutionists call "natural selection" has to do with the probability of survival; and changes such as speciation are examples of "development." So a theology of nature need not ask first and foremost about the meaning of Darwinian evolution, but instead it needs to ask about the meaning of a *universe* whose basic constitution is that of emergent probability.[10]

4. The notion of emergent probability gives a meaning to deep time, spatial expansiveness, and large numbers that would otherwise remain obscure. As I see it, this meaning consists of the fact that emergent probability gives the universe a *dramatic* mode of being that is ignored by mechanistic and materialist (mis)representations of nature. So if someone poses the childlike question of why the universe is so big, so old, and so numerically immense, the answer is that these features are essential for the universe to be a drama.

5. A drama, however, unlike a machine or a mere mass of stuff suspended in space, *may carry a meaning*. The meaning, however, need not be immediately evident. We must wait for it to emerge and develop as is the case with our attending to any story. Since the posture of waiting in hope is the fundamental biblical virtue, and patience one of the main marks of authentic faith, I am arguing in this book that a Catholic theology of nature in an unfinished universe needs to adopt an anticipatory, as distinct from an archaeological or purely analogical, understanding of creation.[11] Since the outcome of the cosmic drama is presently unpredictable and out of sight, we can come to understand it only by anticipation. Applying these ideas to the question of the meaning of an unfinished universe, I want to emphasize that the main features of what Lonergan calls emergent probability are the same as those required for there to be *any* story or drama: (a) time and space for a range of initially improbable things to *emerge*; (b) the selection of some series of emergent patterns for *survival*; and (c) time for the *development* of initial patterns into new arrangements.

Let me comment a bit further on what I mean by the dramatic or narrative character of the cosmos. First, if events in the universe were completely predictable, the design of the universe would be that of a machine rather than a story. Without the possibility of unpredictable or surprising patterns of events and of unpredictable series of arrangements—in which the possibility of the later patterns depend upon the emergence and survival of the earlier ones—the cosmos would allow for no dramatic suspense. Second, however, if a series of events were completely devoid of at least some degree of predictable patterning, it would lack the consistency that ties things together into the form of a story. So nature has to have inviolable constraints or "laws" that place limits on unpredictability. And finally there has to be available a sufficient amount of time for significant development to take place. Emergent probability gives the universe the three qualities essential to existing in the overall pattern of a drama: contingency, regularity, and time for development. It is this threefold pattern that renders the universe dramatic and that allows us to look for meaning in evolution.

In subsequent chapters I will say more about the dramatic quality of life and the universe. Here I want to mention only in passing that after the appearance of *Humani Generis* in 1950, another Catholic thinker, Karl Rahner, made a significant attempt to develop Catholic thought in a manner consistent with an evolutionary worldview.[12] I cannot discuss Rahner's evolutionary theology here,[13] but I want to point out that both Rahner's and Lonergan's appreciation of the need for doctrinal development in terms appropriate to an unfinished universe was preceded by the synthesis of Catholic faith and evolutionary science initiated long before 1950 by Pierre Teilhard de Chardin. I am convinced that Catholic reflection on evolution even today must start with close attention to Teilhard who fully accepted the scientific data present in the fossil record, biogeography, comparative anatomy, and other fields of science tributary to evolutionary theory. Before Lonergan and Rahner started thinking about evolution, Teilhard had already embraced the Darwinian ideas of variation and selection, the statistical play of large numbers, and the necessity of deep time, all of which he took to be explanatory factors in evolution. What he vehemently rejected is the still current—and completely nonscientific—assumption that only a materialist metaphysics can render evolutionary research intelligible. Teilhard argued, as Lonergan did later on and as I maintain throughout this book, that a materialist metaphysics only serves to make evolution ultimately unintelligible.

Teilhard's main preoccupation throughout his adult life was that of how to connect Catholic thought and spirituality to a scientifically informed awareness of life and the cosmos. Ordained a priest in 1911, he became a stretcher-bearer during the First World War and received awards for his courage in battle. It was during his life in the trenches that his transposing of traditional Catholic thought into an evolutionary key began to take definite shape. After the war and the completion of his studies in Paris, he spent about a quarter of a century in China where he became one of the most authoritative geologists in the Far East. There he began to write *Le Phénomène humain*, a large and complex treatise setting forth the groundwork of his lifelong efforts to synthesize a scientific understanding of the world with his faith in revelation and his deep personal commitment to a Catholic understanding of the world.[14] However, both the Vatican and Teilhard's religious superiors forbade the book's publication during his lifetime, and it appeared in print only after his death in 1955.

At the time of his burial in upstate New York, relatively few Catholic thinkers outside of France had even heard of Teilhard, let alone become familiar with his unprecedented ideas. He was highly regarded in scientific circles, but most Catholic theologians knew little, if anything, about him. His immediate superiors and the Vatican had no objection, of course, to his producing strictly scientific papers, but they withheld permission to publish *The Phenomenon* and his other major writings on science and faith. After his death, however, his literary executor submitted Teilhard's manuscripts to eager publishers, and by the close of Vatican II in 1965, his ideas had begun to spread into theological circles and the wider intellectual world.

Today, early in the twenty-first century, most Catholic thinkers no longer consider Teilhard's thought theologically "dangerous," although his ideas have begun to lose some of their earlier popularity, partly because of more recent conservative antipathy to Vatican II. Snubbed by his own Church during his lifetime, this great scientist and spiritual visionary has turned out, in my opinion, to be the most important religious thinker of the twentieth century. Not everyone will share this opinion, but to those of us who believe that Catholicism—for the sake of its intellectual credibility—must come to grips with science, especially with evolutionary biology and cosmology, Teilhard will forever stand as a model of honesty, openness, and courage. The following is a short list of his insights relevant to this book's main theme, topics that I will expand on as we move through subsequent chapters.

1. The whole universe is still coming into being. It is worth pointing out again that Teilhard has the distinction of being one of the first scientists in the twentieth century to have seen clearly that the entire cosmos, and not just life on our planet, is a momentous drama. The universe is not just a stage on which human beings are tested in order to prove their worthiness to gain a heavenly reward. We now know, thanks to science, that humans, along with other living beings, are products of an immensely long and extravagantly creative cosmic process.

2. The cosmic story has a direction. The general drift of the universe has been toward a measurable increase in organized physical complexity over immense spans of time. After giving birth to the spheres of matter and life, the universe has recently exploded into "thought" by virtue of the evolution of complex human brains and the invention of culture here on earth. So, overall, the universe has undeniably made a kind of "progress" measurable in terms of increasingly higher degrees of physical complexity during the course of deep time. As the cosmos has become more complex, it has also become more conscious, at least in its terrestrial precincts. The cosmic process has already gone through pre-atomic, atomic, molecular, unicellular, multicellular, vertebrate, primate, and human stages of increasing complexity-consciousness. Presently, in human beings, who are endowed with exceptionally elaborate nervous systems and brains, matter has attained a proportionately elevated capacity for consciousness. Because of its gradual increase in complexity-consciousness, the cosmos has exhibited an overall tendency to move in the direction of *fuller being*. As a person of faith, Teilhard identified the God incarnate in Christ as the ultimate goal (Omega) of the universe's ongoing creative movement.

3. The cosmic tendency to maximize complexity—and consciousness—is now occurring on a planetary scale as a result of human inventiveness

in the areas of technology, education, economics, and global politics, all connected to new modes of travel and communication. Today the Internet contributes much to the sort of planetary complexity that Teilhard saw occurring at an accelerated pace during his own lifetime. Even in the face of forces of destruction, despair, evil, and death, the earth is now clothing itself in something analogous to a brain. A globe-encircling spread of consciousness, corresponding to the increase in physical and technological complexity on a planetary scale, is now in the early stages of formation. Teilhard refers to this emergent terrestrial phenomenon of planetary complexity-consciousness as the *noosphere*. The emergence of the noosphere is now happening rapidly and explosively, but most scientists, partly because they are still blinded by materialist beliefs, have yet to pay close attention to the phenomenon of "thought" as it intensifies on earth. They fail to see "thought" as a cosmic, and not just a cultural, development. In any case, we should not assume that the universe's trending toward more complexity and consciousness is anywhere near being complete. Life and the universe are open to more creative outcomes in the future.

4. However, the ongoing creation of the universe, at least from a terrestrial perspective, requires on the part of human beings the fervent and persistent practice of faith, hope, and love. An important function of Catholic theology, therefore, is to reflect on how the practice of these virtues, and of moral life in general, contributes to the ongoing creation of the universe. We pray, therefore, for the wisdom and grace to distinguish those human actions that can contribute to the ongoing creation of the universe from those that lead only to destruction. Today, we must add, the ongoing evolution of the world demands special attention on the part of Catholic theology to economic justice and environmental responsibility.[15]

No other Catholic thinker in the post-Darwinian period has done more to integrate evolutionary biology, geology, paleontology, and cosmology into a biblically inspired theological vision than has Teilhard, even though technically he was neither a theologian nor a biblical scholar. Moreover, it is doubtful that any Catholic natural scientist since Galileo has suffered more from unjustified ecclesiastical censorship during his own lifetime. Unfortunately, as I noted earlier, while he was still living, the Vatican had prevented Teilhard from publishing most of his revolutionary writings, and even as late as 1962, the Holy Office was warning seminary faculties and Catholic universities to protect students and prospective priests from exposure to "the dangers" of Teilhard's thought. Teilhard's writings, however, have convinced at least some Catholic thinkers that evolution is not an obstacle to faith but the key in which all theology must now be set and developed. It is within an evolutionary, future-oriented picture of a universe still coming into being that Catholic thought must situate human moral life and spiritual aspiration.

So, in great measure, it is because of Teilhard's pioneering work that at least some Catholic thinkers over the past half-century have come to consider Darwin as a friend rather than a foe of their faith. Why, though, had Teilhard's writings seemed doctrinally dangerous in the first place? Most likely because of his views on original sin. Going beyond the story of Adam and Eve, and the so-called Fall, which could no longer be taken literally after Darwin and modern biblical scholarship, Teilhard had tried, in some of his earliest essays on Christianity and evolution, to think about what redemption by Christ could possibly mean in a post-Darwinian world. The very notion of evolution, he insisted, implies that the world is still in process. This means that the cosmos could never literally have been completed in the past or "in the beginning," nor can it be perfect at any present moment. Consequently, the fundamental "fault" that calls for redemption and new creation is the inevitable incompleteness of our still-emerging universe. The existence of both suffering and human sin are closely related to the fact that the universe is now unperfected. If so, Catholic faith is required to look toward the cosmic future for divine healing. Logically speaking, an unperfected universe, since it is still in process, would inevitably have a dark side in which evil, including human sin, can presently find a foothold. The importance of evolutionary science and cosmology to Catholic theology, therefore, is that by extending the original fault to the entire cosmos, it serves to magnify the scope and healing significance of Christ's redemption so as to include the whole universe and its future.[16]

But what then can we say about original sin after Darwin? In view of the still-emerging universe, original sin, along with our sinful tendencies and moral fallibility, is not literally traceable to a historically identifiable Adam and Eve, biblical figures that modern exegesis had already demythologized. Rather, as I see it, the predicament traditionally referred to as original sin is the brokenness of the world into which each of us is born, a condition to which we humans have contributed throughout our history. In all of its dimensions—personal, social, political, economic, biological, and cosmological—this brokenness stains every human being born into this world. This sinful condition now affects not only humans but also the entire life-world that is now being subjected to human greed and violence. It is a situation that calls out for nothing less than a redemption as wide as the whole created world. Our actual sins, therefore, are rebellions against God's passionate call and creative longing for the universe to become more than it is at present. Only God, whom we believe to have become incarnate in the Christ, can bring ultimate healing and meaning to life's evolution, to the individual's misery, to a history distorted by human sin, and, ultimately, to the entire restless universe.

Here I may be going beyond Teilhard's own speculation on sin, but I believe this interpretation is consistent with his intentions. Far from doing away with a sense of evil and our own need for redemption, as misguided critics of Teilhard have often claimed, this interpretation of evil deepens our sense of the tragedy of human evil and sin by connecting them to the narrative of an emergent universe. The good news is that it also broadens cosmologically the scope and significance of our hope for the redemption accomplished in Christ's incarnation, suffering, death, and resurrection. In any case, Teilhard's inventive theological reinterpretation of nature, sin, and salvation proved too adventurous for both Jesuit and Vatican censors, but as I point out again in the following chapter, only a decade after Teilhard's death, his own Church had become comfortable enough with the new biology to appropriate some of his ideas on sin, faith, and evolution officially as its own.

Summary

Throughout Teilhard's lifetime, Catholicism still adhered to the picture of an essentially static and unchanging cosmos. During the last century, however, Teilhard became one of the very few Christian thinkers to acknowledge that the Darwinian revolution and contemporary cosmology now call for development of the doctrines of creation, sin, and redemption. Such an acknowledgment has several important implications for theology. In the first place, as I have been emphasizing, the sciences have shown beyond any doubt that the universe could not literally have come into being in a state of finished perfection. Second, the figure of Christ and the meaning of redemption must now be understood as having something to do with the fulfillment of the earth and the whole universe, and not just the healing of persons or the harvesting of souls from the material world. And third, after Darwin, Christian hope gets a whole new horizon, not one of expiating an ancestral sin and nostalgically returning to an imagined paradisal past, but one of supporting the adventure of life, of expanding the domain of consciousness, of building the earth, and of participating in the ongoing creation of the universe in whatever small ways are available to each of us. The following chapters attempt to unfold these three proposals in more detail.

Spirituality: From Contemplation to Anticipation

John Donne's famous poem "Anatomie of the World" includes these troubled lines:

> And new Philosophy calls all in doubt,
> The Element of fire is quite put out;
> The Sun is lost, and th'earth, and no man's wit
> Can well direct him where to looke for it.
>
> 'Tis all in peeces, all coherence gone . . .

Donne's dark assessment appeared in 1612, two years after Galileo had published the world's first scientific bestseller *The Starry Messenger* wherein he demonstrated that the heavens are not organized the way people had thought for centuries. In 1543 Nicolaus Copernicus had already invited the sun to change places with "th'earth," but his book *On the Revolution of the Heavens* packaged the news in a way that was not as disruptive as one might suppose. Its earliest readers did not necessarily take the Copernican model as a factual representation of the world. They could read it instead as a mere "hypothesis" useful for making astronomical predictions, drawing up astrological charts, or correcting the Roman calendar. For Galileo (1564–1642), on the other hand, Copernicus's heliocentric model represented the way things really are, and to sensitive Christians such as Donne, the news was not a little disheartening.

It is hard to exaggerate the extent to which a novel understanding of nature can upset our devotional lives. For centuries Christian piety had been tied so tightly to Ptolemaic cosmology that when the Copernican revolution came around, it caused considerable religious anxiety. Similarly, for many Christians today, nothing threatens their sense of religious meaning more dramatically than developments in biology over the last century and a half. Charles Darwin's evolutionary portrait of life is not what the faithful had come to expect from their creator. The randomness, impersonality, and temporal immensity underlying the story of life on earth shattered the benign simplicity of previous conceptions of natural order and divine design.

Donne's disorientation at losing his spatial bearings has now been superseded by the ongoing ordeal of connecting spirituality to evolutionary science and to the new discovery of deep cosmic time.

Spirituality can mean a lot of things, but at the very least, it has to do with the search for a vision of reality that can lift up our hearts and give us a "zest for living."[1] The geocentric model of the universe had functioned spiritually for hundreds of years to elevate the souls of people for whom earthly existence was difficult and deadly. By contemplating the perfectly circular movement of the unchanging heavenly spheres, religious believers assumed they could draw near to a timeless perfection beyond the world of becoming and perishing. Simultaneously they could find in Catholic culture's vertical cosmic hierarchy a negotiable map for the religious journey. Spiritual life was a perilous but rewarding adventure of gradually detaching one's soul from the seductions of matter so as to arrive at eventual communion with an otherworldly God. The prescientific portrait of the universe as a ladder of distinct levels of being still functions as the backdrop for much Catholic devotional and moral life.

Galileo's new method of inquiry, then, launched a cosmological revolution that amounted to a great spiritual loss for many Christians. After Copernicus, modern astronomers, one after the other, forced the stars and planets to undergo a series of demotions that increasingly blurred nature's former transparency to divine perfection. In the ancient world, Aristotle had portrayed the heavens as a quintessential (fifth) kind of reality far surpassing in value the four mundane elements, earth, air, fire, and water. But in early modern astronomy, Tycho Brahe (1546–1601) demonstrated to his disappointed contemporaries that comets and supernovas—both implying change in the heavens—were making their appearance in a cosmic territory previously assumed to be changeless. The heavens were beginning to lose their luster. A bit later, Johannes Kepler (1571–1630) calculated that planets move in ungainly elliptical rather than elegantly circular orbits. And finally, Galileo (1564–1642), inspecting the heavens through his newly upgraded telescope, delivered a decisive blow to the ancient and medieval ideals of celestial excellence. The moon, he demonstrated, is pocked with craters; Venus goes through phases; Jupiter has satellites that do not directly orbit the earth; and the sun is blemished with spots. The heavens are not so exceptional after all. "The Element of fire is quite put out," says Donne, and modern science's "principle of mediocrity" begins to spread over all things visible and invisible.

In a post-Copernican age, therefore, can the spiritual quest discover windows to perfection that may stir us anew to lift up our hearts? Are there any natural openings to a transcendent sacred reality that can expand our souls, heal our anxieties, and give us peace? In the age of science, is there any inspirational equivalent to the flawless heavens that in ages past pointed so palpably to the infinite? One might not think so at first. Modern scientific method, after all, thrives on the belief that what seems remarkable is, underneath it all, quite ordinary. To contemporary scientific secularists, everything in nature, however sacred it might have seemed earlier, is now reducible to mundane material elements governed by impersonal physical laws. According to the outspoken Oxford physical chemist Peter Atkins, for example, whatever in nature seems initially wondrous is really nothing more than elemental matter "masquerading as complexity."[2] So, is there anything in the new scientific understanding of the universe that can recharge us with spiritual excitement and give us a new zest for living?

I believe there is. Even though the birth of modern science called "all in doubt," in the new systems of Copernicus and Galileo, the horizon of a new future for the world came faintly into view, and the spiritual ideal of contemplation began ever so slowly to give way to one of *anticipation*. Presently, as a result of developments in biology and cosmology, science has abandoned for good all static ideas about nature and opened the universe to a vast and previously untraveled domain of new creation now taking shape up ahead.

Few people, however, including most Catholic theologians, seem to be noticing. The cosmos, science has now demonstrated, is still coming into being. This could be spiritually exciting, and not just theoretically interesting, news. Our own existence is part of an enormous and still-unfolding epic of emergent creation. Cosmology is laying out before us a universe calculated to be 13.8 billion years old, and the story is not over. Indeed, it may be just beginning. Nature is narrative to the core, and it still holds the promise of becoming *more*. If so, it may be harboring something momentous for our spiritual and ethical, and not just intellectual, lives. Science is now extending the boundaries of our world, temporally as well as spatially, beyond all previous impressions. In doing so, it offers the opportunity for an unprecedented renewal of spirituality.

Biology, Big Bang physics, and recent cosmological speculation are giving us a picture of nature that allows for the lifting up of hearts not only to the expansive spatial heavens up above but even more to the temporal dawning of a new cosmic future up ahead. Science not only allows us now to enlarge our sense of God spatially beyond billions of galaxies and whatever other worlds there may be, but it also stretches the world out temporally in front of us toward an open future of ongoing creation. Indeed, in spite of pessimistic astrophysical predictions of ultimate cosmic doom, the dramatic understanding of nature that I will be developing in this book allows us to place spirituality on a new footing. It does so not least by allowing us to think of God as the world's absolute future.[3]

Accordingly, my wager here is that Catholic spirituality can now reconnect the natural world more firmly than ever to faith in the biblical God who makes and keeps promises. We may think of God as opening up a new future for the whole universe—and possibly for a multiverse—in the face of all apparent dead ends. The God of Abraham calls not only Israel and the Church but also the whole cosmos into a new future. Together with the prophets and Jesus, we can taste the kingdom of God not so much through contemplation of apparently changeless heavens above, nor in mythic nostalgia for an imagined initial cosmic perfection, as in our anticipation of a future that awaits and will redeem the whole universe.

Vatican II

The Second Vatican Council called for a new synthesis of Catholic spirituality with contemporary science and biblical hope. Those of us who were still young during the Council felt at the time a palpable freshness breaking into our spiritual world. A half-century later we still rejoice in recalling that time of great expectation. The Council and its immediate aftermath seemed to recouple Catholic faith with the wave of hope that had swept over the ancient world at the birth of Christianity. Vatican II left many of us with a deeper conviction than ever that the Church must be forward-looking and that God calls us to move courageously toward an unprecedented future, beginning with the renewal of the earth.

The Council specified in several important ways that the revivification of Catholic spiritual life requires a closer encounter of theology with the natural sciences than had yet taken place. In his "Closing Message of the Council" (December 8, 1965), Pope Paul VI, speaking directly to scientists, acknowledged the indispensability of science for any intellectually robust Catholic vision. "Continue your search without tiring and without ever despairing of the truth," he said.[4] "Never perhaps, thank God, has there been so clear a possibility as today of a deep understanding between real science and real faith, mutual servants of one another in the one truth. Do not stand in the way of this important meeting. Have confidence in faith, this great friend of intelligence. Enlighten yourselves with its light in order to take hold of truth, the whole truth."[5]

Even before the Council came to a close in 1965, *Gaudium et spes* (*The Pastoral Constitution on the Church in the Modern World*) had already called for a fresh encounter of science with Catholic faith and hope. This important document, after noting that the "scientific spirit exerts a new kind of impact" on culture and thought, makes two claims that earlier in the twentieth century would have seemed frightful to most Church officials. The first is this: "The human race has passed from a rather static concept of reality to a more dynamic, evolutionary one. In consequence there has arisen a new series of problems . . . calling for efforts of analysis and synthesis" (#5). The second claim, relying implicitly on the first, adds something else: "A hope related to the end of time does not diminish the importance of intervening duties but rather undergirds the acquittal of them with fresh incentives" (#21). The document then goes on to emphasize that Christian hope must not lead to withdrawal from the world but instead to the "bettering" (#21) and "building" of it (#34).[6] The juxtaposition of these two rather startling propositions provides, I believe, a promising point of departure for Catholic theology in our unfinished universe.

The Council's words, however, may seem so familiar to us now that we could easily forget their revolutionary spiritual implications. Many Christians, including some Catholics, prefer to ignore the two items just cited. Why, they reflect, should we want to reconcile our spirituality with an evolutionary worldview? Isn't evolutionary biology just a cover for materialist atheism? Hasn't Darwin's science been exploited by murderous visionaries to justify unprecedented horrors? So, what "fresh incentives" can an evolutionary picture of the world give to our "intervening duties" as we await the coming of Christ?

I cannot address these questions without calling to mind, once again, the Jesuit priest and scientist Pierre Teilhard de Chardin whom we met briefly in the preceding chapters. In writings still unpublished before his death (1955), Teilhard had already anticipated the spirit of the Council and outlined ways to renew Christian spirituality for a post-Darwinian age.[7] I believe some of his reflections can still guide us as we reflect on the significance of the Second Vatican Council today, early in the twenty-first century. There can be little doubt that *Gaudium et spes* reflects Teilhard's revolutionary ideas. As the celebrated Catholic theologian Henri de Lubac remarked right after the Council, *Gaudium et spes* expresses "precisely what Pére Teilhard sought to do."[8] Robert Faricy, another Teilhard scholar, considers Teilhard's influence on the document to have been "a dominating one."[9] I believe that a Teilhardian spirit of hope, at least tacitly, informed the Council more generally. So it may help us understand its revolutionary exhortations if we look again at Teilhard's efforts to frame an anticipatory spiritual vision for Christians in the age of science.

Teilhard, of course, would lament the Church's present indifference to science. He would see it as not just an intellectual but also a spiritual loss.

Vatican II endorsed, at least in principle, Teilhard's call for the transformation of Christian spirituality from a pre-Copernican contemplation of the heavens to an evolutionary, anticipatory one. Unfortunately, though, relatively few Catholic thinkers during the last half-century have paid much attention to the momentous shift in the spiritual landscape that, according to Teilhard, the new sciences of evolution and cosmology entail. During his own lifetime, few Catholics had even heard of Teilhard, and those who had were often afraid to take him seriously. This is still the case, although unfamiliarity and indifference are now becoming more common than suspicion about his orthodoxy, and most complaints about his doctrinal integrity are the consequence of a failure to read his works carefully.[10] During his lifetime, Vatican censorship had forbidden the publication of Teilhard's unusual reflections on science and Christian faith, and as late as 1962, the same year the Council opened, the Holy Office had distributed to seminary rectors and the heads of Catholic universities a warning (*monitum*) that they should "protect the minds, particularly of the youth, against the dangers presented by the works of Fr. Teilhard de Chardin and his followers."[11] So radical had Teilhard's prescription for the renewal of Catholic spirituality seemed to his religious superiors that they saw to it that he would spend a quarter century of his life doing geological work in China, far removed from the European theological arena where he had already been perceived as too innovative. The long period in China, however, served only to confirm Teilhard's sense of the need for a new Catholic spirituality that would blend contemplation with anticipation.

Church officials, along with many theologians, were initially alarmed by the world-affirming spirituality that Teilhard was building into his evolutionary vision. Remarkably, however, only three years after the *monitum* and a mere decade after Teilhard's death, the Council was acknowledging the need to integrate Teilhard's evolutionary ideas into its emerging understanding of Christian vocation. And by the end of the Council, Pope Paul VI is reported to have remarked that Teilhard's "expression of faith is necessary for us!"[12] In 1967, excitement about Teilhard was reflected in remarks by the influential American TV personality Archbishop Fulton J. Sheen who predicted: "It is very likely that within fifty years when all the trivial, verbal disputes about the meaning of Teilhard's 'unfortunate' vocabulary will have died away or have taken a secondary place, Teilhard will appear like John of the Cross and St Teresa of Avila, as the spiritual genius of the twentieth century."[13] Teilhard died in 1955, but by the beginning of the Council, his ideas on science and Christian faith had become at least vaguely familiar to some of the participants. His spirituality of "divinizing" human action in the world and of "building the earth" is reflected in the

Council's exhortation not to let our hopes for final redemption diminish the importance of "intervening duties" during our present pilgrimage. The Council embraced in principle Teilhard's conviction that what Christians may hope for is no longer reducible to the saving of human souls from a sinful world.

Teilhard, of course, was not alone among Catholic thinkers of his time to integrate secular activity into a sense of Christian vocation, but the intellectual power of his synthesis of evolutionary thought with human action and Christian hope for the world's future was unprecedented. Intellectually as well as spiritually, as Teilhard realized, Catholicism needs to come to grips with science in general and evolution and cosmology in particular, even if this requires an extensive theological makeover. Our spirituality sometimes seems not only pre-Darwinian but also pre-Copernican in its fixation on a static hierarchical model of the universe. Catholic thought tolerates evolution and Big Bang physics in principle, but it has scarcely begun to integrate these scientific discoveries into a spiritual vision that allows us to lift up our hearts anew. Science meanwhile has now made it possible to celebrate the glory of God not just in the splendor of the heavens but also in the astonishing process of organic evolution on earth and in the grander adventure of a whole universe still in process. Science allows us to respond to the threat of spiritual suffocation by lifting our eyes not only to the spatial immensity of the cosmos but also, in the spirit of the apostle Paul, to the future redemption and liberation of an entire universe. More than any other religious thinker of his time, Teilhard realized that the discoveries of the natural sciences can contribute to a bracing new spiritual vision. Even while digging deeper into the geological past, he increasingly understood that the world "rests on the future as its sole support."[14] An evolutionary sense that something big is going on in the cosmos can give appropriate incentive to our "intervening duties," even as it tightens the tie-in between Catholic spiritual life and the biblical theme of promise.

And yet, almost half a century after Archbishop Sheen ventured his bold prediction, Teilhard's synthesis of Christianity and evolution remains largely unknown to most Catholics. Unfortunately, by ignoring the universe, Catholic Christianity has largely failed to undertake the synthesis of science, spirituality, and hope encouraged by *Gaudium et spes*. As I noted in the preceding chapter, when Teilhard began to construct his unique integration of evolution with faith, his own Church discouraged such efforts, clinging instead to pictures of a static universe. However, Vatican II encouraged Catholics to take up the kind of reflection that Teilhard had already inaugurated but left incomplete. In any case, there is no doctrinal or pedagogical reason to postpone any longer the task of exploring what evolution and cosmology now imply for Catholic spirituality. Evolution is the central integrating idea in the life sciences. In the intellectual world, Darwin's ideas have never been more important than they are today, and in cosmology there is no realistic alternative to the unfinished universe associated with Big Bang theory. It is past time, then, for Catholic thought to answer Vatican II's call to connect our spiritual life more closely to the sciences. I can think of no better way to start than by reflecting further on Teilhard's own efforts. Here, and in subsequent chapters, I will not repeat, but mostly apply and build on, the brief summaries of Teilhard's ideas I have already given.

Teilhard's "Analysis and Synthesis"

Evolution and cosmology have profound theological significance simply by virtue of their demonstrating that creation is *unfinished*. After Darwin and Einstein, the universe seems more open than ever to new creation. Looking back over the long cosmic journey, we notice that at each stage something new and significant has always been taking shape, as it were, up ahead. So at the present time also, the universe is open to the emergence of what Teilhard repeatedly calls more being or fuller being. Consequently, when the Council refers to our "intervening duties," it implies that Christian moral and spiritual life must have something to do with our contributing in a human way to making the universe *more* than what it has been and more than what it is presently.

Creation still goes on—no less today than in the beginning. If any of us had been present in the earliest stages of cosmic history, could we ever have predicted back then that the primordial plasma held the promise of eventually becoming stars, supernovae, carbon, life, mind, art, morality, and persons who have the capacity to make and keep promises? Yet, even in its remotest origins, all of these outcomes were already beginning undetectably to take shape "up ahead." Four billion years ago, when microorganisms oozed quietly into the earth's outermost layer, the web of life was already beginning beneath the surface to weave itself into the pattern of a *biosphere*. And after the biosphere had appeared, an even newer sphere of thought, language, art, complex culture, education, moral sensitivity, freedom, scientific research, and technological complexity was already awaiting on the horizon of the earth's future. The noosphere, a new terrestrial envelope, was even then starting to form.[15] Today, theologians and scientists together need to ask what might lie up ahead in the continuing cosmic journey, now that, in the recent appearance of human beings, the universe has at last become conscious of itself?

How, though, does the universe go about becoming more? Only through intercommunion and integration of its individual elements. This is how evolution works. Early on, subatomic units joined up with one another to build atoms; then atoms linked up to create molecules; large molecules eventually came together in living cells; cells coalesced into organisms; organisms built up into communities; and so on. Currently a dominant new evolutionary "layer" consisting of networks of conscious human persons has blanketed our planet. The recurrent pattern of evolution leads us to assume that interpersonal relationships and a shared sense of anticipation among members of our species are essential to prepare the present terrestrial setting for becoming something more. Only mutual love, along with "a great hope held in common,"[16] can bring the distinct personal centers together into an unprecedented planetary super-organic state of fuller being. If so, the cosmic function of Catholic spirituality would include that of fostering human communion and fellowship as a necessary condition for the ongoing growth of the world. A spirituality of anticipation, centered in a renewed eucharistic theology, would acknowledge also that the universe consists of many different kinds of communities and that it attains fuller being not by homogenizing but by differentiating the individual components that make up communities. True union differentiates, as Teilhard puts it.[17] Today this would mean "building the world" with an eye not only to social and economic justice but also to ecological integrity and diversity.

A vision of continuing cosmic creativity, I believe, can serve to lift up our hearts and give new incentive to our spiritual and moral lives after Darwin, Einstein, and Hubble. Contrary to the judgment of cosmic pessimists, as I argue in more detail later on, such hope is completely consistent with the discoveries of science. As Teilhard rightly indicated, there is an obvious general direction to evolution, an ascertainable drift toward more being in the cosmic process up to the present. Evolution as seen through the eyes of a biologist may seem at times to resemble a drunken stagger, for there are many backward movements in the story as well as much standing still.[18] Yet, the long cosmic journey gives evidence of a measurable intensification of organized complexity over time. One can hardly suppress the suspicion, therefore, that this mysterious movement may still have in reserve a future now almost unimaginable. At least, we cannot rule it out. It is easy, Teilhard admits, to be pessimistic when looking at human history over the last several thousand years during which "civilizations crumbled one after another into ruin." "But," he adds with his usual habit of taking a long view of things, "it is surely far more scientific to discern once again, beneath these successive waxings and wanings, the great spiral of life always irreversibly ascending, but by stages, along the dominant lines of its evolution."[19]

In cosmic history so far, as the cosmic stages of development have become increasingly more complex, a vein of subjectivity or "insideness" has intensified in proportion to outward physical complexity.[20] The recurrent pattern of evolutionary advance, having recently brought human consciousness onto the cosmic stage, gives us every reason to suppose that the universe's appetite for more being and deeper interiority has not yet been fully satisfied and that the world is still being invited to become *more* by organizing itself inwardly as well as outwardly around an always new and higher center. Ultimately this center, as far as Catholic faith is concerned, is nothing other than the God who has become fully incarnate in matter and who still, by the working of the Holy Spirit, gathers the folds of the emerging cosmos into the body of Christ.

And Christ still has a future. For Teilhard, the incarnation of God in Christ continues even now to stir up the world. Eventually, one ventures to hope, the entire process of cosmic creativity will find its ultimate destiny in the everlasting redemptive compassion of God. So even if the physical world will eventually "die" of energy exhaustion, as astrophysicists predict, nothing in the cosmic *story* is ever lost or forgotten by God. Our belief in bodily resurrection, whatever else it may mean, includes a hope that the entire cosmic drama, along with the narratives that shape our individual identities, is all saved and redeemed forever by its assumption into God. Evolution, viewed theologically, means that creation is still happening and that God is creating and saving the world not *a retro*, that is, by pushing it forward from out of the past, but *ab ante*, by calling it from up ahead.[21] All events that make up the cosmic story are still being brought together in the Christ who is coming. From beginning to end, therefore, the whole of creation is constantly granted the opportunity of renewal by God, in Christ, through the power of the Holy Spirit.

Our action in the world matters, therefore, because it contributes both to the deeper incarnation of God and to the redemptive gathering of the whole world, and not just human souls, into the body of Christ. The exhilarating Pauline intuition of a universe summed up in Christ (Col. 1:13-20; Eph. 1:9-10) matches our scientific understanding of a world struggling to become more.[22] Our spiritual hope, our "resting on the future," therefore, is simply the flowering and prolongation in human consciousness of what has always been an anticipatory universe. At present, through our own longing for truth, goodness, and beauty, the universe demonstrates that it is still restless for more being. Surely this must all mean something momentous for our spiritual lives.

Finally, attuning one's mind and heart to a doctrine of creation reconfigured in the context of our new awareness of cosmic evolution should also have a bearing on the meaning of worship. As Teilhard writes, "To worship was formerly to prefer God to things, relating them to him and sacrificing them for him. To worship is now becoming to devote oneself body and soul to the creative act, associating oneself with that act in order to fulfill the world by hard work and intellectual exploration."[23] Such an understanding of worship, Teilhard goes on to say, "has no taint of the opium which we are accused with such bitterness (and not without justification) of dispensing to the masses."[24] Teilhard's reinterpretation of worship in the light of evolution and cosmology has seemed too radical for many Christians, but he was right to insist that the intellectual integrity of Catholic tradition depends on our giving a cosmological accent to our understanding of both worship and morality. Viewing all phenomena in the temporally expansive context of evolution, moreover, Teilhard could not exempt his own faith tradition and its theology from undergoing the disturbing phase transitions that occur in other evolving systems. In 1933, he wrote: "I believe Christianity to be immortal. But this immortality of our faith does not prevent it from being subject (even as it rises above them) to the general laws of periodicity which govern all life. I recognize, accordingly, that at the present moment Christianity (exactly like the mankind it embraces) is reaching the end of one of the natural cycles of its existence." And, he adds, this is "an indication that the time for renewal is close at hand."[25]

Life: From Design to Drama

Is the theological vision outlined in this book intellectually defensible? Today many scientifically educated people doubt it. An increasing number believe that evolutionary biology provides so complete an understanding of life that theology has no place in the world of right understanding. "Evolutionary naturalism," as we may label this relatively new but confident creed, claims that natural selection of random adaptive changes in organisms over an immense period of time can account in an ultimate way for all living and behavioral traits, including human intelligence, moral aspiration, and religious longing. After life on earth arose spontaneously almost four billion years ago, the aimless Darwinian mechanism for evolutionary development took over the job of creating organisms and species, a task that religion had formerly assigned to God.

The impersonal evolutionary engine of creation is said to be powered by three mindless ingredients: accidental organic variations (now understood to be caused mostly by genetic mutations), blind natural selection of heritable traits, and an enormous amount of time. This simple three-part Darwinian recipe, according to the evolutionary naturalists, can account all by itself for *every* aspect of life. Descent, diversity, adaptive design, suffering, death, sex, human intelligence, morality, and religion are all now subject to an exhaustively Darwinian explanation.

For example, according to evolutionary naturalists, the exquisite "design" of organisms requires no divine intelligent designer. Chance, selection, and deep time are enough. Furthermore, if organisms had been designed by "a beneficent Creator," writes biologist Jerry Coyne of the University of Chicago, they should have no "design flaws." A perfect God would have created an impeccably engineered world. Yet, organisms are not perfectly built, and so God cannot possibly exist.[1] After Darwin, says the University of Washington evolutionist David Barash, the scientific understanding of life rules out any place for theological accounts of life.[2] Life's designs do not have to be planned, so there is no job for a creator to do. Mindless natural selection is enough to explain every evolutionary outcome, no matter how "intelligently" put together it may appear. Rendered superfluous by Darwin, the designer-deity can now be forgotten for good.

Dramatic patience

By linking the whole issue of God's existence to the question of how to account for complex organic design, the evolutionary naturalists share a lot more than they are willing to admit with their anti-Darwinian religious adversaries. God, for Darwinian atheists and ID advocates alike, must be a "designer" to fit their joint job description of an acceptable deity.[3] Both anti-Darwinian theism and evolutionary atheism, however, fail to observe that life, deep down, is a *story* before it is a display of intricate structures. And it is the *dramatic* shape of life, not the exquisite architecture of living cells and organisms, that most merits theological attention.

Unlike design, the drama of life demands that observers *wait* until an entire series of events has played itself out before deciding whether it makes any sense. In a staged comedy or tragedy, to carry the analogy further, spectators do not insist that the production wrap everything up neatly in the first or second act. Watchers have to wait. And so it is with the stream of life. Presently, we cannot know for certain where the drama is going. It is not unreasonable, therefore, to approach it in a spirit of expectation. If life is a drama, we should be looking for narrative coherence, not mechanical virtuosity. Appreciation of a drama requires tolerance of present ambiguity for the sake of maximizing the impact of the whole since a drama's unfolding will be circuitous, indeterminate, and perhaps inelegant in the short run. The dramatic flow of life, I suggest, requires that we view it presently not as perfection but as promise. Only those who wait will not be put to shame (Isa. 49:23).

A theology of evolution, moreover, will be interested in what transpires throughout the whole cosmic narrative, not merely in the biological chapters that take up the last four billion years. A scientifically informed theology of nature, therefore, will not complain that adaptive design is imperfect—which it surely is—but will instead wonder why the whole natural world is endowed with the capacity to unfold as a story at all. Theologically speaking, what is most remarkable about our unfinished universe is not its pageant of patterns, but its dramatic way of being. If the universe carries a meaning, it would come to expression in narrative development rather than instantaneously perfected organization. Stories, not isolated physical or biological constructs, are the mediators of meaning. For this reason we must be critical of both evolutionary naturalists and ID devotees for the narrowness of their search for God in improbable instances of cellular and organic complexity. ID proponents profess to have found in cells and organisms a kind and degree of order that requires an intervening supernatural causal agency. Meanwhile their hyper-Darwinian opponents, no less obsessed with the search for perfect design, consider the absence of efficient engineering in organisms to be irrefutable proof of God's nonexistence. Look, they exclaim, at the ungainly way in which the components of our ears and digestive systems are assembled. Would an "intelligent designer" devise such convoluted and inefficient contraptions? And wouldn't a competent mechanical engineer do a much better job?[4]

A dramatic understanding of nature, I suggest, can tolerate evolution's errant experiments. These are completely consistent with life's unfolding as a suspenseful epic in which significant outcomes such as mind, language, and moral aspiration are permitted to appear only gradually, in keeping with the world's overall allowance for emergent probability. Ancient and medieval metaphysics, including the impressive Thomistic synthesis and the long Catholic tradition of natural theology, knew nothing of nature's lengthy temporal emergence, and for that reason they are ill-prepared now to deal theologically with questions about the meaning of it all. We rightly embrace the Thomistic sense of the mystery of being and classical theology's astonishment that the world exists at all, but after Darwin and Einstein, we have to wonder also why nature has a narrative disposition when for all we know it might not have had one. In addition to ontological shock at the sheer givenness of being, there is now room for "narrative shock" at the fact that the cosmos has the shape of a story still unfolding.

If the universe has anything like an overall way of presenting itself to human understanding today, it is not that of mechanical elegance but of *narrative anticipation*. Someone obsessed with design, whether Dawkins or an ID devotee, feels compelled to ask why the universe was not perfectly finished at the start in an instantaneous act of completed creation. If an intelligent designer exists, why so much waste of time before getting around to the creation of life? Why is the cosmos so extravagantly immense and so old if a deity is in charge?

In response I propose that the "design" of the universe—with its blend of deep time, spatial immensity, large numbers of elements and opportunities, and its mix of predictability and probability—is that of a story somehow aroused and powered by what is *not-yet*. What seems most remarkable about the universe, apart from the fact that it exists at all, is that it is a long, unfinished story still open to new and indeterminate outcomes. Understanding evolution, therefore, means looking for a narrative meaning that holds the universe together from up ahead. To those who are willing to wait, twists and turns in the cosmic process that seem erratic when measured by current human standards of engineering efficiency may turn out to be consistent with a narrative coherence that can emerge only in a future still out of sight.

Again, it is not instances of design but instead the dramatic character of the cosmos that is of primary interest theologically. Why so? First, because the cosmic story, like all stories, may in principle carry hidden meanings in spite of all suffering, perishing, and death, and, second, because the story may presently be far from over, thus opening up a horizon of hope and final redemption for the whole of creation. Even though we are still in the dark, the story may have a meaning or meanings that can be approached only through hopeful anticipation.

The news that the universe is an *unfinished* story is so recent and undigested that traditional Catholic theology, with its cult of an absolute conceived of as an eternal present, has barely begun to think in depth about what the cosmic drama might mean for our understanding of God, Christ, redemption, and other theological themes. Only yesterday did we learn that life and evolution long ago jumped astride an already existing narrative movement of matter. Evolution, we now understand, did not take off from a Democritean swarm of indifferent atomic units destined to be aimlessly shuffled and redistributed across the ages. Rather, the emergence and transformations of life linked up with a cosmos disposed from the start to be a dramatic performance.

Three ways of looking at the cosmos and evolution

Is this narrative universe, however, compatible with a biblically based hope that the story has a permanent significance? Since the story is still unfolding, theological speculation can be only tentative. Indeed, the provisional and revisable status of both scientific and theological speculation is itself consistent with the story's being unfinished. If there is a meaningful story being told, in any case, the only direction in which to look for its full intelligibility is that of the future. Only on the horizon of the not-yet could cosmic coherence begin to show up, if at all. Hope then is the epistemic risk that the human quest for understanding has to take if the universe is now unfinished. Only by adopting the attitude of watchful expectation could we ever detect even the faintest manifestations of meaning. I call this vigilant posture of expectation "cosmic hope" to distinguish it from the allegedly more realistic disposition of "cosmic pessimism" espoused by scientific naturalists, and from the "otherworldly optimism" characteristic of traditional Catholic spirituality.[5]

My question then is whether cosmic hope is an intellectually plausible stance for Catholic thought to take in view of contemporary science. For centuries, cosmic hope, the first strains of which emerged in Abrahamic religion, has had to contend, on the one hand, with the oppressive gravity of cosmic pessimism and, on the other, with the escapist levity of otherworldly optimism. Cosmic pessimism, as espoused by the majority of scientists and philosophers today, is convinced that the universe is headed toward a far-off and final extinction, and that eventually it will be as though life, consciousness, and culture had never existed at all. Otherworldly optimism, in contrast, looks forward to each personal soul's escaping from the physical universe and finding an eternal home in heaven. Cosmic hope, for its part, looks toward a final redemption not only of human persons but also of all life and the whole cosmic story to which life is inextricably connected.

These three ways of looking at the cosmos and evolution, as sketched briefly in Chapter 2, may be called, respectively, the archaeological, analogical, and anticipatory visions of nature. Let me now expand on this triad, especially because it will become increasingly important to both my critique of evolutionary naturalism and my more specific proposals in subsequent chapters for the renewal of Catholic theology.

1 The archaeological vision (metaphysics of the past)

The archaeological vision seeks to understand the present condition of the universe, and to predict the cosmic future, by digging back as far as it can into the cosmic past and then imaginatively retracing the series of blind causal steps that have led up to the present. This retrospective way of looking at the world is the characteristic mind-set of scientific modernity. It interprets present and future realities as simply the uncoiling of earlier physical states governed by uncaring *laws* that will ultimately drive the whole cosmic mass toward an abyss. The archaeological vision fosters a style of inquiry and, in the academic world, a standard of research that looks primarily to what has already happened to find the key to understanding everything that is taking place right now and that will occur in the future.

This archaeological mode of inquiry typically assumes that the appropriate way to comprehend the world is by breaking down present complexity into its simpler elements.[6] In the context of Big Bang cosmology, the intellectual and experimental decomposition of complex entities into their elementary constituents is simultaneously a journey into the far distant past. Scientific analysis follows the cosmic trail back to an epoch when the universe existed only as dispersed subatomic units. Philosophically speaking, this archaeological approach comes to rest in a "metaphysics of the past" according to which what is "really real" consists of elemental bits and fixed laws operative in the earliest phases of natural history.[7] It rules out not only the existence of God but also human freedom.[8] In this intellectual setting, the universe is not a narrative but instead an aimless movement of mindless material stuff across vast periods of time.

Evolutionary naturalism with its reductively materialist understanding of Darwinian biology adheres implicitly to a metaphysics of the past insofar as it interprets all physical occurrences, including the eventual emergence of mind, as the outcome of inviolable physical routines mixed in with chance occurrences and an unfathomable enormity of time. Adhering rigorously to this formula, strict scientific materialists in effect deny that anything truly new can ever happen. Whatever is going on now or whatever will occur later—even if it seems new at first—is not really so. To cite Peter Atkins once again, it is merely past simplicity "masquerading as complexity."[9]

2 The analogical vision (metaphysics of the eternal present)

Otherworldly optimism, the second rival to cosmic hope, follows the still influential metaphysics of the eternal present that for centuries has shaped Catholic thought and spirituality. I refer to it as the *analogical vision* since it views earthly and temporal things as imperfect analogies of a changeless supernatural or archetypal perfection. In spite of its explicit rejection of tragic pessimism, the analogical vision shares with the archaeological vision a tendency to suppress what I am calling cosmic hope. It is optimistic about the soul's destiny but pessimistic about where the cosmos will end up. The salvation to which it aspires is one in which the human soul is liberated from matter, space, and time. According to this static and vertical understanding of human destiny, the phenomenal world is a mere shadow of a heavenly realm immune to transience. All things "here below" are relatively deficient in being and value. They receive their significance only in proportion to their degree of temporal participation in a timeless absolute. Accordingly, all that gets accomplished in time and human history, apart from growth in personal sanctity, is eventually nullified by being absorbed into an eternal oneness and sameness. By constantly measuring the results of human accomplishment and effort against the backdrop of timeless perfection, the analogical vision can make the dramatic texture of our own earthly lives seem insignificant except as preparation for entry into a fully spiritual realm of being. As we shall see later on, it may therefore lend support to a moralistic perfectionism that leads in turn to a religious cult of shame and expiation.

The analogical vision has been the main conceptual setting for traditional Catholic sacramental spirituality. Its metaphysics of the eternal present has accompanied the Church's religious devotion for centuries. Even today it remains compelling for the simple reason that it responds directly to human anxiety about perishing. By offering an eternal refuge from the erosions of time and the terrors of history, and by providing tidy answers to the questions raised by death, evil, and human suffering, a metaphysics of the eternal present continues to enjoy considerable appeal, both spiritual and ethical. Unsurprisingly, some of its most stalwart devotees care little or nothing about evolution, the destiny of the universe, or even the long-range accomplishments of human history. In contrast to a biblically inspired cosmic hope, a purely analogical vision sponsors spiritual withdrawal from the world instead of preparing it for the coming of God.

3 The anticipatory vision (metaphysics of the future)

I am arguing that Catholic theology in a post-Darwinian world must now pay close attention to science as well as to the deepest—and that means biblical—origins of our theological traditions. The biblical discovery of the future may now link up with the world revealed by cosmology and evolutionary biology. Together, the biblical sense of promise and the scientific discovery of an unfinished universe provide the foundation of an "anticipatory vision" that can serve as the conceptual framework for contemporary Catholic theology. This third perspective, one that understands the cosmos as a drama still in process, expects the world's intelligibility—its narrative coherence—to emerge only "up ahead" in the future renewal of *all* of life and the *whole* of creation in God.

We can understand the world most realistically, therefore, by adopting the posture of anticipation and hope, not by retrospective analysis or vertical flight. The universe hangs together not from behind but from up ahead. Breaking things down analytically in an archaeological or atomistic manner without simultaneously turning our attention toward yet unrealized future possibilities leads only to a sense of nature's ultimate dismemberment. The further back we journey imaginatively into the cosmic past, in other words, the more things fall apart. In contrast, as I am claiming here, whatever hints we may get of the world's intelligibility will show up only by our looking in the direction of the future, in other words, by putting on the habit of cosmic hope. Cosmic hope is not an illusory escape from "reality," as cosmic pessimists take it to be, nor is it comfortable with a piety that treats the physical universe as a temporary training ground for human souls. Rather, cosmic hope is the steady turning of our hearts and minds toward the horizon of the cosmic future in search of possible meanings arising now only uncertainly.

Consequently, what deserves to be labeled illusory is not cosmic hope but the academically endorsed belief that scientific analysis alone can make the universe intelligible. Analysis can help us retrace the stages in the cosmic story up to the present, but by itself it cannot tell us what the story is about or where it may be going. Only a patient, long-suffering hope, not tragic resignation or mystical flight, deserves to be called realistic as long as the universe is still on its way. Teilhard provides a helpful image of the direction in which we need to look for cosmic meaning:

> Like a river which, as you trace it back to its source, gradually diminishes till in the end it is lost altogether in the mud from which it springs, so existence becomes attenuated and finally vanishes away when we try to divide it up more and more minutely in space or—what comes to the same—to drive it further and further back in time. The grandeur of the river is revealed not at its source but at its estuary.[10]

This futuristic approach looks downstream in the direction of the cosmic delta. It is therefore confluent with the Abrahamic traditions in which God comes to meet and redeem the world from out of the future. New developments in biology and cosmology reveal an emergent universe that renders the themes of promise and hope consonant with our new scientific sense of the cosmos. Even while twentieth-century biblical theology was rediscovering Jesus's passionate longing for an earth-transforming kingdom of God, Teilhard was exploring the continent of the cosmic future—a future *for* this world, not an escape from it. "Seeing" the world in this way shifts our theological search for the real and the intelligible away from grounding in the past or an eternal present, and toward the perpetual dawning of the world's future.[11]

Again, I am calling this third approach an "anticipatory vision" to distinguish it sharply from the archaeological and analogical approaches that may have seemed to exhaust the possible ways of interpreting the universe. As I recalled in the preceding chapter, it was one of the great accomplishments of Vatican II to have exposed Catholics, however fleetingly, to a new sense of the world's promise based on our growing awareness of an evolutionary universe. Unfortunately, the Council's forward-looking way of understanding God and the world has yet to take deep root in Catholic intellectual and religious life. Part of the reason for this reluctance is that most Catholic thinkers probably find it hard to imagine how the still unavailable future can function as the *foundation* of the cosmos and life. How can the future be the "sole support," as Teilhard calls it, of the entire universe? Doesn't it make more sense to look to the fixed past or an eternal present for the most stable and immovable ground on which to base our intellectual, moral, and spiritual lives? How can the future, which is not yet present, really be foundational?

My response will take more than a few pages. Let me begin, though, by observing that Teilhard himself struggled throughout his life to find something imperishable in which to anchor not only his inquiring mind but also his religiously anxious temperament. It is wrong to accuse him of being indifferent to perishing, evil, and suffering, as a careless and often secondhand reading of his voluminous writings has sometimes concluded. His whole life was a search for a way to address the fact that nothing seems to last. Even in early childhood he had looked to iron and rocks to find stability in the midst of what he already took to be a universal perishing.[12] Later on, in early adulthood, he was tempted to calm his restlessness by merging his personality with pure materiality. What could be more permanently grounding, after all, than losing oneself in the eternal bosom of impersonal matter?[13] The fact that Teilhard chose rocks as his field of research is consistent with his natural longing for what endures. Since the past is already fixed and cannot change, scientific analysis seems, at first sight, to provide a physical consistency in which the restless mind and soul can drop anchor. Teilhard could appreciate, therefore, why many of his fellow scientists leaned toward materialism. Mystical fusion of the human self with lifeless and mindless matter can be an irresistible lure, offering the bliss of oblivion to those who are weary of life, crushed by the demands of the present and uncertain about the future.

Teilhard was also aware of his own disposition to live in the past, one of the characteristics of a natively melancholic temperament. Yet he came to realize that the further scientific analysis took him into the terrestrial and cosmic past, the more the world dissolved into dust instead of delivering the stability for which he longed. The deeper he journeyed into geological prehistory, the more removed he felt from the splendid realms of personality, cultural creativity, moral aspiration, and religious longing—all instances of what he called "spirit"—that have emerged only as the cosmos has moved narratively from a fixed past toward an indeterminate future.[14]

Materialism appeals to that undeniable part of us that longs to merge with a purely objective realm of being where no subjects or persons are around to shock us into life.[15] All of us, as existentialist philosophers have appropriately observed, feel the impulse to shed our freedom by immersion in the sphere of the purely objective. Teilhard too was aware of the ease with which one can relax into the impersonality of mere matter, but he came to realize that neither emotional nor spiritual fulfillment will be found by moving in that direction. Even more important for my purposes here, however, Teilhard rightly perceived that the evolutionary naturalist's metaphysics of the past is unsatisfying intellectually. While many humans experience the lure of the impersonal in the guise of sensuality divorced from personality, Teilhard knew of a parallel temptation in the realm of the mind. He called it the analytical illusion, the fiction that we can arrive at a final understanding of reality by breaking everything down, including organisms, cells, and persons, into irreducibly lifeless and impersonal physical elements.[16]

A mysticism of pure matter may appeal to our instinct for simplification but not to our nobler search for what is really real. Only by looking toward the future can we discover the fullness of being. A close correlation exists, in other words, between an anticipatory turn to the future and a view of nature that allows for emergent freedom and personality. This is why Teilhard grew increasingly dissatisfied with a purely analytical excavation of nature and life. Even though he had earlier sought in iron and rocks the kind of solidity that would place his world on an unmoving foundation, by the 1930s he was feeling at times a strange sense of nausea when digging into his treasury of fossils. Increasingly, he thought of himself as a "pilgrim of the future" making his way back "from a journey made entirely in the past."[17] His forays into the past, though scientifically essential, left him unsatisfied intellectually as well as spiritually. As scientific research takes our thoughts deeper into the remote cosmic past, he continued to argue, nature becomes more diffuse since the primordial scattered atomic bits we find there lack tight linkage to a unifying center. The deeper the mind ventures into the cosmic past, the more the world it finds there becomes decentered and lapses into indefiniteness and deadness. This is why Teilhard always found it more interesting to talk about outcomes than origins.

To be clear, the Jesuit geologist allowed ample room for archaeological analysis in any purely scientific understanding of the world. He was never an opponent of the reductive *method* of natural science, only of the reductionist metaphysics that granulates everything real into dunes of unconsciousness. He maintained an enthusiastic intellectual interest in geology throughout his life even when that field of research was no longer his central preoccupation. He realized that by looking into the past, science has unwittingly gifted us with data that allow us to think of nature as a drama. Without scientific excursions into geological, biological, and cosmological prehistory, our understanding of nature and life—as well as of God—would be considerably impoverished. As the result of analytical science, we are now able to appreciate, more than our ancestors did, the long struggle of life that led to our ability to walk upright, to swing our arms freely, to communicate by language, and to cooperate morally with our fellow humans. Scientific journeys into the past have brought us a deeper sense than ever of the magnificent, but also tragic and sacrificial, narrative of nature that lies behind and beneath our physical, intellectual, moral, and religious lives. However, remaining in the past once our thoughts have traveled there, and expecting a full account of life to burst forth simply from retrospection, will only distract us from the pursuit of being, intelligibility, and truth. These transcendentals, compounded with the note of futurity, beckon from up ahead. Both mind and soul are restless until they allow themselves to be grasped by the horizon of the world's future and try to fathom how fuller being emerges only there in new, unpredictable, and ultimately redemptive ways.

Interpreting life

How, then, if we adopt an anticipatory vision and a futurist perspective of the world, are we to make sense of evolutionary phenomena such as descent, diversity, design, death, suffering, sex, intelligence, morality, and religion?[18] What will life look like if we search for its intelligibility not in the temporal past or eternal present but in the future opened up by hope? Since the drama of life is not yet complete, the items on our list may have meanings that an excavation of the past or a contemplative glance at the eternal present cannot uncover all by itself. In a universe that is still coming into being, after all, nothing makes complete sense except in the long run. What follows then is a brief look at the life-world as examined from an anticipatory frame of reference. To get a glimpse—since this is all we can expect—of what an anticipatory vision of the life-world may discover, however, let us begin, for the sake of comparison and contrast, with a brief summary of how the analogical and archaeological visions interpret the nine features of life listed on page 55 above. Here, for historical reasons, I start with the analogical.

The analogical vision

Descent. Why do so many species of animals closely resemble one another? The answer often given by the classical, pre-evolutionary philosophy of nature is that family resemblances, for example those that exist among different species of primates such as monkeys, chimps, baboons, and humans, exist because they are all versions of an archetype residing eternally in a Platonic heaven or in the mind of God. The many earthly versions "descend" vertically—by virtue of divine creation—from a heavenly analog, and they participate by different degrees in the timeless sacred original. Descent, in other words, implies a relative deficiency of terrestrial forms in comparison to their celestial models. The earthly renditions participate in the heavenly world, but only imperfectly.

Diversity. Why are there so many different kinds of life? To adapt the medieval perspective of Thomas Aquinas, living diversity exists so that what is lacking in one kind of life in analogously manifesting the divine generosity may be supplied by another, and what is lacking in the latter may be supplied by something different from that, and so on. Thus the diversity of life helps compensate for the imperfection of earthly instances of descent by multiplying natural sacraments that collectively bring to expression the infinite ingenuity and generosity of God in a hierarchically ordered way.[19]

Design. Why are organisms adapted so exquisitely to their particular environments? It is because of an eternal divine wisdom that permeates nature and orders everything to its appropriate goal. Design is never perfect, but whatever imperfection organisms have is not the fault of their creator. Finite beings can represent only inadequately the perfection that exists on high. Wherever design seems imperfect, it may also be because of sin and the world's estrangement from God.

Death. Why did death come into the world? Ultimately, because of sin. Nevertheless, the analogical vision offers the comforting news that at death, each person's immortal soul may attain final liberation from the earthly veil of tears and, because of the sacrificial death of Christ, arrive at a climactic union with God. The theme of bodily resurrection is also part of classical Catholic belief, but it has usually taken second place, at least in the spirituality of most of the faithful throughout the ages, to the idea of the soul's immortality. As we shall see in Chapter 9, a renewed theological understanding of the tight connection between our bodies and the cosmos, and of cosmic destiny to our personal redemption, becomes possible with the arrival of evolutionary biology and the new cosmology.

Suffering. Suffering makes sense in traditional Catholic thought as expiation for human sin. The pain we experience is ultimately the result of a primordial human fault that ruined an initially paradisal creation. Our actual sins participate in the original sin against God. Suffering, therefore, is somehow justified since a proportionate amount of pain is needed to compensate for sin. The expiatory vision, as we shall call it, requires atonement for sin by a suffering savior. Catholic tradition, of course, offers other ways of interpreting suffering, but the Church's theology, as expressed, for example, in St Anselm's satisfaction theory of redemption, has made suffering intelligible to countless people throughout the ages by way of the myth of expiation. It still does. We examine this theology of expiation more closely in Chapter 7.

Sex. Sexual activity is the way in which human beings and other living creatures implement God's Edenic commandment to "be fruitful and multiply." This pre-Darwinian understanding of sexuality still prevails in official Catholic moral teaching, which has been dominated more by the theme of fertility than concern for personal development and interpersonal intimacy. An obsession with fertility is symptomatic of a natural law theory that, partly because of its reliance on a metaphysics of the eternal present, has had the effect at times of diminishing the value not only of nature but sometimes, in my opinion, of persons and the quality of personal relationships as well.

Intelligence. The experience of our minds' restless longing to understand the world has been accounted for in classical Catholic thought by the assumption that creation participates sacramentally in a transcendent divine intelligence. It is the world's finite mirroring of an unrestricted divine light that lures the human mind to seek an ever deeper understanding of things. Human reason, however, has been vitiated by sin, and so revelation is needed to compensate for the clouding of our minds by evil.

Morality. According to the analogical vision, our inner experience of moral aspiration can be accounted for sufficiently if there exists an infinite and transcendent goodness that arouses in us the responsiveness we call conscience. The closer the soul comes to the infinite goodness of God through the practice of virtue, the more liberated human desire becomes from purely this-worldly attachments. The life of virtue suffused with a sense of detachment from the material world is essential preparation for final union with God. However, neither virtue nor final union with God can be realized without the supernatural assistance known as sanctifying grace.

Religion. The restless human heart (*cor inquietum*) makes it impossible for us to adjust fully to a world of becoming and imperfection. Religion exists ultimately, therefore, because God's timeless beauty and goodness have already quietly touched each soul, awakening in it a longing for final union with the divine, a marriage that also requires an ethic of detachment.

The archaeological vision

Descent. To evolutionary naturalists, the family resemblances among species, instead of being distinct versions of a perfect archetype existing eternally in the mind of God, are nothing more than the outcome of accidental modifications of ancestral organisms preserved by blind natural selection and laws of heredity operating invariantly in life's evolutionary past.

Diversity. The millions of species that exist today constitute only a small percentage of the total number of living experiments churned up by evolution during ages past. That so many different experiments have occurred, according to evolutionary naturalists, is testimony to the fact that evolution is essentially random and blind. The impersonal mechanism of natural selection never had any particular outcomes in mind from the start. Our own existence is also the unintended outcome of an aimless evolutionary process.

Design. The appearance of adaptive design in living organisms, according to Darwinian naturalists, has nothing to do with divine wisdom. In evolutionary history, most attempts at adaptation failed, and the "fit" ones we observe today are only a tiny remnant of the total number of impersonal experiments. Moreover, countless "design flaws" exist, and no adaptation is ever perfect, thus rendering the idea of a divine designer unnecessary.

Death. Death makes good sense because of evolution's need for genetic variety. Since most genetic variations are nonadaptive, each individual must eventually die and make room for others as a way of guaranteeing a numerically sufficient population of adaptive organisms. If organisms never died, there would be insufficient genetic variety. Death increases the probability that enough random variations will occur to permit adaptation and reproduction by a lucky few. We humans are mortal, therefore, not because of sin but because we are a species that has evolved in the same way as others.

Suffering. The capacity for suffering in living organisms becomes sufficiently intelligible if we understand it simply as an evolutionary adaptation. Suffering warns a sentient organism when it is in danger of being injured or killed, thus enhancing the probability of that organism's surviving and reproducing. Even this adaptation, however, is always imperfect, another indication to the evolutionary naturalist of the superfluousness of religious ideas of divine intentional design.

Sex. By allowing not only for reproduction (which in simple organisms can take place asexually) but also for a sufficient variety of genetic combinations, evolution chanced upon sex. Humans today invest sex with multiple meanings, of course, but originally sex had no other meaning than that of providing a sufficient number of genetic possibilities for the adaptation, survival, and reproduction of a few fortunate organisms.

Intelligence. The human mind with its exceptional capacity for understanding and knowing exists today because large complex brains capable of reflection and prediction happened to give our remote ancestors a reproductive advantage over organisms less richly endowed. Their rapidly developing brains and nervous systems gave our evolutionary predecessors the cleverness to escape predators or to devise shelter and weapons. We have inherited the adroit brains of our ancestors, but our own capacity for thought (even when shaped by culture) is *ultimately* no less the result of blind natural selection than any other living trait.

Morality. The fact that humans have a tendency to care morally for one another can be accounted for by tracing the evolution of cooperative instincts back into our animal prehistory. Morality first came into the story of life faintly when various ancestral species accidentally developed mutually cooperative instincts that increased their probability of surviving and reproducing. So there is no need to explain or justify human morality or conscience by bringing in the idea of an eternal goodness or divine command as a source and standard of behavior. We can adequately understand morality by tracing its origins back to altruistic, self-sacrificial behavioral tendencies that just happened to be adaptive in the evolutionary past and that were then passed on through genetic rules of inheritance.

Religion. Since, according to evolutionary naturalists, God does not exist, there can be no plausible theological explanation or justification for religion. Religion can be accounted for in purely natural, evolutionary terms. Likewise the *persistence* of religion, including the staying power of the idea of God, has a purely natural explanation. People are religious only because in the remote human past some of our ancestors found life more endurable in harsh natural and social environments when their genes, now inherited by their descendants, accidentally tricked them into believing in supernatural powers that made their lives seem worthwhile and that provided a (seemingly) supernatural system of rewards and punishments that, in turn, promoted adaptive moral conduct.[20]

The anticipatory vision

Descent. We may discover the true meaning of all aspects of life, including descent, only by looking toward the cosmic future. Without in any way denying evolutionary *science,* an anticipatory interpretation of life's descent notices that each organism, including each human person, is born into a dramatic current of life that is still flowing. Instead of looking only upstream (with the archaeological approach), or pointing vertically beyond the stream (with the analogical approach), cosmic hope looks downstream toward the delta of evolution and hence toward a cosmic fulfillment that now lies out of sight. Cognizant of our present kinship with all other species in the wide river of living experiments, an anticipatory theology of evolution is enchanted not only with the grandeur of it all, as was Darwin, but even more with the prospect that the whole current of life is still flowing toward future creation. The anticipatory vision wagers that fuller being—and final redemption—is even now taking shape "up ahead." We are free, however, either to reject or to embrace the lure toward more being—that is, the call toward deeper consciousness, freedom, relationality, and love.

Diversity. Fully aware of Darwin's three-part recipe for life—accidents, natural selection, and deep time—an anticipatory perspective views organic diversity as an expression of life's dramatic groping toward increasing differentiation, more intense being, and wider beauty. Divine generosity consists of opening the unfinished universe to a new future symbolized, for example, by Jesus's proclamation of the coming kingdom of God and his longing "that all may be one." Along with the universe's overall convergence toward unity, there is also a general movement toward increasing complexity, novelty, and nuance. True union or convergence simultaneously individuates and differentiates the converging units.[21] The ultimate *unity* toward which

God, the goal of evolution, summons creation coincides with creation's maximum differentiation, which in the human sphere means maximum *personalization*.

Design. The overall "design" of the universe is that of narrative anticipation. From an anticipatory point of view, the important question is not whether complex adaptive design points to deity but whether the drama of life carries a meaning. Specific instances of cellular and organic design are essential steps in the emergence of increasing complexity and consciousness, but we do not grasp their meaning as long as we try to understand them apart from the larger drama of life. Appreciation of this drama, in turn, requires patience and putting on the virtue of hope. The imperfections that exist in all particular instances of living design are consistent with the uncertain dramatic flowing of life toward possible future narrative coherence. The icy glaze of design has to thaw if the universe is to open itself toward more being and richer intelligibility. Again, it is only by expectation, not by objectification, that we may presently begin to sense the full reality and ultimate destiny of life and the universe.

Death. Scientifically speaking, death makes sense as a prerequisite for genetic diversity in life's evolution, as Darwinian science rightly indicates. From the point of view of an anticipatory metaphysics, however, the death of individual organisms must be situated—more broadly than evolutionary naturalism allows—within the drama of a universe still coming into being. In a fully finished and completely intelligible universe, death has no legitimate place: "Death will be no more" (Rev. 21:4). However, the universe is not yet finished, so death finds a foothold in the darkness of a still imperfect world.

Suffering. Darwin observed rightly that suffering is an evolutionary adaptation, but it is much more than that. It is part of the drama of life's struggle toward "more being." Like death, suffering has no intelligible place in a fully finished creation, but in a still-emerging universe, suffering arises in company with sentience, striving, and subjectivity. Suffering is not primarily expiation or pedagogy (see Chapter 7). It is an inevitable aspect of a dramatic universe that is only now awakening to consciousness, freedom, and the capacity to love.[22]

Sex. Sexual activity can be understood scientifically as both a necessity for reproduction and a rich source of genetic variety. Traditionally, Catholic theology has interpreted sexual fertility as a sacrament of divine love and creativity. To suppress fertility has seemed, in traditional Catholic teaching, equivalent to turning our backs on the divine commandment to be fruitful and multiply. An anticipatory metaphysics, however, moves the discussion of sexuality away from preoccupation with issues of fertility and from matter-despising versions of the archetypal vision of existence. It is also critical of the inevitable tendency of materialist philosophy to depersonalize sexuality by first depersonalizing the universe. The anticipatory vision interprets the emergence of persons as a vital part of the cosmic drama. It seeks to redeem human sexuality from the dualism of classical, otherworldly theology as well as from the impersonality that accompanies a materialist metaphysics of the past. An anticipatory reading of human mating, for example, might interpret sexual communion not only as a sacrament but also as a promise of final intimate union of the cosmos with its creator.

Intelligence. Through the awakening of our own inquisitive minds, the universe anticipates a future condition of emerging coherence. To the Darwinian naturalist, human intelligence is simply an evolutionary adaptation, and in the classical hierarchical vision the human mind is an imperfect reflection of divine intelligence. From the point of view of a metaphysics of the future, however, the emergence of intelligence is a crucial chapter in the drama of a universe opening itself to a future of "more being." "To be" is good. "To be more" is even better. To be conscious is good. To be more conscious is even better.[23] An anticipatory worldview, therefore, understands our mental activity as more than just an adaptation or an imperfect temporal participation in a timeless divine wisdom. Our individual cognitive striving is also, at a deeper level than we usually notice, a function of the whole cosmos groping through our minds toward a climactic union with infinite being, meaning, and truth. This striving can stay on course, however, only if it is animated by faith, hope, and love.

Morality. To the evolutionary naturalist, human morality is a highly developed instance of the adaptive requirement for members of a species to cooperate. Cooperation has enhanced reproductive possibilities in life's evolutionary past, for example in social insects. In a metaphysics of the eternal present, on the other hand, human moral aspiration points us toward the perfect goodness from which we are presently estranged (because of sin) but to which we are still mysteriously bound here below. An anticipatory perspective, for its part, views moral inclination as a free human response to the infinite God who calls the whole cosmos toward the goal of new creation. The anticipatory vision locates the source of moral obligation proximately in the stream of cosmic becoming into which each of us is born, and ultimately in God's calling creation toward a new future. The ethical life consists not of spinning our moral wheels in a squirrel cage of ethical challenges, nor merely of pedagogical or ascetic practices devised to improve our moral character. The good life, more fundamentally, is one that responds to the call to contribute, even in excruciatingly monotonous ways, to the great work of ongoing creation in a still-unfinished universe. Any moral aspiration that is not energized by cosmic hope, therefore, lacks sufficiently serious motivation to be sustainable throughout many generations.

Religion. To the evolutionary naturalist, religion, like morality, is merely an adaptation or a by-product of other adaptations. And the analogical vision views our religious restlessness as the human heart's response to the hidden presence of the infinite in all created beings. However, an anticipatory metaphysics, without denying the insights of either biology or traditional theology, understands religion to be the characteristic way in which the cosmos, now become conscious of itself, opens itself through our prayer, gratitude, fidelity, and worship to the inexhaustible source of more being up ahead, to the God who is the world's absolute future. This book argues that this third perspective can provide the framework for an "anticipatory" Catholic theology that is both deeply rooted in the Bible and fully aware of scientific method and discoveries. Subsequent chapters will expand on the sketch just given.

Evolution: From Outcomes to Opportunities

As I have just argued, the most appropriate place for Catholic thought to engage biological science is not on the question of how to explain organic "design," but on that of how to make sense of the dramatic blend of predictability, contingency, and temporal duration that allows life to be a story rather than a senseless series of mechanical states. The basic "design" of the universe—if such a term is not interpreted too narrowly and statically—is that of allowing events to unfold narratively, that is, in the mode of a story. And stories can carry meaning.

Any narrative requires a blend of accidents, regularity, and time. So does evolution. *First*, the accidents occurring in genetic mutations and natural history keep the course of life from being a foregone conclusion. Accidental events, since they are unpredictable, give to life the essential narrative aspect of indeterminacy and, hence, openness to surprise. *Second*, the regular functioning of natural selection, along with subsidiary physical and chemical "laws," gives coherence and continuity to the series of events that make up the story of life. In line with the metaphor of life as a drama, the predictable physical routines in nature may be thought of not as laws—a metaphor derived too narrowly from juridical experience—but as analogous to "grammatical rules" to which the story must adhere if it is to be the expression of meaning. The metaphorical reference to laws fits perhaps the obsolete deterministic, archaeological vision of nature in which everything is driven by past mechanical causes. But now that nature is seen to have the format of a narrative, a change of language seems necessary when depicting what gives consistency to the dramatic sequence of events.

Scientific discourse can no more avoid the use of metaphors than religions can, so now that science has uncovered the dramatic texture of our unfinished universe, it is more appropriate to think of the required regularity along the line of syntax rather than deterministic laws. The inviolable "mechanism" of natural selection, for example, functions in the story of life analogously to the way syntactical regulations function in the writing of a literary narrative. All of life has to fall within the "grammatical" constraints of natural selection, but this rule still allows for unpredictable outcomes as the story moves along. A metaphorical shift from law to grammar is appropriate to a dramatic universe whose meaning, whatever it may be, is not determined by the past but is open instead to an unpredictable future patterning. The emergence of new and deeper meaning does not violate the grammatical rules but employs them as enabling conditions for the expression of new narrative content. Third, and finally, the enormous amount of time required—nearly four billion years— gives the story of life on earth a narrative breadth and depth that previous ages of religious reflection knew nothing about.

Today, evolutionary biologists debate the respective roles that accidents, natural selection, and deep time play in the evolution of life. The late paleontologist Stephen Jay Gould, for example, theorized that accidents in natural history are the main engine of evolutionary invention.[1] Richard Dawkins, on the other hand, claims that natural selection, understood deterministically, is the main cause of evolutionary change and diversity.[2] And both Gould and Dawkins view time itself or, more precisely, a great abundance of time, as somehow explanatory of the evolutionary outcomes I listed in the preceding chapter. Anyway, whatever the respective roles assigned to chance, law, and time may be, all three ingredients show up in one degree or the other in every evolutionary account, thus, at least tacitly, presupposing the fundamentally narrative character of life.

It seems fitting, therefore, that a theology of evolution will direct its attention primarily to the question of the religious meaning of the three-pronged suite of factors that allow life to be a story at all. The blend of probability, regularity, and time endows nature, broadly speaking, with a narrative constitution that was already operative in the cosmic process long before the actual emergence and evolution of life. The interesting theological issue, therefore, is not first of all why divine providence permits so much randomness and so much impersonal blind necessity in the life-world. Rather, the relevant question is why the basic structure of the universe is that of an unfolding drama rather than a pointless battle of chance against necessity.[3]

In recent decades, science has expanded enormously our sense of the spatial immensity of the natural world and the temporal magnitude of the cosmic story. Typically, however, scientific naturalists have taken the lengthening of time and the widening of space as proof of human insignificance and, above all, as "evidence" of the nonexistence of God. Citing what they call the Copernican Principle, they have insisted that terrestrial human existence is trivial and insignificant when placed against the backdrop of science's ever-expanding sense of time and space. However, from this book's perspective, the large numbers, spatial distribution, and enormity of time underlying evolution and the cosmic process give to nature an overall narrative makeup that science has generally failed to notice or ponder.[4] A universe spread out over deep time and spatial immensity, in combination with an incalculable number of physical units and temporal moments, is a universe in which significant things may eventually take place when viewed from a narrative point of view. In this new cosmic context, human existence, seemingly crushed by the enormity of space and time, may in principle carry a *dramatic significance* that fails to show up on a purely materialist map of the universe.

Although Bernard Lonergan does not highlight the narrative quality of nature as explicitly as I am doing here, his notion of emergent probability gives to the unfathomably expansive temporal and spatial properties of the physical universe a dramatic intelligibility that mechanistic philosophies of nature fail to notice.[5] For materialists, the insurmountable theological difficulty raised by evolutionary biology and Big Bang cosmology is why, if God (usually understood as an "intelligent designer") really exists, the universe has to be so wastefully old and extravagantly immense. If a creator exists, and if this creator is interested in bringing about life and consciousness, why so much temporal duration and spatial excess prior to the emergence of living and thinking organisms in nature—and perhaps on only one lonely planet at that? Evolutionary naturalists, who almost invariably follow a materialist metaphysics of the past, attribute whatever takes place in nature to "chance" and "necessity," as though these abstractions could somehow be the main agents of evolutionary outcomes. My point here, instead, is that from a narrative point of view, the physical and biological indeterminacy depicted by the word "chance," and the lawful regularity of nature referred to by materialist biologists as "necessity," when blended with the seemingly wasteful enormity of space and time, become remarkably intelligible as essential ingredients of narrative or drama. And we need to remember, once again, that it is narratives, not mechanical constructs, that are the primary carriers of meaning.

The mystery of matter, then, is somehow the mystery of its narrativity. The physical universe has from the start played host to dramatic occurrences. Understanding nature as narrative, of course, does not tell us what the story is all about, since an essential feature of any story, short or long, is that spectators must wait for its meaning to emerge. Likewise a dramatic understanding of the universe requires that we wait for its intelligibility to arise on the horizon of the future. Contrary to the pervasive cosmic pessimism that rules over current intellectual culture, such a dramatic vision of nature leaves room for hope. It is significant to theology then that beneath the surface of life and its evolution there resides a more fundamental cosmic narrative matrix. Even before living beings ever appeared in natural history, the physical setting out of which life eventually emerged had already connected openness to the future (made possible by contingency) and the inviolable grammatical rules (referred to imprecisely as the laws of nature) into an irreversible flow of time, thus giving nature a rich narrative-historical weave. And even if nature is construed broadly enough to include a multiverse, this in no way removes, but only magnifies, its fundamentally narrative way of being and becoming.

I conclude, then, that it is not from the interplay of blind chance and necessity but from the narrative womb of nature that life and its evolution have come to birth. Theology does not take this narrative amalgam for granted but, going beyond the limits proper to scientific inquiry, asks why the universe (or multiverse) would be graced at all with the potential for being a drama. To avoid asking this question at all, or to dismiss it as silly, would be a stultifying repression of the desire to know. Once the question of cosmic purpose is asked, however, theology adds the caveat that our coming to an awareness of whatever meaning may be lurking in the drama requires a patience that can survive only in an atmosphere of hope. Unlike scientific naturalism, an anticipatory theology is willing to wait, since "hope that is seen is not hope" (Rom. 8:24).

A contemporary Catholic theology of nature

The cosmic drama may be read at many different, noncompeting levels. Astrophysics reads it one way, but chemistry, geology, and biology read it in other ways. Each reading level leaves something out, and each offers a different sense of what is going on in the story of nature and life. And yet the various readings need not oppose or contradict one another. Attempting to read the universe theologically, likewise, need not compete or conflict with scientific readings. Catholic theology, for example, will scan the drama of life without taking its eyes off the revelatory image of God given in biblical and traditional portraits of Christ, but this focus in no way stands in opposition to scientific readings.

One way of reading the universe theologically is suggested by centuries of Christian reflection on the picture of Christ as the revelation of God's humility or God's "descent."[6] In this reading, the image of a humble God whose very essence is self-giving love supplants all ideas of a divine potentate or engineer that cosmic pessimists have in mind when they talk about "God" and "design" or when they complain about blind chance and impersonal necessity in nature. For Catholic theology, moreover, the image of God's humble descent is not optional but central to our understanding of the ground and source of all being. It should also be the lens through which we look at the story of life.

Scientific naturalists no less than ID proponents, on the other hand, typically think of God as a cosmic engineer or architect. Yet, as Pope John Paul II recently testified in his encyclical *Fides et Ratio* (1998), the God of Catholic faith and theology is, in fact, an unreserved love which, in creating and redeeming the world, undergoes a dramatic *kenosis,* that is, a self-emptying. This dramatic understanding of God's descent comes from a long tradition of prayerful meditation on the Cross and the self-sacrificial obedience of Jesus. Hence the chief purpose of Catholic systematic theology, as Pope John Paul claims, is to highlight the divine *kenosis.* The humility or descent of God is a "grand and mysterious truth for the human mind, which finds it inconceivable that suffering and death can express a love which gives itself and seeks nothing in return."[7] When we read the story of life theologically, therefore, we need above all to connect it to the drama of God's self-emptying love as revealed in the image of the obedient and crucified Christ.

To make this connection, theologians must begin their work by dispelling any lingering doubts about the self-emptying love of God. In my own conversations with scientific naturalists, however, my highlighting this understanding of God is sometimes an obstacle to mutual understanding. The most significant stumbling block to faith in God after Darwin, I have found, is not the "design flaws" in evolution that make naturalists doubt the existence of a designing God. Rather, it is the shocking idea of God as a self-humbling love that allows nature to be dramatic rather than mechanically put together. The response of evolutionary naturalists to such a proposal is that God, if God exists, *must* be a competent engineer—a magician, really—who should have made the world perfect in the beginning. This diminutive idea of God, of course, has come partly from their exposure to biblical literalism, ill-formed natural theology, and ID advocacy with which they typically confuse Christian theology. Catholic theology, however, is not obliged to defend the idea of the intelligent designer against which evolutionary naturalism directs its animosity.

Regretfully, the classical Catholic metaphysics of the eternal present has also often grounded its theology of nature in the notion of divine *order* rather than in the drama of divine *kenosis.* An anticipatory theology, on the other hand, approaches the question of the meaning of evolution by looking at nature while simultaneously embracing the startling revelation of God's descent as the deeper narrative underlying the creative process. The astounding picture of a self-emptying God, I believe, is a fruitful starting point for Catholic theological reflection on the meaning of an unfinished universe. By allowing our reflections to be shaped by the deeper drama of divine descent, we discover that the results of evolutionary research pose no real intellectual or spiritual threat to the substance of Catholic faith. Our approach still allows ample room for trust in the unfathomable divine wisdom and power that underlie everything, but divine wisdom is eternally furled in humility, and divine omnipotence transfigured by an infinitely self-sacrificing love.

Of course, the image of a self-emptying God, according to the authoritative interpreters of Christian faith beginning with St Paul, can be appreciated only if we are personally drawn into its transformative power. There can be no true encounter with the God of Jesus Christ without allowing the Gospels to restructure our lives and our sense of what constitutes true being and genuine power. What usually passes as reason and logic is not enough to bring about this personal conversion. As the apostle Paul observed, and as Pope John Paul recently reaffirmed, the image of God's humble descent is inaccessible to philosophical or scientific understanding. The idea of a self-emptying God fits no conventional conceptual scheme devised by human speculation. It fits least of all the idea of God as an obsolete *scientific* hypothesis, an idea of "God" that Richard Dawkins enthrones as central to his understanding of Christian theology and then tries to depose in his version of the New Atheism.[8] Nor does the image of divine descent find a comfortable home in intellectual systems devised by great philosophers such as Plato, Aristotle, Plotinus, Descartes, Kant, or Spinoza.

The new picture of an unfinished universe, however, can accommodate comfortably both the theology of God's descent and the Abrahamic sense of divine futurity that I have been highlighting all along. Catholic theology, in its conversations with science, may even think of God's descent and God's futurity as two sides of the same eternal divine self-gift to a still-emerging universe. The *kenosis* of God is not an occasional but an eternal dimension of God's self-giving identity. The humility of God not only opens up room for the creation of a world that is *other* than God, but it also allows that same created world to have an always new future. In the wide clearing opened up by an infinite love, creation is permitted to unfold narratively toward an open future rather than being driven coercively toward a predetermined end.

The Christian revolution in God-consciousness points to a love that calls the world into being as something distinct from the Creator. The image of divine descent, therefore, challenges the idea that God creates in the manner of Aristotelian efficient causation. To think of divine action simply as efficient causation would place theology in competition with science. The divine mystery may instead be thought of (metaphorically, of course) as the goal and future of the cosmic process, inviting and not compelling creation to actualize new possibilities relevant to every stage of its emergence. If God is self-giving love, then God wants the creation to become something *other* than God, and ultimately it is God's love of otherness that allows creation to be dramatic. So, to arrive at full otherness vis-a-vis its creator, the world's significance would consist, in part at least, of hosting the drama of emergent life, consciousness, and freedom. Then, with the emergence of freedom comes the associated capacity for morally motivated conduct and religious longing, but also the possibility of enormous evil and estrangement from God.

Evolution as opportunity

In this theological reading of the cosmic story, evolution is not so much a set of blindly determined outcomes as a matrix of opportunities. God does not mechanically manufacture entities in a completely finished state of being. The eminence of divine creativity consists not of pushing the world forward from out of the past but of calling it toward more being from up ahead in the future. God's creative love is both a lure and a letting-be. It longs to open the world to always new possibilities of being—including the finite kind of freedom that we humans cherish and, at our best, seek to share with others. Human freedom is in a sense "uncaused" since it could not be freedom if it were the consequence of the application of deterministic "laws." Freedom is not so much outcome as opportunity, and in a wider sense, so also is evolution. What I have been calling a metaphysics of the future provides a setting that is intellectually and theologically suitable for both evolution and human freedom. It features opportunistic openings that are inconceivable in terms of the deadening determinism that accompanies a materialist metaphysics of the past. The universe, at least as cosmic hope sees it, is grounded ultimately in an eternal drama going on in the inner life of God, a drama that leaves an opportunity-space for creation in general and human freedom in particular. Moreover, as I argue in the following chapter, a Catholic theology of evolution must make no claims about God that ignore the struggle, loss, and suffering that have accompanied the *whole* story of life's evolution and not just human history.

Predictably, of course, scientific naturalists will protest. In nature and evolution, they claim, there are really only physical outcomes, not narrative opportunities. Nature, so the pure physicalist believes, is no drama but simply an impersonal chain of events governed by inviolable laws acting blindly on mindless material units. Since stories require openness to surprise, a materialist or determinist view of nature forbids anything to happen narratively. In that case, evolution is simply necessity disguised as drama. Everything that happens in nature is the outcome of (efficient) causal necessity, and the job of science is to cut through the apparent drama to the determinism beneath. Freedom, like the idea of God, therefore, is an illusion.

This denial of freedom flies in the face of everything conscious human subjects, including determinists, know intuitively to be the case. Yet it meets only weak opposition in a scientistic intellectual world. Even though, as I argue in Chapter 10, materialist metaphysics implicitly contradicts the very minds that entertain it, it remains the dominant setting for contemporary intellectual conversation. It can be debunked, I am convinced, only by a *conversion*—and that is exactly what it will take—to a metaphysics of the future that requires our putting on the virtue of hope.

Unfortunately, more often than not, Catholic thinkers have expressed their opposition to materialism and determinism ineffectively. They have sought refuge in a classical metaphysics that separates the realm of matter from that of spirit. Classical theologies have connected human consciousness, freedom, and faith directly to an eternal present residing in an ontological space cut off from the temporal world. This traditional metaphysics, however, concedes too much to the materialists by tolerating the idea that a mindless and lifeless material world exists objectively "out there" and that it is linked only tenuously, if at all, to the world of subjectivity "in here." Even more problematic from a theological point of view, however, is that a metaphysics of the eternal present clips the wings of hope by virtually negating the dramatic achievements of time and history. Like materialism, the analogical worldview fails to appreciate the narrativity of nature in which life, mind, and freedom can become intelligible as emergent chapters in a larger story still going on.

A metaphysics of the future, by contrast, makes room for both freedom and divine creativity by first training our minds to view nature dramatically. God's selfless creative love provides an immensity of time and a wideness of space for creation to *become itself* as something clearly distinct (though not separate) from its creator. God's sustaining of the narrative structure of nature, therefore, is a much deeper and more intimate kind of involvement in the world than would be the case if divine action consisted essentially of engineering or tampering with things in the direct manner that evolutionary materialists, creationists, and ID advocates consider appropriate to their idea of a masterful, magical deity. Again, the theological position I am laying out here understands God's relationship to the universe in a manner analogous to the way in which Jesus related to others, namely, by opening up a new future in the face of what would otherwise be dead ends. God is not one actor among others in the cosmic and evolutionary drama, but instead the ground of what we may call the "narrative cosmological principle." God acts presently with respect to evolution and the cosmic process by creating (and becoming incarnate in) the narrative loom on which an indeterminate and still-unfinished cosmic drama continues to be woven. The idea that God directly and simply engineers creation is inconsistent, I believe, not only with science but also with the revelatory image of God in Christian faith.

Because of our faith in the presence of the Spirit of God, we may view the narrative of nature as in some sense God's own story. Exactly how the story will turn out we cannot say, for God's creative will includes enabling the world to create itself—even permitting it to make mistakes in the process. A universe deeply loved by its creator will always have some degree of autonomy or else it would lapse from story into stone. So the randomness in evolution is not contrary to divine providence. Even during the universe's long prehuman run, and in its microcosmic makeup, there is room for spontaneity, a quality highlighted by contemporary physics. Without the narrative ingredient of contingency, the universe could never have been the great adventure that it is. Nor could it ever have been a universe at all, theologically speaking. It would have been an ornament attached passively to God's being rather than a reality distinct enough from its maker to become alive, conscious, and free.

Accordingly, if Darwin is right, then the classical religious idea of a perfectly ordered world divinely molded by its creator in every detail from the very beginning would make little sense theologically. A universe imagined to be created instantaneously by God could not even be a world at all. It could hardly stand dialogically in relation to a personal God. Nor could creation be perfectly laid out in every detail from the start. Nature, says the evolutionary philosopher Henri Bergson, "is more and better than a plan in course of realization." "A plan," he continues, "is a term assigned to a labor: it closes the future whose form it indicates. Before the evolution of life, on the contrary, the portals of the future remain wide open."[9]

A creation truly distinct from its God is given leave to experiment with a wide, though not unlimited, range of possibilities of "becoming more," even if God's creative latitude also opens up the possibility of tragedy. Are suffering and death, then, inevitable aspects of an unfinished universe? And why would God create a universe without finishing the job immediately, hence eliminating the prospect of suffering and death from the outset? Here we can only speculate, but it seems to me that an instantaneously complete original creation would leave the world devoid of life, freedom, and a real future. Such a world would be an outcome stripped of opportunity. A world devoid of the possibility of becoming more—that is, one incapable of the self-transcendence essential to life and freedom—would be less significant and certainly less interesting than the one we have. Theologically, any creation called into being by a humble, self-giving, and promising God could not spring into full bloom immediately but would take its time, becoming actualized dramatically rather than magically, as it responds to its creative calling.

If so, the probabilistic portrait of life evolving through the play of chance, regularities of nature, and large numbers spread out over the vastness of space and time is consistent with the reality of a caring and compassionate God. The narrative pattern of evolution fits comfortably into a worldview that features as its ground, center, and future a self-giving God who offers the universe—and perhaps a multiverse—an open future in which to become actualized in new, though also dangerous, ways. The appropriate stance toward such a universe on our part would be that of patience, a posture that is not fully distinguishable from faith and hope. Patience, however, is not one of the virtues congenial either to ID advocacy or contemporary scientific naturalism's requirement that the universe be perfectly designed here and now, once and for all.

The suffering of sentient life

But can an anticipatory theology of nature make sense of the ruthless and often painful way in which natural selection transforms life? Suffering, from the point of view of natural science, makes sense as an adaptation that enhances an organism's probability of surviving and reproducing. Darwin himself thought that suffering is "well adapted to make a creature guard against any great or sudden evil."[10] Even though suffering is as imperfect as other adaptations, it can often signal when an organism is in danger and thus help it survive long enough to have descendants. Yet, the degree of suffering often seems out of proportion to its adaptive value, and this is one of the reasons why Darwin understandably rejected the idea of divine design. He sensitively speculated, for example, that a benign providence could not have willed that wasps should lay their eggs inside healthy caterpillars so that their larvae upon hatching could feed on living tissue. Other evolutionists are no less disturbed than Darwin by nature's allowing so much suffering. Richard Dawkins, for example, complains about the "pitiless indifference" of a universe that allows life to develop in the way Darwin depicts.[11] The late biologist George Williams referred to nature as a "wicked old witch" for permitting so much pain and struggle.[12] And the paleontologist Stephen Jay Gould declared that because of evolution's amoral insensitivity to pain, humans may no longer reasonably look to nature for ethical guidance.[13]

Keep in mind, however, that these avowedly atheistic protests against life's excessive suffering come from sensitive persons who are part of the whole chorus of humans crying out for a world devoid of pain and death. No less than deeply religious people, they have tacitly allowed themselves to be grasped in the depths of their own moral consciousness by the value of compassion. And they believe in the absolute *rightness* of their moral protests. The problem is that their materialist worldview cannot justify this assumed absoluteness. Materialism by definition, after all, reduces everything ultimately to a state of total lifelessness, mindlessness, and valuelessness. For the materialist, there is no transcendent domain of absolute goodness that could conceivably ground the unconditional quality that their protest against pain requires if it is to be taken with complete seriousness. For if the protest, like the pain, is merely an evolutionary adaptation, or at best a product of the protestors' cultural conditioning or temperamental inclinations, there would be no firm ground to support it, and we would not be obliged to take it seriously.

By contrast, an anticipatory metaphysics can provide a solid foundation for the protest. It does not look back to the world's past for justification but allows us instead to be grasped by the world's absolute future. Indeed, the ageless human cry for redemption is possible at all only because this future—where pain, tears, and death exist no longer—is already taking us into its embrace. I believe it is essential, therefore, to look at the suffering of all sentient life, and indeed the whole of biological evolution, in terms of the dramatic, unfinished universe in which the threefold Darwinian evolutionary recipe comes into play. Recalling what I said earlier, a world without accidents would be painless, but it would also be lifeless, futureless, and devoid of freedom. Everything would be fixed in place permanently from the start. Likewise, in the absence of reliably functioning grammatical rules (so-called laws of nature), the world would have no narrative coherence and hence would remain unintelligible. An atomistic assembly of unrelated bits of matter suspended timelessly in space, if this could even be imagined, would be a world without pain. But such a world, it goes without saying, would be flat and featureless in comparison with the mountainous one we have. Finally, a world that is not endowed with ample temporal opportunity to unfold experimentally and incrementally would also be unremarkable in comparison with an evolutionary one. Such a counterfactual world is much less attractive, at least to those who love life and freedom, than the hazardous Darwinian world that allows life to be dramatic. For in removing all of the drama from the cosmos, we would be robbing it of its matrix of meaning as well. Whether life's suffering has a meaning, however, and how Catholic theology is to approach this question in the context of an unfinished universe, are topics for the following chapter.

Suffering: From Expiation to Expectation

Catholic thought still struggles to make sense of the four billion years of life's evolution. Our theologians renounce scriptural literalism, of course, but Catholic religious instruction generally reflects a prescientific understanding of cosmic and human origins. Teachers and homilists continue, at least unconsciously, to imagine the universe as having been made perfect by an almighty Creator in the beginning. They may accept in principle the traditional doctrine of ongoing creation (*creatio continua*), but from all that I can tell, they usually fail to reflect on the opportunities for theological renewal resident in Darwin's revolutionary understanding of life.

Moreover, our theological anthropology has failed to ponder the gradualness of *human* evolution.[1] Even though Catholic theologians do not turn away from the undeniable trail of evidence for human evolution, as do creationists and other opponents of Darwin, our understanding of sin, suffering, evil, and redemption still generally ignores scientific accounts of how modern humans came to be on earth during the last 200,000 years. Even though paleontological evidence for the slow and ragged arrival of anatomically modern humans out of a primate and hominid ancestry is now abundant, theologians and catechists habitually speak about the creation of human beings as though it occurred instantaneously at some definite moment in the remote past. *The New Catholic Catechism* reflects this literalism.[2]

Although a plain recital of biblical narratives of origins may have pedagogical suitability for the young, educated Catholics require a more sophisticated understanding of biblical texts that deal with origins. In the religious formation of adults, Catholic teaching generally turns a blind eye to the scientific information essential to an educated vision of the natural world. Secular thinkers assume, therefore, and not always without reason, that Catholic faith requires of scientifically educated people a stultifying sacrifice of intellect. This is a scandal, both theologically and pastorally. Departments of theology routinely fail to deal head-on with evolution and other scientific discoveries, and science education is seldom part of the training of priests and religious educators. In my own experience, the closest most Catholic pastors come to paying attention to Darwinian science is in their granting permission to lay adult religious educators to hold lectures or sponsor study programs on topics related to science and faith. Having offered numerous lectures and workshops on evolution and theology in American Catholic settings over the last several decades, I now recall only a handful of occasions where local clergy participated. Furthermore, the theological mind-set of most Catholic bishops remains largely untouched by science except for issues relating to human fertility, technological advances, and (occasionally) environmental abuse.[3] Even though Catholic history includes periods of expansive openness to lively intellectual discussion, substantive ecclesiastical conversations about evolutionary science are uncommon today.[4] Consequently, many scientifically educated Catholics now struggle intellectually to hold onto their faith.

As long as theology, preaching, religious education, and official Church documents fail to connect the promises of Jesus or the Church's sacramental vision to the fascinating new portraits of an unfinished universe, Catholicism cannot be an inviting spiritual home for many educated seekers. The timidity with which official Catholic thought typically engages evolutionary science shows up, for example, in Pope Benedict XVI's 2007 encyclical *Spe Salvi*. Commenting on a text from St Gregory Nazianzen, the Pope writes that

> at the very moment when the Magi, guided by the star, adored Christ the new king, astrology came to an end, because the stars were now moving in the orbit determined by Christ. This scene, in fact, overturns the world-view of that time, which in a different way has become fashionable once again today. It is not the elemental spirits of the universe, the laws of matter, which ultimately govern the world and mankind, but a personal God governs the stars, that is, the universe; it is not the laws of matter and of evolution that have the final say, but reason, will, love—a Person.[5]

Inspiring as his profession of faith may be, Benedict does not address here, or anywhere else that I am aware of, the questions educated readers will ask about how divine "governance" overrules "the laws of matter and evolution." Unintentionally, Benedict even seems to place theology into a competitive relationship with science. It is not essential that an encyclical engage in extended theological argument, of course, but scientific readers will certainly wonder how it is that the laws of matter do not have "the final say." Even if Benedict personally sees no conflict of science with faith, the fact is that countless scientists, philosophers, and other educated people do. After Darwin, the idea of a personal God who providentially "governs the stars" seems less believable to them than ever. And even though Albert Einstein and other physicists may have dimly discerned an "intelligence" behind the laws of physics, it is not easy for secular thinkers to discern any religious meaning at all in the fog of evolutionary accidents, waste, and wild experiments.

One thoughtful evolutionary philosopher who has commented explicitly on Pope Benedict's theology of nature is Philip Kitcher who speaks for many philosophers and biologists today in claiming that "a history of life dominated by natural selection is extremely hard to understand in providentialist terms." Puzzled by the long and painful evolutionary struggle of life on earth, Kitcher concludes that "there is nothing kindly or providential about any of this, and it seems breathtakingly wasteful and inefficient. Indeed if we imagine a human observer presiding over a miniaturized version of the whole show, peering down on his 'creation' it is extremely hard to equip the face with a kindly expression."[6]

The question of evolution's compatibility with divine providence has been central to conversations in theology and science ever since Darwin's day, but Catholic theologians have only occasionally dealt with it directly and systematically. They have been content to comment vaguely that science does not contradict the teachings of the Church, but they have undertaken little sustained investigation of the relationship between theology and evolutionary biology. Even Pope John Paul II's 1996 endorsement of evolutionary biology refrained from addressing the difficulty scientists and philosophers have in reconciling the randomness or contingency in evolution with trust in divine providence.[7] A 2004 International Theological Commission, working under the supervision of Cardinal Joseph Ratzinger who later became Pope Benedict XVI, took up the issue of contingency and divine governance, but it assumed that classical Catholic philosophy and theology, especially that of St Thomas Aquinas, is intellectually resourceful enough to make good sense of the accidents in evolution. It failed to consider the possibility that Darwin's science requires a much more sweeping overhaul of theological understanding than a prescientific metaphysics allows.

"According to the Catholic understanding of divine causality," the Commission summarily remarked, "true contingency in the created order is not incompatible with a purposeful divine providence." Yet, the document made no attempt to address the sort of difficulties that Kitcher and many other scientists and philosophers have flagged. It simply asserted that accidents in nature fall "within God's providential plan for creation." It appealed for support to Aquinas, citing the *Summa Theologiae*: "The effect of divine providence is not only that things should happen somehow, but that they should happen either by necessity or by contingency. Therefore, whatsoever divine providence ordains to happen infallibly and of necessity happens infallibly and of necessity; and that happens from contingency, which the divine providence conceives to happen from contingency (*Summa Theologiae*, I, 22, 4 ad 1)." The Commission then went on to say that "neo-Darwinians who adduce random genetic variation and natural selection as evidence that the process of evolution is absolutely unguided are straying beyond what can be demonstrated by science. Divine causality can be active in a process that is both contingent and guided."[8] Finally, the Commission stated that "an unguided evolutionary process—one that falls outside the bounds of divine providence—simply cannot exist because . . . [according to Aquinas] 'all things, inasmuch as they participate in existence, must likewise be subject to divine providence'" (*Summa* I, 22, 2).

Here the theological question of *how* to reconcile contingency in the world with divine providence is left hanging. The document rightly admits that true accidents exist in nature, but from the point of view of critics such as Kitcher, the real issue still remains: What does it say about God that the randomness in evolution and the undeserved suffering of sentient life fall under divine providential governance? Kitcher, along with most other contemporary scientific skeptics, cannot imagine how the idea of providential "guidance" makes any sense at all in view of natural evolutionary processes. He even quotes St Basil the Great (as cited by Pope Benedict XVI): "Some [Basil writes] . . . deceived by the atheism they bore within them, imagined that the universe lacked guidance and order, as if it were at the mercy of chance."[9] But as far as Kitcher and many other critics of theology are concerned, Darwinian science has simply restored to respectability what Pope Benedict considers to be the pagan, pre-Christian fatalistic view that nature and life are indeed at "the mercy of chance."[10] Countless other honest people also find it hard after Darwin to embrace the Christian exhortation to trust in a providential God.

As "faith seeking understanding," Catholic theology must try harder to understand how natural processes can be both contingent and "governed," to use Pope Benedict's term, or "guided" as the International Theological Commission states. Are "governed" and "guided" the most appropriate terms in which to speak of how providence relates to the meandering, experimental, and ungainly, not to say cruel, ways of evolution? Reference to providential governance and guidance in a world riddled with misery seems to exacerbate the problem of theodicy, that is, the persistent question of how God's capacity to order events could also be consistent with an infinite love. Moreover, if governance and guidance entail a "plan" or "design," critics of theology rightly wonder how such terms protect the Creator from the accusation of complicity in the excessive suffering of sentient life. Designations such as governance, guidance, design, order, or plan, when associated with divine providence, raise serious questions about the adequacy of traditional Catholic metaphysics to deal with the undeniable degree of accident and indifference in Darwinian process.

It seems to me, moreover, that such terms as "guidance" and "order," when associated with the idea of divine providence, are too closely tied to the perfectionist metaphysics of the eternal present to frame a contemporary Catholic theology of evolution. For this reason I am arguing that a shift from the metaphor of divine governance toward that of God as goal—in accordance with a metaphysics of the future—is more appropriate to a theology for an unfinished universe.[11] Accordingly, the place for theology to engage evolution is not on the question of the origin of design but on that of the meaning of life's drama. In this chapter I argue that an exclusive theological reliance on the metaphors of design, guidance, and order in our depictions of divine action also lends too much weight to theologies that interpret suffering primarily as *expiation*.

Order and expiation

Our new awareness of an unfinished universe, one whose internal arrangement has never been fixed or finalized, raises serious questions about the meaning and value of expiatory theologies of suffering and redemption. There is a close connection, after all, between the idealization of order or design on the one hand and the demand for expiation on the other. Biology and cosmology, however, now render both the metaphysics of the eternal present and the ancient expiatory understanding of suffering theologically questionable. Although he did not develop the point in systematic detail, Teilhard was rightly sensitive to the tie-in between expiatory theology and the theological assumption of a perfectly ordered initial state of creation. In 1933 he wrote:

> In spite of the subtle distinctions of the theologians, it is a matter *of fact* that Christianity has developed under the over-riding impression that all the evil round us was born from an initial transgression. So far as dogma is concerned we are still living in the atmosphere of a universe in which what matters most is reparation and expiation. The vital problem, both for Christ and us, is to get rid of a stain. This accounts for the importance, at least in theory, of the idea of sacrifice, and for the interpretation almost exclusively in terms of purification. It explains, too, the pre-eminence in Christology of the idea of redemption and the shedding of blood.[12]

An expiatory understanding of suffering survives and thrives in the shadows of an idealized cosmic order. It presupposes a metaphysics in which change means the defilement of an initial integrity, and in which development often appears to be a violation of order that may need to be compensated by suffering. The theme of reparation by paying a penalty in pain can lead at times to hopelessness and self-hatred. Yet it still lives on in contemporary Catholic religious education and popular piety. The recent controversial film *The Passion of the Christ* produced by actor Mel Gibson represents an approach to the problem of evil and suffering that many Catholics still find redemptive: the more serious the moral offense, the more intense the suffering needed to expiate it. So by portraying in the most graphic images the stripes of Jesus, the innocent victim, the film's message is that the faithful can now be assured of full atonement for their sins. Order has been restored through suffering.

Expiation, it needs to be said, is not the only way in which Catholic theology has understood what God is doing in the incarnation, crucifixion, and resurrection of Jesus. Citing the writings of St Irenaeus and Duns Scotus, theologians have also connected Christ's significance to the doctrine of creation and not solely to that of redemption.[13] Today Roman Catholic theologians are also paying closer attention to Eastern Christianity's theme of divinization as more central to the work of Christ than satisfaction, reparation, or expiation.[14] Nevertheless, the idea that an originally perfect order was disturbed by a sinful human act of rebellion against God *in the beginning,* and that expiation is required to make things right again, continues to provide much of the dramatic backdrop of Catholic intuitions about Jesus's significance.

The order/expiation theological formula, when taken alone, implies that the work of Christ is essentially atonement for an initial transgression. Here the Cross is a necessary condition for repairing a state of divine and cosmic order that was soured by human sin in the beginning. When it is taken literally, the expiatory vision of suffering turns human moral effort into a project of restoration. Virtue along with suffering then has the meaning of repairing a lost perfection instead of contributing to the growth of the world or the emergence of something truly new.[15] It follows that wherever expiation has been theology's main way of addressing the question of suffering, nostalgia for a state of initial cosmic perfection easily becomes a substitute for genuine hope. The supplanting of hope by nostalgia then gains support liturgically wherever eucharistic theology interprets the Mass as *mainly* a reenactment of Christ's expiatory sacrifice rather than as a foretaste of new creation and future communion of humanity and the whole cosmos with God.

If, as I have just supposed, expiatory theology is inseparable from the perfectionism that accompanies a theological metaphysics of the eternal present, it is not surprising that adherents to this ancient worldview usually ignore evolution or at least play down its significance to faith. Evolutionary biology, if correct, excludes the possibility that the biblical story of the Garden of Eden and the sin and punishment of Adam and Eve can ever again be taken literally. Proponents of an expiatory theology of atonement, however, fear that if Darwin is right, the redemptive significance of Jesus—insofar as it is taken to be expiation for the sin of our first parents—will be diminished or lost. So their ongoing infatuation with a theology of expiation helps explain why biblical literalists are the most vocal anti-Darwinians today.

Even Catholics who say they accept evolution have yet to abandon all traces of such literalism, and so they fail to think out consistently what the new scientific setting implies for Christology and soteriology. Catholic theodicies, moreover, have concentrated almost exclusively on human misery, and they have typically construed our own suffering as the penalty for our sin. However, biological and paleontological awareness of the millions of years of life's innocent suffering prior to the recent evolutionary emergence of humans clearly challenges both the traditional emphasis on expiation and the metaphysical assumptions that underlie it. Since there is suffering in all of life, and not just among sinful humans, Catholic theology now needs to bring the prehuman epochs of innocent suffering, death, predation, disease, and extinction formally into its reflections on the problem of evil and its understanding of the meaning and scope of redemption. Expiatory theology is too narrow insofar as it is still usually tied to a tacitly Edenic literalism as well as to a metaphysics of the eternal present, sometimes to the point of denying that a larger-than-human arena of innocent suffering even exists at all. What then would Catholic theology look like if it considered more straightforwardly the evolutionary fact that the universe is still an unfinished creation and that most of life's suffering is completely innocent?

Any response to this question needs to investigate the theological meaning of *order*. By ignoring the wider story of life's suffering, expiatory theology construes the world in such a way that (divinely established) order can be restored only if a sufficient price in suffering is paid to repair the fault that befouled the original design. As the philosopher Paul Ricoeur has pointed out, there is a close relationship between the demand for expiation, on the one hand, and the perfectionistic craving for stability and order, on the other.[16] The religious imagination spontaneously devises sacred cosmologies on the model of, and for the sake of legitimating, a given social order. So whenever violations of the sanctioned social order occur, suffering is invited in to preserve or mend it. Over the last century and a half, however, science has been demonstrating, at least to those who bother to look, that life's suffering cannot be rendered broadly intelligible in terms of punishment. Suffering spills over and extends far beyond the reach of an exclusively expiatory vision of evil and perfection. For countless evolutionary scientists and philosophers today—Kitcher being only one among them—the excessive and absurd suffering of sentient life vindicates the ancient tragic interpretation of existence and decisively refutes Pope Benedict's providential theology.

Nevertheless, I believe that Catholics who embrace evolution and who also take the biblical theme of promise seriously can find in the roots of our tradition a compelling alternative to both cosmic pessimism and theological perfectionism. We may situate life's innocent suffering in the context of an anticipatory universe and a metaphysics of the future consistent with the powerful biblical motif of promise. An open-eyed scientific awareness of our unfinished universe, taken together with belief in the promise of new creation, allows theology to transfer its understanding of suffering and sacrifice from the framework of expiation to that of *expectation*. After Darwin, fortunately, the long reign of expiatory theology is now challenged, at least in principle, by a Christian sense of God as "calling" the world into being rather than simply "causing" the cosmos to exist. Our theology may now undergo a transformation that is consistently Abrahamic and that encourages us to think of God more as goal than as "governor" of creation.

As long as we had assumed that creation was instantaneously complete in the beginning, the only way we could make sense of present evil and suffering was to posit a secondary distortion. But this picture of things opened up the possibility of interpreting suffering essentially as punishment, and it fostered an ethic of retribution. Such a view, one that still infects social life everywhere, can only render expiation an interminable affair, thereby robbing suffering of the possibility of being interpreted as part of the process of ongoing creation itself. "A primary disorder," Teilhard says, "cannot be justified in a world which is created fully formed: a culprit has to be found. But in a world which emerges gradually from matter there is no longer any need to assume a primordial mishap in order to explain the appearance of the multiple and its inevitable satellite, evil."[17]

Evolution, to recall our theme, means that the world is still coming into being. If so, we cannot justifiably expect creation to be perfect yet. A creation that is still in the process of struggling toward its goal is *inevitably* defective in some way and to some degree at any moment prior to its fulfillment in God. Redemption, therefore, if it means anything at all, must signify the healing not only of the evil caused by human guilt but also the *cosmic* fault coexistent with the reality of an unfinished universe. Especially in view of Darwin's unsettling portrait of the life story, one that exposes previously unknown epochs of life's suffering and struggle, it would be negligent indeed on the part of theologians to perpetuate the one-sidedly anthropocentric and retributive notions of redemption that fit more comfortably into pre-evolutionary pictures of the world.[18]

Before Darwin, the idea of an initially complete world residing in a distant Eden or in the eternal present, hovered judgmentally over our sense of the empirically given world. Measured by the time-suppressing perfectionist metaphysics of the eternal present, each human life, as Friedrich Nietzsche reminded us, is rendered quite pointless if our sense of dignity depends in any way on our capacity to create something new. So, if the world had already been fashioned fully in the beginning, any apparent novelty that we could introduce into it would seem to be a defilement of perfection, easily leading to a sense of hopelessness that seeks relief in interminable acts of expiation and retribution.

Humans, to be sure, will always need unattainable ideals that call us to nobility of life, but these ideals can be enlivening only if they steer us toward an unprecedented future rather than a hypothesized initial or timeless perfection. Imagine that the created universe had at first been completely perfect in every conceivable way. Then the evil that we experience here and now would have to be attributed to a contingent occurrence that somehow spoiled the primordial creation, causing it to lose its original integrity. This, of course, is how evil and suffering have often been accounted for by religions, including Catholic Christianity. Accordingly, any "history of salvation" runs the risk of being interpreted as a process of restoring the original state of affairs. And although the restoration may be garnished at its edges with flashes of novelty, it will be understood ideally as the reestablishment of an aboriginal fullness that has now been lost.

The central biblical intuition is that salvation involves much more than the restoration of a primordial fullness of being, but the influence of Platonic philosophy on Catholic soteriologies has led theologians to subordinate the thrill of being surprised by the discovery of God's open-ended promises to one of contentment at the recovery of pristine perfection. The fact of evolution, on the other hand, no longer allows us to imagine that the universe was at any time a fully rounded-off state of being. This is why Darwin's science is potentially such good news for a biblically grounded theology. As we look back into the universe's remote evolutionary past with contemporary science, we see a world accompanied at its birth by an almost imperceptible straining toward a future that even now remains to be finalized. For this reason, a scientifically informed theology may no longer plausibly make themes of restoration or recovery dominant. The notion of an unfinished universe happily opens up the horizon of a healing future and, in doing so, allows for an end to expiation. After the emergence of evolutionary biology and cosmology, the theme of being's futurity begs as never before to be brought deliberately into ontology, theology, and cosmology. Any idealizing of being, in other words, must be layered over with a sense of what is not-yet and still-to-come.

Providence and pain: From expiation to expectation

Unfortunately, however, along with the idea of direct divine governance of the universe, the expiatory understanding of suffering is still so deeply embedded in Catholic spirituality that it seems nearly ineradicable. Expiatory theology began to take shape in the prophetic traditions long before the birth of Christianity, most notably in biblical narratives about the spoiling of an original cosmic perfection by free human acts of rebellion. Even though the Bible and especially the teachings of Jesus struggle to overcome a purely expiatory understanding of evil, the prophetic and Deuteronomic literature, along with the Genesis account of the expulsion from Eden, reflect the intuition that suffering is needed to expiate human guilt.[19] Partly as a result of this myth's influence in both religious and secular settings, whenever suffering or misfortune occurs, people tend to look for culprits. The assumption that a price in suffering must be paid for the defiling of creation's primal purity still undergirds the entrenched human habit of victimizing the innocent and helpless. It continues to legitimate the sad human history of torture and scapegoating that only prolongs the reign of misery.[20]

Back then to Kitcher's question: What sense can the doctrine of divine providence make in view of Darwin's divulging the longer story of life's suffering? Any adequate theological response begins by reaffirming the belief that God truly cares for the world. Indeed, Catholic tradition stands or falls with the credibility of our belief that God is *interested* in redeeming the *entire* world. If we are serious about it, our trust in divine care and redemptive compassion must be extended to cover the nonhuman experience of pain and death, as well as our own suffering. So vital is the notion of general divine providence for Catholic faith that it functions comparably to the way in which the central core of a theory works in science. Scientists typically cling to a theory as long as its main point seems unassailable, but when new observation or research challenges it, its defenders devise "auxiliary hypotheses" to save the theory's central core.[21] Eventually, however, the auxiliary hypotheses may prove too weak or unbelievable, and then the whole theory collapses.

Could something parallel to this sort of breakdown be happening to the doctrine of providence after Darwin? Doesn't the flood of information from evolutionary biology and cosmology now threaten the idea of divine governance, as Kitcher claims? To draw out the analogy to scientific inquiry a bit further, recall what happened to the ancient Ptolemaic, geocentric theory of celestial motion. Central to that theory was the picture of heavenly bodies revolving uniformly in perfect circles around the earth. However, observations seemed to indicate that planets move backward for long periods of time relative to the movement of other heavenly bodies. So to save the central core of the Ptolemaic theory, models had to be found to account for the retrograde movement of the planets. One proposal hypothesized that the earth is not exactly in the center of the cycling heavens. Another speculated that planets revolve in "epicycles" around imaginary points on their main orbit of the earth. For many centuries, the auxiliary hypothesis of epicycles helped save the central core of Ptolemaic theory. However, after Johannes Kepler concluded that planets move in elliptical orbits, and Galileo provided observational data suggesting that the earth revolves around the sun, the auxiliary hypothesis of epicycles eventually became superfluous. The geocentric system had to be abandoned.

So let us assume that the core teaching of Catholic faith is that there exists a providential God who is faithful, concerned about saving us and the whole universe, and hence deserving of our trust. To hold onto the "theory" of divine care in the face of suffering, theologians have entertained a whole set of "auxiliary hypotheses." One of these has been the expiatory theology that tries to make sense of suffering by attributing it solely to sin. The myth of expiation strives to give meaning to suffering by postulating that all guilt deserves a proportionate punishment. Wherever there is guilt, in other words, there must be a matching penalty paid in the currency of suffering. Some version of this myth shows up in almost every society, for example in the law of karma in Indian culture. The belief that guilt must be expiated by suffering, as Ricoeur suggests, serves the cause of preserving order, whether cosmic, religious, or political. Think, for example, of how societies justify beatings, imprisonment, maiming, and killing as punishment for crimes that disturb the social order.

What happens to the auxiliary hypothesis of "suffering as expiation," however, when theology encounters the waywardness and waste in evolution—and especially the innocent suffering of nonhuman life? The suffering of nonhuman life is like the retrograde movement of Venus, which astronomy could interpret in terms of epicycles only until closer observations demonstrated the need for a whole new scientific paradigm. Analogously, I am asking whether the expiatory vision of suffering is any longer serviceable as an "auxiliary hypothesis" supportive of the doctrine of providence. How long can theology continue to ignore the Darwinian discovery that most of life's suffering (and death) has nothing to do with guilt?

In John's Gospel, the disciples ask Jesus whether a man born blind was so afflicted because of his own or his parents' sin. Jesus answers by removing suffering from having to be understood as penalty: "Neither this man nor his parents sinned; he was born blind so that God's works might be revealed in him."[22] Similarly, St Paul's theology strains to remove the meaning of suffering from having to be determined any longer by the myth of expiation. And the main message of Letter to the Hebrews may well be that "the age of expiation is now over" since Christ entered the temple of sacrifice once and for all.[23] Evolutionary science is theologically important, I suggest, partly because it pressures Catholic theology to divorce our sense of divine providence more decisively than ever from the motif of expiation and oversimplified ideas such as divine design, order, guidance, and governance. In view of the fact that Darwinian biology has exposed the complete innocence—and indeed tragedy—of most of life's suffering, the expiatory motif of redemption has become as problematic as epicycles in astronomy. Science has demonstrated that the earth could never have hosted an originally paradisal order since the universe is still coming into being. And if no ideal initial order ever existed historically or cosmically, it makes no sense to try to restore it by expiation. The whole universe, as I have been proposing, may now be understood as anticipation, and God may be understood as creation's ultimate goal and absolute future instead of governor and overseer of a hypothetical initial cosmic order. Authentic faith too may now be seen as epitomizing the element of anticipation that coincides with the movement of an entire universe. Correspondingly, sin is not so much a disturbance of an initial cosmic integrity as a refusal to hear the call of God and hence participate in the world's ongoing creation.

Another traditional theological proposal, I should point out in passing, has attempted to shore up the idea of divine cosmic governance by interpreting human suffering as pedagogy. This interpretation tries to make sense of suffering by moving it from the horizon of expiation to that of education. It argues that the meaning of suffering lies in its being part of a divine discipline for the development of character or "soul." Our sufferings, accordingly, are not counter-evidence to the central "theory" of divine governance but instead indications that providence is watching over us by deliberately setting up the natural world as a rugged school essential to our growth. Evolution makes sense in this pedagogical perspective as the curriculum of a "soul school" that challenges us to develop spiritual backbone and moral fiber. Thus God can be excused for "chastising" those whom God loves.[24]

This proposal has received strong support from the Christian philosopher John Hick, and it deserves a closer study than I can provide here.[25] After Darwin, however, one has to ask how applicable the theme of education is to the suffering of all of life. The idea that evolution is theologically justifiable as divine pedagogy and that such an idea could save the notion of providence seems especially crude. Kitcher refers to this kind of theodicy as "ambitious providentialism," observing that it cannot justify all the suffering of nonhuman life or the existence of human freedom without making God seem monstrous:

> When you consider the millions of years in which sentient creatures have suffered, the uncountable number of extended and agonizing deaths, it simply rings hollow to suppose that all this is needed so that, at the very tail end of history, our species can manifest the allegedly transcendent good of free will and virtuous action. There is every reason to think that alternative processes for unfolding the history of life could have eliminated much of the agony, that the goal could have been achieved without so long and bloody a prelude.[26]

In view of the evolutionary picture of life, not to mention such human horrors as the Holocaust, both expiation and education seem to have spent most if not all of their theological utility and can no longer function satisfactorily to support providential theology. Just as the ongoing accumulation of fresh astronomical data led to the acceptance of a heliocentric system that at one time had seemed inconceivable, so also the evolutionary portrayal of life's long epochs of suffering now provides data that call for a drastic reconfiguration of the Catholic theological heavens.

The unfinished universe and the end of expiation

Unfortunately, instead of offering a good reason to trust in God, the "auxiliary" ideas of expiation and education still sometimes serve to legitimate suffering rather than providing the motivation to defeat it. And if theology ties the ideas of God and creation tightly to these two themes, such an association may end up legitimating suffering rather than offering hope of redemption from it. Fortunately, however, Catholic theology has available to it an alternative way of dealing with suffering. This option has long been lurking in the pages of Scripture where for centuries it has been struggling to emerge from the shadows. That alternative is a theology of *expectation* that can subordinate and relativize and—at least to a considerable extent—replace the alternatives of expiation and education. Within a truly biblical horizon, suffering can be directly addressed primarily by hope in the God who is the world's final goal and liberator, a God who creates, sustains, and redeems the universe from out of the future. Within the anticipatory horizon of Abrahamic expectation, suffering has finally no legitimate place. Suffering is part of an unfinished universe, as we have seen, but such a universe is not yet fully intelligible or real. Here and now the world's intelligibility can only be anticipated, not possessed. Consequently, theology's central core, the doctrine of divine care, now calls out for another kind of support than that of expiation or education. It can find this support in the setting of what I am calling cosmic hope and a corresponding metaphysics of the future.

It will not be easy, of course, for Catholic thought to undergo the metaphysical makeover I am proposing. The expiatory vision still functions, at least tacitly, to forestall a fully open embrace of evolution and its implications for our understanding God as creation's goal. Expiatory theology over the course of time has shifted away from being an auxiliary satellite circling the sun of divine promise and fidelity, and has at times become instead the center around which a diminished idea of providence has been forced to orbit. Consequently, the conviction that providence is essentially an ordering principle has ended up supporting a theological obsession with expiation.

There is always need for order, of course, but if evolutionary science has taught us anything, it is that the cosmos is not a fixed order. It has always been in the process of becoming, and so there is no reason to suppose that it is now, or ever has been, virtually finished. Evolution implies that along with order there is also novelty, and novelty cannot become actual unless present order somehow gives way. Since novelty can bring unrest, the idea of providential governance has often been seized as a sanction for sustaining static and unrealistic ideals of decent order, whether of nature, by suppressing evidence of evolution, for example, or of social existence, by ignoring the unsettling voices of those who protest the injustice of the status quo, or of ecclesiastical structures that appeal for support to obsolete vertical, hierarchical (essentially patriarchal) models of the universe. The idea of providence as a plan or design has unfortunately given a fictitious aura of necessity to repressive visions of social and ecclesial order by absolutizing pre-evolutionary conceptions of nature and being.

It is noteworthy, then, that Israel's religious thought also struggles to deliver suffering from a purely expiatory interpretation. When Job objects to the unfairness of his predicament, his friends attempt to bolster their trust in divine governance by assuming that Job has suppressed the memory of the guilt that justifies his suffering. Their reasoning is that after his guilt has been acknowledged Job's suffering can make sense as expiation, and then the good order of his life and the cosmos may be restored. Yet, even as these expiatory arguments are exposed as empty, the idea that Job (or we) can have a clear sense of any divine "plan" is also revealed as equally shallow (Job 38).[27]

In spite of protests by Job and other innocents that suffering is unjustified, the expiatory vision of redemption still exercises great power over our souls. I believe it also sanctions a religious culture of shame. The compulsive need to punish others and/or ourselves gains legitimacy from the motif of expiation. This is deeply ironic from a Christian point of view, especially since Jesus's own life and preaching reach beyond the expiatory vision toward an ennobling God whose love overtakes us while we are "still in our sins." It is a love that falls indiscriminately on the just and unjust alike. Instead of crushing the life out of sinners by demanding expiation, divine love as revealed in Jesus opens up the possibility of new life unceasingly. This is what Christianity means, at the very least, by its belief in "the forgiveness of sins." Heralding the possibility of new life, in any case, is a much more gladdening incentive to effective moral action than is the threat of punishment. Hence, it is only after our ideas of providence have been transfigured by the notion of God as self-giving and promising love that Catholic theology will be in a position favorable to the linking of the idea of providence to the fact of evolution.

Summary

It is no coincidence that expiatory interpretations of sacrifice find sanction in myths that suppose a primordial paradise. A sociologist might even speculate that the cultural infrastructure of expiation and victimization generates ideologies that project perfection onto an imagined paradisal past and thus lend religious approval to entrenched habits of violence and compensatory sacrifice. I am asking once again, then, what the consequences for theology would be if we were to think out consistently the implications of the evolutionary claim that an original state of complete cosmic integrity has never been an actuality. By ruling out any past epoch of created perfection, our religious aspirations may henceforth be turned away from regret and remorse and set more resolutely in the direction of hope. If, as science has demonstrated, the universe and life have emerged only gradually, and no actual cosmic epoch of paradisal perfection has ever occurred, then our religious attention could turn more freely toward the world's future in God, the only arena in which the fulfillment of our longing for meaning, coherence, perfection, and new creation could conceivably become actualized. Such a pivot would finally align our theology more explicitly with the biblical leitmotifs of promise and hope, not to mention with the unfinished universe of contemporary science.

Science, I am suggesting, has providentially delivered theology from the impossible burden of fitting the fact of suffering onto the grid of guilt and punishment. Again, the real, though humanly unanswerable, question remaining then is why God would call into being an unfinished, imperfect, evolutionary universe in the first place rather than forcing it to be complete and perfect from the start. Could it be that a truly good and powerful God has no choice? After all, as I concluded in the previous chapter, a completely ordered universe, one forever devoid of accidents, would be frozen so stiff that there would be no room for life, freedom, or anything new to happen at all. Moreover, the allegedly "unfair" impersonality of natural selection need not conflict with a promissory sense of divine providence, for without inviolable grammatical routines (usually called laws of nature), the world would lack the consistency and continuity to have any future at all. And, finally, the fact that evolution takes so long—at least from our human calendrical point of view—is not inconsistent with a sense of divine providence that is caring enough to grant the world ample time to experiment with a rich array of possible new forms of being and in this way participate in the drama of its own creation.

After Darwin, then, we may speak in a more biblical way than ever of divine providential care as operating in the mode of *promise*. God's providential activity is, before all else, that of providing a vision (a dream?) of how the world may become new, of keeping a space open for life and human freedom, and of inviting conscious and free beings to awaken to a life of patient hope and active contribution to the fulfillment of all things.

Dignity: From Static to Dramatic

Prior to the scientific revolution, Catholic thought presupposed a static, vertical, and hierarchical understanding of the cosmos. The universe was pictured as a relatively unchanging ladder of distinct levels of being. Starting from "matter" at the bottom, the Great Chain of Being ascended vertically through the successively higher realms of plants, animals, human beings, and angelic spheres up to the infinite unchanging perfection of God on high. This immobile scheme of things (*scala naturae*) allotted humans a special place of honor within the whole domain of created being. Since human consciousness lies lower than God in the classic hierarchical arrangement, people of faith cannot comprehend God, but they may speak of the divine mystery by way of symbols, analogies, and metaphors. It is in this context that the Catholic sacramental vision of nature traditionally finds its home. Nature can reveal God to us in many different ways, but in theistic traditions, an indispensable symbol for representing God is that of personhood. God is a "Thou" and not an "It," and the personality of God grounds our human dignity and rights since we are created "in the image and likeness of God." We too are each a "thou" and not an "it." If, therefore, we abandon the belief that God is personal, as scientific naturalism advises us to do, this would in effect remove the eternal ground of our own personal value as well.

What happens to the Catholic affirmation of human dignity, however, now that the classical hierarchical picture of the universe has given way to that of a horizontally unfolding and still-unfinished universe? At the very least, the Great Chain of Being has now been "temporalized."[1] And if, as science has taught us, the universe is still in the making, doesn't this call for a new way of understanding human dignity and identity? Geology, biology, paleontology, genetics, neuroscience, astrophysics, and other sciences combine now to give us a picture of the universe that seems to have flattened the vertical theological worldview that had previously upheld Catholic sacramentalism and our sense of special human worth. After Darwin, says the evolutionary naturalist Steven Pinker, the whole idea of human dignity is "stupid."[2] What then can Catholic theology say in response to such claims while still remaining fully abreast of science?

Contemporary cosmology and personal dignity

Our universe began with a Big Bang approximately 13.8 billion years ago. To get a sense of the scale of the cosmic story, it may be instructive to imagine that you have a set of thirty big books, each 450 pages long, and each page of every book standing for one million years of cosmic history. The Big Bang takes place on page 1 of volume 1, and the first twenty volumes are taken up with the story of lifeless astrophysical, chemical, and geological transformations. Clearly life and mind are not in a hurry to come into this cosmic narrative. Earth and other planets spin out around the sun in volume 21, about 4.5 billion years ago, but the first signs of cellular life do not show up until around 3.8 billion years ago (in volume 22). Life remains relatively uncomplicated until almost the end of volume 29 when the Cambrian explosion occurs (around 520 million years ago). After that, living organisms become more complex at an accelerated pace. Dinosaurs eventually appear around the middle of volume 30 and go extinct on page 385, probably because of the earth-chilling effects of an enormous asteroid impact. This leaves only the last sixty-five pages of volume 30 to cover the development and flourishing of mammalian life. When do we humans show up? Our hominid ancestors appear a few pages from the end of volume 30, but anatomically modern humans do not arrive until page 450. Reflective thought, ethical aspiration, a sense of personhood, and religious longing finally enter the cosmic story only toward the bottom of the last page of the whole set.

Are the emergence of minds and persons, therefore, anything more than cosmic afterthoughts? Once the first living cells appear in volume 22, Charles Darwin's recipe for the evolution of life comes into play, but only at the end of volume 30 does the slowly simmering life-process cook up human beings and thrust us into a challenging natural environment that supports us for a brief span but then leaves us to die. Is this a picture of things that can give us much of a sense of self-worth? In the light of science, isn't the idea of human dignity "stupid"?

Nowadays scientists see no sharp breaks in the cosmic story between humans and our animal ancestry. We are just the latest products, it would seem, of an impersonal process of blind natural selection. The traditional vertical cosmic hierarchy that for centuries nurtured our sense of human dignity has collapsed. Lifeless matter, the lowest level in the traditional hierarchy, is now the dominant feature in the new picture of the universe. The origin of life is an accident, evolution a morally indifferent process, and the emergence of mind an unintended appendix to a long and mindless course of events. Finally, our ideas about God, meaning, and values seem now, in the light of Darwinian science and naturalist philosophy, to be nothing more than adaptive illusions invented by populations of ancestral human genes to improve their prospects of surviving into subsequent generations.

Science, furthermore, has not only flattened the classic vertical hierarchy of values but its analytical method of inquiry has also atomized the prescientific hierarchical picture of the universe, leaving only a heap of mindless elemental bits of matter. The theoretical dissolution of life and mind into inanimate and unconscious micro-units is a major part of the intellectual background of the claim that the idea of human dignity is groundless. Scientific thought strives to simplify our understanding of the natural world by reducing it to indivisible components and reductive algorithms, and its granulation of life seems to undermine our sense of personal value as well. Atomism, we recall, has long been a temptation for human thought, represented in antiquity especially by the philosopher Democritus who declared that reality consists of only two components, atoms and the void. In most Catholic thought prior to the modern age, however, atomism receded into the intellectual background because of the dominant influence of Plato and Aristotle in the shaping of our theologies. Scorning atomism, the two greatest philosophers of Western antiquity insisted that nature makes no sense apart from formal and final causality. Only if everything has a determinate essence and a fixed goal can it be intelligible.

For centuries Catholic philosophers and theologians have agreed that attempts to understand the world simply by breaking everything down into mindless bits of stuff is both morally offensive in the case of living beings, and intellectually incoherent as far as our understanding of physical reality in general is concerned. Nevertheless, during the modern period, beginning with the particles-in-motion cosmos of Galileo and Newton, materialist atomism returned and has picked up unprecedented intellectual momentum ever since. Contemporary scientific materialists instruct us that we can understand everything from cells to brains only by decomposing them into constituent atomic and subatomic units. So entrenched did materialist atomism become in modern thought that after Darwin's *Origin of Species* appeared in 1859, it became increasingly tempting to view the evolution of life itself simply as the reshuffling of physical elements across an enormous span of cosmic time. As a result of the atomizing, temporalizing, and horizontalizing of nature, the traditional lines that distinguished one level of being decisively from others in classical theology's vertical hierarchy have become blurred. It is easier now than ever for scientific naturalists to declare that the whole idea of human dignity, supported earlier by the hierarchy of being and the sacramental vision of creation, is intellectually obsolete.

The atomizing approach to nature is especially provocative to Catholic thinkers who strive to make a satisfying space for the affirmation of human dignity in today's intellectual climate. How, then, can we meet the challenge posed by science to the hierarchical view of the universe, a picture that for so long has grounded our sense of dignity and our belief in a personal God? Since it would take more than one book to develop a theology of human dignity, I must be content here simply to highlight two important developments in science itself over the past half-century that now allow, at least in principle, for a reaffirmation of Catholic tradition's intuitions concerning the special value of human life. The first is science's relatively recent discovery of the role that *information* plays in the natural world. The second consists of twentieth-century *cosmological* discoveries that have solidified our sense that the universe is still undergoing a dramatic self-transformation. Information science and Big Bang cosmology together provide a fresh intellectual environment for the renewal of a credible theological sense of human distinctiveness in a post-Darwinian world. These two developments cannot by themselves establish an adequate foundation for a contemporary Catholic theology of human dignity, of course. What they can do, however, is allow us to reaffirm the sacredness of life and the inviolable dignity of the human person in a way that is at least consistent with biology, cosmology, and other scientific fields of research.

I The significance of "Information"

With the arrival of life in cosmic history about four billion years ago, there occurred what Holmes Rolston III refers to as a second Big Bang— an explosive introduction of *information* into the cosmos.[3] In the realm of living beings, information means the encoding and transmission of messages in patterns of "letters" of the genetic code. The DNA molecule in the nucleus of the eukaryotic cell is composed of letters of an "alphabet"— the four nucleotides known as A, T, G, and C—that can be arranged in a wide variety of informational sequences. Physical and chemical processes translate the "messages" coded in DNA sequences into corresponding patterns of amino acids out of which proteins are made. In ways that scientists are still trying to clarify, DNA sequences provide directions for the building of informationally rich chains of proteins into three-dimensional structures that collectively make up the diverse body types (phenotypes) of living beings. Without specific informational sequences of DNA in the nuclei of cells, there would be no instructions for making proteins, no living diversity, and no distinct species of life, including human beings.

The discovery of the chemical basis of life may seem at first to support an atomistic worldview. Citing the significant role that nucleic and amino acids play in living cells and organisms, both Francis Crick and James Watson, the codiscoverers of the double helix formation of DNA, claimed that biology is now reducible to chemistry and physics.[4] Further reflection, however, shows that this atomistic assumption is logically misguided. What gives rise to different species and unique individual organisms is not simply the physical and chemical processes at work in living cells but the *specific sequence* of letters in their DNA.[5] What makes one organism a carrot, another a monkey, and another a human being is the differing strings of letters taken from the genetic alphabet. DNA, as we now realize, carries a considerable amount of "junk" segments that have little if any direct informational function, and the signaling that occurs in the cell's development is more complicated than Crick and Watson thought. Nevertheless, the presence of junk segments and informational complexity in no way diminishes the fact that a discernible message is inscribed in the overall sequence of letters in a DNA molecule.

By disclosing the essential role of information in the life process, science has now encountered a previously unsuspected facet of nature, one that frustrates the atomistic dream of reducing life to its chemical and physical components. Information in living beings is real, even though it is nonmaterial. To atomists and materialists, the DNA molecule may seem to be just chemistry, but at a deeper reading level, information science allows us to make out something more. Information is logically and ontologically distinct from the material processes it informs. Because the arrangement of letters (nucleotides) in the DNA molecule is informational rather than material, life cannot be understood in terms of purely chemical or physical laws and activity, even though it relies for its functioning on predictable physical and chemical routines.[6] Different living beings like alligators, rabbits, and humans may rely on similar metabolic and chemical processes, but at the level of their nuclear DNA, even small informational differences are enough to make one species qualitatively distinct from others. Even if the respective genomes of humans and chimpanzees differ only fractionally from each other—chimps, for example, are said to share around 96 percent of the human genomic content—this small quantitative informational difference is enough to allow for large qualitative differences between the respective phenotypes and behavioral tendencies of each species. We need not overlook the atomic and chemical continuity that exists between humans and other species of life, but as we stand back and read the story of life in a multilayered way, we observe that infinitesimal informational differences can make each species and each member of a species sharply distinct from others as the drama unfolds.[7]

Even though our new awareness of the informational coding of life is not by itself enough to support a theological affirmation of human dignity in the age of evolution, at least it allows us to demonstrate that the idea is not stupid. New awareness of the role information plays in the world of life allows us to question atomistic claims that science has now pulverized the hierarchical framework that traditionally served as a basis for our discernment of different grades of value in the natural world. By taking into account the fact of information, we may justifiably reject the assertion that molecular biology and biochemistry have reduced life to chemistry, or human personality to lifeless chains of atoms and molecules.[8] One must read life, after all, not only at the level of its chemical makeup but also at the level of its different informational arrangements. Science's relatively new discovery of the effective functioning of information in living beings, therefore, is not irrelevant to the question of whether evolutionary theory and molecular biology have jointly destroyed any basis for affirming human value and dignity. Even though evolutionary, atomic, molecular, and biochemical continuity ties humans tightly to all other living beings, and beyond that to the whole physical universe, the fact of information differentiates us ontologically from all other species, and them from us.

The discovery of information is another indication that an archaeological metaphysics of the past cannot account for every aspect of life. Even though the physical and chemical processes in the living cell function now in the same way as they did in the past, the specific informational arrangement in presently living beings is not predictable by physics and chemistry. Information slips through the wide nets of any purely physical dredging up of the fixed cosmic past. Those who embrace a metaphysics of the past try to reduce all present complexity to elemental simplicity. Ignoring the cosmic information explosion that occurred with the emergence of life, they fail to notice anything dramatic about the universe at all. Life and mind for them are merely the products of a senseless reshuffling over a long period of time of the same material and atomic stuff that has always been around.

The fact that a metaphysics of the past is not conditioned to notice information at all helps account for why information's discovery has been accompanied by so much intellectual confusion, ambiguity, and even denial. I believe this is the case because information, one of the most distinguishing marks of life, arrives on the wings of the future. Only an anticipatory worldview can make a place for it.[9] A simple analogy may help clarify this point. In writing the chapter you are reading now, I am using the same alphabet, lexicon, and grammatical rules that I used in earlier chapters. Nevertheless, the specific sequence of letters and words that defines the content of this chapter is new in comparison with sequences employed in the previous ones. You would not be able to predict what I will be saying here and in future chapters simply by digging back into previous chapters and gathering up the letters, words, sentences, and grammatical rules you find there. The message in the sentences and paragraphs in front of you at the moment resides not in the letters or words but in their particular arrangement. This arrangement is not determined in advance by phonetic, lexicographical, or grammatical rules, nor is it predictable in terms of them, even though the rules remain inviolable.

Furthermore, without bending any of the rules just mentioned, even slight changes in the sequences of letters, words, and sentences can make major differences in the content or meaning of what I am writing now. Analogously, even quantitatively minute differences in the sequences of letters and "words" in the respective genomes of species such as chimps and humans can, in principle, allow for disproportionately large differences in their specific identities. An informational perspective, in other words, provides a corrective to the analytical illusion and the narrow atomism that profess to have reduced life to chemistry and physics, and that have devoured much biology since the time of Mendel and Darwin.[10] On the other hand, our new awareness of information fits comfortably into a metaphysics of the future. DNA's openness to an endless variety of arrangements means that life is not determined by the past and that it logically allows for sharp formal discontinuity among species even where there is physical and chemical continuity. To return to this book's main metaphor, then, I suggest that each species and each individual may be the expression of a special new "meaning" in the ongoing *drama* of life. Thus the informational dimension of life leaves ample logical space for theological readings of what it means to be specifically human as well as for ongoing affirmations of human dignity.

II The soul and cosmic transformation

One of the main ways in which Catholic faith has traditionally upheld our sense of the intrinsic dignity of persons is through its belief in an exceptional creation of each human soul directly by God. The notion of the soul has been central to Catholic teaching about the uniquely precious value of the human person in the eyes of God from the moment of conception in the womb. In a broader historical sense, for centuries belief in the existence of the soul has been essential to declarations concerning the rights and responsibilities of persons everywhere. Belief that the soul is created immediately by God has protected the intrinsic dignity of the mentally and physically disabled, of the impoverished and those who have been discriminated against for reasons of gender, race, nationality, intellectual ability, and other qualities. The notion of the immortal soul has been an influential democratic norm in Catholic moral teaching while also providing a reason for hoping in the prospect of each person's eternal communion with God after death.

However, from its beginning modern science has raised serious questions about the intelligibility of the idea of the soul, and especially so after Darwin. René Descartes (1596–1650) had transformed the traditional distinction between body and soul into a strict dualism of mind and matter, and his separation of the two spheres seemed at first to protect the idea of special human value. In fact, however, just the opposite has occurred. After Descartes, materialist philosophers decided that mind does not really exist and that it is simply a name for an interesting combination of physical elements and chemical processes in the human organism. Only lifeless and mindless matter is real. As a result of the expulsion of mind from matter, there remained in nature no place for the soul or for the influence of God. Any eternal foundation for our sense of special human rights and dignity seemed to crumble. And today, as materialism has become ever more closely alloyed with evolutionary biology, the traditional ideas of human freedom and dignity seem to evolutionary naturalists such as Pinker to be more fictional than ever.

In its concern to shield human personal dignity and freedom from the materialist intellectual onslaught, modern Catholic teaching and theology have insisted all the more earnestly that the human soul exists in a spiritual domain ontologically distinct from mindless and soulless nature, at least as the latter is understood by materialism. The problem with this reaction, however, is that it concedes too much to the materialists who have reduced nature as a whole to lifeless and valueless stuff. We are left then with the question of how Catholic theology can now stitch human persons seamlessly into the realm of physical reality and the new cosmic story without dragging them back into the mud of materialist mindlessness.

I believe our theology may do so by first dislodging the whole cosmic drama from its comfortable intellectual setting in materialist metaphysics, and second, by thinking of human dignity in terms of the special role we humans have in the unfinished, anticipatory universe of which we are a part. In previous chapters I have already begun to undertake the first task by trying to liberate the entire story of nature from imprisonment in a metaphysics of the past and by re-situating it in the context of a metaphysics of the future. Here I want to contribute further to the second task by connecting human dignity to our cosmic responsibility for contributing to and intensifying the remarkable drama of cosmic awakening now going on.

Let us begin by looking with science at what it takes to make the human minds that are the main instruments of that awakening. For minds to have emerged at all in volume 30 of the cosmic history pictured at the start of this chapter, there first had to be brains of sufficient complexity to make the leap into thought. However, for these brains to exist, a rapid evolutionary process was required several pages before the end of volume 30, the last book in our set. There had to occur a sharp acceleration of cerebral complexity sufficient to allow self-reflective thought to come into the universe around page 450. Of course, for evolution to happen at all, there had to be life, and for life to exist, there had to be planetary conditions and just the right set of chemical components to allow for the emergence of the large molecules essential for life. Among these chemical elements, carbon is central since it has the bonding properties that allow for the existence of complex organic molecules. However, carbon was not present in the early universe. For carbon to exist in our Big Bang universe, there first had to be massive stars hot enough at their cores to "cook" primordial hydrogen and helium into heavier elements. This physical process required not only massive stellar ovens but also several billion years of cooking time for carbon to be created. Even more massive stars, those that eventually exploded as supernovas, were necessary to convert simple forms of matter into still heavier elements, including those essential to the building of ever more complex organisms with brains that could burst into consciousness.

Each chapter of this mind-making story, however, required that initial cosmic conditions and constants in our Big Bang universe be fixed with remarkable precision from the time of cosmic origins. The astronomer Martin Rees claims that for carbon-based life and mind to exist in the universe, at the time of cosmic origins the mathematical values of at least six physical constants (for instance, the cosmic expansion rate and the gravitational force) had to be "just right." However, the chances that these six numbers, none of which is necessitated by the others, would come together at the first moment of cosmic origins are extremely small. So, how are we to explain this coincidence? It is tempting, theologically speaking, to assume that the remarkable coincidence of the six cosmic numbers is ultimately due to divine intention, but in his role as a scientist, Rees rightly refuses to read the universe theologically. Instead, in his justifiable search to exhaust all natural explanations, he posits the existence of a *multiverse* as the backdrop for the improbable universe we live in. Statistically, he assumes, if there are enough universes "out there" (even if they are not observable to us) the probability of at least one of them having the requisite six numbers would improve in proportion to the multiplication of universes.[11] So far there is no empirical evidence that any other universes besides our own exist, but an increasing number of physicists maintain that the idea of a multiverse is theoretically compatible with current physical ideas such as cosmic inflation and string theory.[12]

Here I need not enter into the question of whether our life-bearing universe entails divine design, interesting as the pursuit of this question may otherwise be. Instead, I would just note with Rees and other scientific thinkers that our Big Bang universe has always held the promise of bursting into life and of blooming into mind. Science itself, it is enough to say for now, allows that at least our own universe has at no time ever been essentially mindless. The process of giving birth to mind—and that means us—began during the first microsecond of this universe's existence. The emergence of mind is not a cosmic afterthought after all, nor is the birth of "thought" on our planet the intrusion of something fundamentally alien into the universe. Even though the Big Bang universe has awakened into consciousness only recently, the narrative prelude to this emergent wonder was playing from the start. During the earliest moments of cosmic existence, our minds (and souls), in other words, were already stirring at the very heart of matter.

However, in light of contemporary astrophysical speculation, the question of whether humans are special now brings along with it the question of whether our mind-making Big Bang universe is special. The topic of human dignity is now inseparable from that of whether our own particular universe is exceptional if it is only one of many universes. Again, we have no direct evidence of a multiverse, but even if there are countless other worlds the idea of an unfinished universe and the narrative approach I have adopted in exploring the meaning of evolution and life in our own universe may now be extended in principle to embrace any conceivable wider totality of worlds. We live, perhaps, in an unfinished *multiverse story* that may not be directly engineered by God but which may overall still have an anticipatory bearing and may be carrying a wider narrative meaning than theology or science has ever previously supposed. Even if mind emerged only in one lonely universe, Lonergan's notion of emergent probability, introduced in Chapter 3, would still be applicable here, and the totality of worlds may, therefore, still cohere narratively, even if it does not presently correspond to narrow mechanistic notions of divine design.

My point then is that even in the context of a supposed multiverse, the cosmic awakening of consciousness that is occurring in us human beings in our own Big Bang universe does not in any way lessen our status or dignity within the total scheme of things, as scientific naturalists often claim. On the contrary, our own human dignity may even be all the more distinctive when placed within the dramatic setting of multiple emerging universes. Whatever additional vocations we may each personally have, therefore, we may assume, cosmically speaking, that our special role and responsibility include that of being agents and instruments of an ongoing cosmic awakening. To participate in the adventure of intensifying consciousness gives our lives a meaning, and the universe—or multiverse—a grandeur that we had not previously suspected.

Along with the cosmic emergence of consciousness, of course, other human propensities associated with mind and soul, such as freedom, creativity, the ability to form deep relationships, and the capacity to make and keep promises, have also recently arrived in the universe. In spite of the claim by Darwinian materialists that the high degree of accident and blind necessity in biological evolution renders humanity nothing more than a cosmic anomaly, the narrative cosmological perspective proposed throughout this book provides a higher point of view and a necessary corrective. For if it takes a multiverse to make only one consciousness-producing universe, this in no way detracts, *dramatically speaking*, from our significance and responsibility. The relatively small size of human bodies, or the spatial mediocrity of our planet and the Milky Way, does not matter, dramatically speaking. In and through human persons, the universe—which you may henceforth read as "multiverse" if you prefer—has at last become conscious of itself. Even if nature is largely uninhabited by living and conscious beings, we and any other such beings existing elsewhere in nature may be quite special when seen from a narrative-dramatic point of view. The overall immensity of the Big Bang universe consisting of over two hundred billion galaxies, and the even more staggering numerical enormity of a possible multiverse, may be a statistically necessary backdrop for the *narrative* coherence I have been proposing as the criterion of cosmic meaning or purpose. A scientifically educated impression that each of us is the outcome of such an unfathomable cosmic drama should do nothing to lower our self-esteem. Since stories require as their backdrop an extravagantly immense field of possibility and contingency, the emergence and evolution of a conscious species is anything but the trivial occurrence that entrenched materialists and cosmic pessimists have taken it to be. If you want a soul, as Teilhard says, you first need a universe. If you want a soul-bearing universe, I now suggest, you may first need a multiverse.

As I indicated earlier, the Second Vatican Council, in its *Pastoral Constitution on the Church in the Modern World*, explicitly embraced the picture of a universe in evolution and recognized that Catholics need to think carefully about what this means for our faith and moral lives. The Council also urged Catholics to take the biblical basis of their faith more seriously than ever. What these two sets of instruction mean in the age of science is that the God who declares the world good is the same God who still creates from out of the future. The word of God that hovered over creation in the beginning is the same word that came to Abraham in the form of an eternal promise that opened up the future for him and his descendants. Both cosmologically and theologically, therefore, our distinctiveness, dignity, and responsibility consist in part of our being the chapter in nature's history when the universe (or multiverse) has finally begun to open itself consciously, prayerfully, and gratefully to the coming of God, the absolute future, the goal (and not just the originator) of all creation.

Each human soul, therefore, is inseparable from the cosmos out of whose creative narrative it has been spun. The soul is not separable from the universe, as I will explain in the following chapter. Rather, each human soul *is* the universe (or multiverse) in an exceptionally intense state of anticipating its ongoing creation and fulfillment in God. In terms of our new cosmological understanding, human dignity is grounded not only in our participation in uncreated being but also in our hopeful *anticipation* of the God who is simultaneously coming from the future and calling the universe into new being. Our sense of self-worth, therefore, is understandably felt most fully in moments of hope, that is, in our heightened capacity for anticipating the coming of God into a creation that has always been a story of awakening to its future. The soul that longs for God "as the deer longs for streams of fresh water" (Psa. 42:1) has the function of bringing to conscious expression the anticipatory leaning of all creation, no matter how broadly construed, in its journey into God.

In summary, human dignity consists, at least partly, of our capacity to let the world's future arrive ever more fully in each present moment. Nature is promise, and our original sin is the defilement of our vocation by turning our backs on—and failing to respond to—the arrival of the future. This turn away from the future has been systematized in secular thought's archaeological vision. It is scientific materialism's metaphysics of the past and the implied ontology of death that permit partisans of that narrow worldview to dismiss the sense of human dignity as a stupid idea.

Unfortunately, the turn away from the future has also been given theological legitimacy in the analogical vision insofar as it thinks of God exclusively as an eternal now rather than also as the world's absolute future. In either case, it is in turning away from the horizon of a new future that we lose our souls. Somehow, it seems, the root of our sin and self-degradation is rooted in a failure to trust that the world can be made new and that its identity is always that of a coming-into-being. Robust pursuit of virtue requires, then, that we first open ourselves to the promissory word that heralds the coming of a new future full of yet unrealized possibilities and corresponding responsibilities. Failure to sense this openness, I suspect, is why we feel anxious and oppressed whenever the past limits and closes in on us. Clearly, an atomistic and materialist worldview, based on a metaphysics of the past, cannot ground a sense of dignity or motivate us to the pursuit of virtue since it formally eclipses the universe's aspiring toward new possibilities and "more being." Cosmic pessimism tries to convince us that everything that seems new has already been determined by a fixed past, and that there is nothing new under the sun. The materialist universe provides no reason for hope nor a basis for affirming human dignity. However, once again we need to ask whether Catholic theology's persistent clinging to the eternal now (the *nunc stans*) of classical metaphysics may not also have stifled the biblical sense of the futurity of God, the fundamental reason for hope's full flowering and the most favorable framework for our claim to human dignity.

Narratively understood, in any case, the arrival in natural history of human consciousness, freedom, and moral sensitivity reveals something essential not just about ourselves but also about the universe (again read *multiverse* here if you like). Having become, in us, explicitly conscious of itself, the creation now demonstrates that it has the reserve to become even *more* in the future. The fact that we humans can contribute in diverse ways to the process of the universe's becoming more implies that we now have a new basis for understanding our special standing within the whole of creation. We all share the honorable calling to contribute, both as one human family and each in our own modest ways, to the ongoing creation of a now-awakening universe. In our creativity, which often consists only of intensifying our relationships to the world and other persons, in our capacity to act responsibly and to worship, and in our private struggles and suffering, the whole universe anticipates fuller being and allows human persons to mirror the image of God in a variety of ways.

While other species may be to some degree sentient and even conscious, there is no evidence that they perceive themselves as having freedom or responsibility. They do not appear to possess a self-conscious concern about who they are, about what they should be doing with their lives, or about their ultimate destiny. Although their own modes of sentience and awareness often surpass our own in detecting some aspects of the sensible world, it is clear that their consciousness does not allow them to ask questions such as "what is *really* going on in the universe, and does it have a purpose?" Consequently, it seems not only theologically but also scientifically unreasonable to maintain, as Pinker does, that science has now made the idea of human dignity unbelievable. The dangers of an exaggerated anthropocentrism are still present and subject to criticism, of course, but instead of undermining our sense of self-worth, the new scientific cosmological perspective has the potential to renew it.

In conclusion, I want to add that it is now possible for Catholic theology to take more seriously than ever the Apostle Paul's belief that *all of creation* has been promised the redemption proclaimed by Christian faith. In Christianity's foundational phase, devotees of Christ did not separate either their redeemer's or their own destiny from that of the rest of creation. Contemporary cosmology, I suggest, provides Catholic thought with an opportunity to recapture and magnify the early Christian belief that the entire creation participates narratively in the fulfillment promised by Jesus—and hence in the resurrection of the dead. There is no good excuse for Catholic theology and religious instruction to separate the question of human dignity and destiny from scientific efforts to understand the universe through which God has made a promise to us and now calls us toward new creation.

Destiny: From Individual to Cosmic

During all the centuries in which Catholics have assumed that God's bright creation is darkened by sin, hope for everlasting life has usually meant each soul's being transported after death to a realm of perfect, changeless being beyond the natural world. Nature, though good in itself, is no lasting home and must be left behind as the soul migrates into the beyond. Even though biblical studies have corrected the extreme otherworldliness of traditional eschatological expectations, a dualistic spiritual sensibility dividing "this world" from the next still hovers over contemporary Catholic preaching, devotional life, and theological reflection.

What then can our belief in the resurrection of the dead and our hope for everlasting life mean if the universe is still in the process of being born? And now that the cognitive sciences have demonstrated how deeply our conscious self-awareness depends on the proper functioning of our physical brains, what are the prospects of subjective survival of death? I believe the possible answers to these questions run parallel to the three visions of the universe we have been examining all along: cosmic pessimism, otherworldly optimism, and cosmic hope. Keeping in mind that these three options match up respectively with the archaeological, analogical, and anticipatory ways of interpreting nature, let us look at each of them again, this time with the question of personal destiny as our guiding concern.

Cosmic pessimism, to start with, considers all loss, including the death of human persons, permanent and final. Science, it claims, has now ruled out the possibility of any subjective survival of death. Since our own consciousness is a function of how our material brains are organized, when this organization disintegrates, so does the capacity for thought. Not only our personal lives but also everything else that has ever occurred in the universe will come to rest in a state of total unconsciousness in the end.

How, though, can cosmic pessimists be so sure that this bleak outcome awaits us? Isn't it more natural to expect that a part of us lives on after death? It must have seemed so to most of our human ancestors, but scientific naturalism now interprets our ancestral flirtation with immortality as nothing more than wishful thinking or evolutionary adaptation, or both. Along with natural science has come the end of hope for personal survival of death. This is not always as uncomfortable a thought for cosmic pessimists as most Catholics might think. By resigning themselves to the inevitability of a final obliteration of mind, some pessimists even profess to feel a sense of relief, if not bliss, at the prospect of eventually merging with the mindlessness they associate with pure matter. By allowing us to unload the burden of personal existence, accepting the finality of death may even evoke a sense of gratitude, as captured by the nineteenth-century poet and contemporary of Gerard Manley Hopkins, Algernon Charles Swinburne (1837–1909):

> We thank with brief thanksgiving
> Whatever Gods may be
> That no life lives forever;
> That dead men rise up never;
> That even the weariest river
> Winds somewhere safe to sea.[1]

Other pessimists, however, look at death differently. They see no escape from death's finality, but the bravest among them find solace in the self-esteem that comes from resisting the inevitable as long as they can. While they have the strength, they rage against the limits cast by the prospect of death, and their indignation is energizing. Realizing that the battle will be lost in the end, the courage of combat makes them feel more alive than those who passively submit. Shaking their fists at the gods, as it were, they feel superior to their fate. One can be a cosmic pessimist, therefore, without submitting only passively to the inevitable.[2]

Still other cosmic pessimists profess to experience sufficient fulfillment in their present lives even while living without hope for final personal redemption. I know a number of scientific naturalists, including many philosophers I have met, who are absolutely certain that the universe will end badly. They expect an eventual cosmic catastrophe, and they do not hope to survive death personally, but they still find the transient natural world sufficiently delightful. Life's evanescence gives nature a delicacy that heightens their aesthetic appreciation of each passing moment. Some scientific naturalists take pleasure, as did Einstein, in the mystery of a universe that human inquiry can at least partially illuminate. Their present life, however, is enough for them, and they do not seem terribly bothered by the prospect of their own consciousness eventually being reduced to zero along with everything else.

Another species of scientific naturalists, however, is not so buoyant. It includes serious thinkers who are saddened rather than sparked by the thought that unconsciousness will win out in the end. They would prefer a universe responsive to the insatiable human craving for fuller life, meaning, justice, and imperishability. They would prefer, if they could, to look forward to the resurrection of the dead and a final cosmic rescue. However, once again, science has made such expectation intellectually impossible for them. They are grateful for occasional feelings of well-being during their journey toward the abyss, but these moments, they realize, are only occasional bursts of light in an encircling gloom.[3]

How then may contemporary Catholic theology address these various expressions of cosmic pessimism without contradicting scientific knowledge? I suggest we start by observing once again that cosmic pessimism is usually the logical consequence of a prior intellectual commitment to a metaphysics of the past. This presumptively realistic worldview, as we have already seen, traces life back to a past series of lifeless physical causes. It assumes that the cosmic present and future have been deterministically set in stone from the start, and that all evolutionary outcomes are nothing more than the mindless uncoiling of earlier material states. For cosmic pessimists, mindless and lifeless matter is the most real, fundamental, and intelligible state of being. Neither God nor freedom can find a home in such a world.

A metaphysics of the past, as I noted earlier, is equivalent to what both the theologian Paul Tillich and the eminent Jewish philosopher Hans Jonas call an ontology of death.[4] It is the product of removing every trace of our own felt aliveness from the nonhuman natural world. In the wake of modernity's post-Cartesian expulsion of mind from nature, all that remains is pure lifelessness. Although the impression of nature's fundamental deadness is the result of endowing mathematical abstractions with a false sense of concreteness, modern materialism has taken only what is measurable to be fundamental, concrete reality.[5] Even though this assumption is a product of what Teilhard calls the analytical illusion, as far as cosmic pessimists are concerned, atomized matter is the foundation of all being. What is dead, past, and particulate, in other words, is more real, more fundamental, and easier for our minds to grasp than what is alive and conscious. It is hardly surprising, then, that this understanding of nature would be inhospitable to the hope that we can survive death.

In its response to cosmic pessimism and the ontology of death, however, Catholic theology need no longer fall back on a defensive dualism that emphasizes the immortality of the soul, since this approach still tolerates the idea of an essentially mindless universe existing outside the sphere of our own minds. It yields too much to the ontology of death. Instead, what Catholic reflection on human destiny now requires is not so much an analogical as an anticipatory view of the cosmos. Bringing the scientific sense of an unfinished universe into contact with the tradition of Abrahamic hope, we may now consider the possibility that what is most intelligible and real is not the elemental physical past, as materialists believe, but a still-dawning future whose fullness can be approached only through hope. Only by synthesizing our religious concern for what happens to each person after death with a more comprehensive hope for the entire cosmos and for *all* of life can we address the question of personal destiny in a theologically satisfying way. More on this below.

A second response to the question of personal destiny is *otherworldly optimism*. It acknowledges the fact of corporeal death and perishing, but it claims that humans have immortal souls that are infused immediately by God into each human being. At death, the soul—the seat of conscious, moral, and aesthetic life—is released from its terrestrial body. Once it is sufficiently purified of sin through (expiatory) suffering, the soul will find its final destiny in blissful and eternal contemplation of God. In the meantime, sacramental reminders of the eternal divine goodness are available to each of us in the passing world as emblems of Eden or as imperfect analogies of the eternal now. A grateful appreciation of earthly tokens of eternity keeps our hearts trained on what lies above. We can accept the world's transient fragility only because faith persuades us that created beings participate temporally in an eternal fullness presently hidden from direct view. Our personal salvation can be assured then if we concentrate on what lies above while being both grateful for and detached from the seductive goodness and beauty of the material world.

This sacramental religious optimism, one or another version of which may be found in many religious cultures, adheres to a metaphysics in which an eternal permanence is said to exist beneath, within, above, or behind the transient flow of worldly events.[6] For the religious optimist, the physical universe is a "veil" which, due to the souring of sin, temporarily conceals the timeless divine beauty whose enjoyment is the soul's final destiny and deepest desire. Accordingly, salvation means eventually embracing death as a gateway to the empirically inaccessible world of the infinite God, a sphere into which science cannot penetrate. A metaphysics of the eternal present separates the world of temporal existence sharply from what its devotees take to be the "really real" domain of timelessness. It includes an anthropology that distinguishes decisively between the human soul and its perishable body. It implies that our lives here and now should be motivated by a longing to grow increasingly closer to the imperishable realm of divine reality. Since temporal process leads eventually to loss, otherworldly religious optimism neutralizes the future by absorbing time into eternity. Although it is more

Platonic than biblical, this dualistic view has greatly influenced traditional Catholic speculation on personal destiny.

Catholics who idealize an eternal present are often educated and scientifically informed, but they generally consider modern science religiously insignificant. Evolutionary biology and astrophysics, for example, may be intellectually interesting to a few of them, but the unfinished universe, if they notice it at all, is theologically inconsequential. If the only world that really matters, after all, is one that lies completely outside the reach of empirical method, why should they be terribly concerned about the less important world discoverable by science? Attraction to a metaphysics of the eternal present, I suspect, partly explains why there is a relative dearth of elite Catholic scientists and why our seminaries care little for the scientific education of the clergy. Unfortunately, it also helps account for why many formerly devout Catholic scientists and students are now experimenting with agnosticism and even atheism as a condition for embracing a career in biology, archaeology, cosmology, and other scientific disciplines.[7]

A third way of dealing with destiny is *cosmic hope*. It incorporates religious concern for what happens to each person at death into the setting of an anticipatory cosmology and a corresponding metaphysics of the future. Cosmic hope is fully aware of the world's perpetual perishing, and it remains abreast of new scientific discoveries, but it rejects the pessimists' claim that perishing is final and the universe "pointless." It is also critical of otherworldly religious optimism for failing to pay sufficient attention to natural history and for being indifferent to nature's forward flow. Cosmic hope feels deeply the dramatic quality of nature, and it trusts that the emergent universe of matter moves at least haltingly in the general direction of more being. It is concerned not only with the individual's survival after death but also with the destiny of the entire universe. It links a natural concern for the cosmic future with a biblical hope for the coming of God and the transformation of all creation. In contrast to both cosmic pessimism and otherworldly optimism, cosmic hope requires a patience that follows closely the course of events that make up our unfinished universe. It embraces the new scientific awareness that human consciousness is tied closely to brain functioning as well as to the evolution of life and the long cosmic process that gave rise recently to organisms capable of thought. Cosmic hope does not look upward to an eternal now that nullifies the passage of time and releases souls from their ties to natural history. Instead, it looks forward to a new creation of the whole universe and the renewal of all life, including our personal, subjective consciousness, in God who is the world's ultimate goal and absolute future.

Even though from the point of view of physics and cosmology, the universe (or multiverse) will eventually run down completely, Catholic eschatology may now be bold enough to hope that the totality of cosmic events, including the whole history of tragic suffering, will somehow find redemption in the eternal compassion of God. Even though individuals and species perish, and temporary physical patterns sooner or later dissolve, it is conceivable to cosmic hope that the whole narrative trail of events, including the evolution and development of consciousness, resides forever in God's intimately personal, ever-renewing care for creation.

Such a prospect lies outside the scope of scientific inquiry, of course, since science sees and understands things only in terms of what is predictable in terms of past and present observations. But cosmic hope is not incompatible with science. It rejects nothing that is scientifically established, but it is not obliged to swallow the pessimistic claim that the awakening of consciousness in the cosmos has no ultimate significance and that mind is destined for eternal death. Cosmic hope awaits not the destruction but the transformation of our minds, hearts, and souls along with the whole universe that has given birth to us. What is permanent to the eyes of cosmic hope is not an eternal divine stillness lurking outside the flow of time, but a fully incarnate deity who suffers and struggles along with all of life and who ultimately saves the cosmic drama from absolute loss by weaving it everlastingly into the divine life. Cosmic hope entails both openness to the coming of what is new and a refusal to view the present and future only in terms of what has occurred in the physical past. It looks forward to the convergence of all things in a future cosmic redemption that retrieves and reconfigures all events into an ever widening pattern of meaning, goodness, and beauty.

Ancient precedents

Cosmic pessimism, otherworldly optimism, and cosmic hope all flow historically from three parallel ancient ways of looking at the world. The first is prefigured in ancient Stoicism, atomism, and Greek tragedy. Pessimism is appealing to contemporary scientific naturalists because it seems more "realistic" than the other two options. It refuses to deviate from the tragic assumption that physical dissolution will eventually swallow up and terminate everything good and lovely. Its sober vision of life sees the world as essentially capricious and only accidentally and fleetingly gracious. In the ancient world, I might add, even parts of the Bible—for instance, Ecclesiastes and Job—never banished every shadow of suspicion that absurdity might win out in the end.

Religious optimism, the second way of addressing the question of personal destiny, is foreshadowed in Platonic thought with its emphasis on an unchanging ideal world existing above time, untouched by transience and perishing. This attractive, but often escapist, option has seemed to offer a decisive way of surmounting the suffering and death that threaten life and human existence. However, its negative view of material reality conspires unconsciously with cosmic pessimism to rob nature of intrinsic value and dramatic meaning. Otherworldly optimism, moreover, is not innocent of the charge that it has contributed much to the devaluation of nature that underlies contemporary ecological irresponsibility.

Our third option, cosmic hope, has ancient origins in the Abrahamic, prophetic religious traditions with their sense that the whole of creation, even in all its transience, is seeded with the promise of a fulfillment beyond all present reach. Cosmic hope follows the central biblical motif of promise by viewing the stream of perishable events in nature and history as a path *toward* God, not obstacles to be overcome on a soul's solitary excursion into eternity. Cosmic hope reads the world of becoming as a universal stream into which we may confidently insert our own lives and particular callings. The living God is to be sought not so much beneath, above, or behind the flux of time as up ahead, calling the temporal world into being from out of the future.[8] God is intimately involved with the world and our personal lives here and now not by absorbing each temporal moment into an eternal now (*nunc stans*), but by offering to the world and persons unprecedented opportunities for renewal or becoming more in each present moment, including the moment of death. It is in the context of cosmic hope, therefore, that Christian theology locates the resurrection of Christ and our own personal hopes for new life beyond death.

Cosmic hope, at least in the context of an unfinished universe, associates God not with an unchanging completeness untouched by the flow of perishable events but with a future fulfillment of all time, history, and creation. This hope has its own asceticism, but the detachment it encourages is not that of separating our souls from nature but of conquering our backward-looking tendency to define ourselves and the natural world only in terms of what has been rather than of what will be. Metaphysically speaking, as I have mentioned several times earlier, cosmic hope transposes the so-called transcendentals of classical Catholic thought (being, goodness, unity, beauty, and truth) into the key of futurity that biblical faith associates with Yahweh, the God of promise. What gives value to all that passes is not so much vertical participation in eternity as present anticipation of the arrival of God.

I believe that in addressing the question of our personal destiny, we are each faced with the option of choosing one or the other of the three positions I have just laid out. In terms of this book's inquiry, however, we need to ask which of the three appears most consonant with the natural sciences that have given us a universe in process or what theology takes to be a creation whose true being and meaning are not yet clearly in sight. Of course, in each person's experience, there may exist hybrid versions of the three options. Cosmic pessimism may be tinged with optimism, optimism with hope, and hope with tragic sobriety. However, upon close inspection, genuine hope appears incompatible with both cosmic pessimism and otherworldly optimism. Cosmic hope, instead of taking a headlong leap into a heavenly realm untouched by time, stays with the world process, waiting patiently across many generations, across billions of cosmic years—perhaps involving many undetectable worlds—for the dramatic flow of events to carry the entire creation, and not just our personal lives, toward fulfillment in God.

But is cosmic hope realistic? By adopting such a long and patient posture are we facing toward or away from reality? Scientific naturalists, who claim that nothing can escape the eventual death of the universe, consider both optimism and hope to be useful adaptive fictions at best. Not only will our own subjective consciousness be extinguished at death, they claim, but also ages from now, the entire physical universe will sink into the permanent oblivion of energy exhaustion.

So, isn't it unrealistic to hope? A metaphysics of the past, it goes without saying, will judge both religious optimism and cosmic hope as unintelligible and "irrational" because, for its many disciples, a primordial state of lifelessness, as Jonas says, is "the intelligible par excellence." The archaeological vision can, in principle, allow for no everlasting future personal survival because it cannot even allow for the *first* arrival of life, mind, and personality as ontologically new and distinct phenomena in cosmic process. Cosmic pessimism permits no true opening for posthumous personal existence since it has no serious opening for any future whatsoever. The past alone is the really real. Scientific naturalism's giving ontological priority to lifeless matter prevents it from acknowledging as real or intelligible anything outside of the devitalized and quantifiable zone of the cosmic past. In such a metaphysical perspective, human destiny can be thought of as nothing other than a return in the end to the lifeless and mindless stuff from which everything began.

In the following chapter, I attempt to expose what seems to me to be the irrationality and logical incoherence of a metaphysics of the past, especially insofar as it tries to account for human intelligence in purely materialist terms, so I will not preview my argument here. Suffice it to say at this point that if the elemental past is taken to be the privileged realm of the real and intelligible, there are no grounds for life and mind to have any ontological standing or special value even now, let alone in the future. Nor does our second option, otherworldly optimism, provide adequate grounds for the valuing of minds and persons. Indeed, it clings to an impoverished understanding of both personality and the universe. By divorcing the soul from its cosmic matrix, it ignores the long cosmic drama that has gone into the fashioning of personal existence. Thinking of personhood in terms of a soul that belongs essentially to a nonphysical realm of being leads the religious optimist to ignore as irrelevant the anticipatory universe that gave birth to beings who live on hope. Indifferent to the long-term cosmic future, otherworldly optimism diminishes our being by narrowing the horizon of human expectation. In doing so (as I indicated in the previous chapter), it also undermines the cosmological foundations of a scientifically informed theological sense of human dignity.

Most academic philosophers today consider cosmic pessimism to be the only one of our three options that can realistically claim the backing of science and reason.[9] However, a reasonable critique of this tragic "realism" begins by recalling that if anything can justifiably claim the backing of science today, it is our new awareness that the universe is still coming into being. Genuine realism cannot ignore the fact that in some sense the cosmos is not-yet, and if the cosmic narrative is still unfinished, we cannot expect to arrive at clarity here and now about what, if anything, the cosmic story is finally all about. As in the case of any dramatic series of events, we have to wait. Waiting in hope, it seems to me, is the most realistic epistemological stance available to those who seek to make sense of both the unfinished universe and personal destiny.

It is the discipline of patience that differentiates genuine religious faith from both otherworldly optimism and the naively impatient archaeological search for solid ground in the elemental cosmic past.[10] But, of course, we are impatient. We prefer not to wait for the world to become wider and deeper. It is hard for any of us to bear the uncertainty of an unfinished cosmic drama, so we try to round it off in the noontime of our own brief spans, and sum it up in categories sculpted solely in accordance with past and present experience. Cosmic pessimists think of the world as mere simplicity "masquerading" as complexity, and otherworldly optimists consider deep time metaphysically irrelevant. And even though religious optimists and cosmic pessimists seem far apart in most respects, they share a restiveness that refuses to let the world ripen. One of the constant temptations of all religions is an obsession with present doctrinal certitude, but scientific naturalists nurture a similar trance in their impatience for present clarity. They prefer a metaphysics of the past because they can accept only what is resolvable into the fixed and familiar. As far as consistent scientific naturalists are concerned, there can be nothing new under the sun. They will simply not allow it. This uncompromising certitude leads to claims such as those of Duke University philosopher Owen Flanagan:

> If you wish that your life had prospects for transcendent meaning, for more than the personal satisfaction and contentment you can achieve while you are alive, and more than what you will have contributed to the well-being of the world after you die, then you are still in the grip of illusions. Trust me, you can't get more. But what you can get, if you live well, is enough. Don't be greedy. Enough is enough.[11]

If we were sure that the present state of the universe is nothing more than the fatalistic working out of what was in the cards from the start, as Flanagan believes to be the case, we might reasonably bow to his demand for an end to all ambiguity about personal destiny. However, as long as the world is still coming into being and our personal stories remain tied into an unfinished universe, we cannot honestly expect at present to make out clearly what is in store either for us or for the universe. Again, there is room for hope.

Anyway, uncertainty about our personal destinies is itself inseparable from the current incompleteness of the universe. Before science revealed to us that the natural world is a process of development, questions about personal fulfillment could be easily divorced from the question of cosmic destiny. As long as the material universe was thought of as a prison for the exiled soul, religious optimists did not worry about what would eventually happen to the cosmic detention center after they escaped from it. But now we expect that the universe has an incalculably long future ahead of it, and even if energy exhaustion will eventually prevail, we can no longer flippantly separate our personal hopes from concern about the cosmic future. Since our conscious subjectivity is intimately woven into the historical unfolding of an entire cosmos, we cannot help but be concerned about the eventual perishing of the cosmos that has given birth to us. If the universe as a whole is drifting toward some kind of extinction, the significance of our own lives is placed in question along with it. Today, then, theological discussion of personal survival beyond death meets up more meaningfully than ever with the question of whether the universe, or the multiverse if there is one, is in some sense permanently redeemable.

So, what about the eventual cosmic apocalypse predicted not only by the Bible but now also by astrophysics? Isn't cosmic pessimism the only option that fits "realistically" the prospect of the eventual death of the universe? Such questions are unavoidable. Cosmic hope, however, is not obliged to settle for the impatient and groundless certitude that Flanagan possesses.

It understands our admittedly uncertain religious longing for final personal redemption to be an expression, at the level of human emergence, of the anticipatory straining toward the future that has carried our whole universe along for billions of years. It wants to stay connected to the cosmic drama. Consequently, it expects to find what is real and what is "intelligible par excellence" not in the dead cosmic past but in the long-term future where ample metaphysical space remains available for an unpredictable narrative coherence. It can only be in the realm of the cosmic future, therefore, that our souls are ontologically most at home, and it is only in hoping for a *cosmic* fulfillment that our minds are epistemologically best adapted to reality.

Here again, our narrative approach to nature, in keeping with the modern (re)discovery of time, allows for new ways of thinking realistically about destiny, both personal and cosmic. Cosmic hope's expectation that the *whole* scheme of things has a meaning, and that the cosmos can be saved in God, may be taken seriously, however, only if we first learn to think of the universe narratively, that is, as composed fundamentally of temporal events rather than spatially distributed chunks of physical stuff. Elemental physical units, imagined in accordance with modern atomistic materialism, eventually disperse, but events can add up over time into a story whose possible coherence requires, cognitively speaking, a patient posture of expectation on our part. Unlike material elements, temporal events can accumulate, each narratively linked to the preceding ones, so that whatever has happened in the past is still resident, at least faintly, in the present state of things and will remain ingredient in the future as well.[12]

There is something lasting, in other words, about the stream of events that build up into our currently unfinished cosmos. A metaphysics of hope thinks of God as both the inspiration and the everlasting recipient of all the events that make up the larger cosmic story. So, if we follow the spirit of Jesus's promises, it seems entirely appropriate for Catholics to trust that God's assimilating the cosmic story into the divine life includes and cherishes also the specific dramas that give each of us our personal identities.[13] A metaphysics of the future allows us to hope that our personal stories, along with that of the unfinished universe to which we belong, abide imperishably in God's everlasting love and remembrance where even the hairs of our head are numbered (Lk. 12:7).

It is hard to fathom how such imperishability would not also include the survival and renewal of our own subjective consciousness. The cosmic pessimist, of course, will ask for evidence. But the only kind of evidence the pessimist is willing to look at is the kind that conforms to the assumed ontological lifelessness and mindlessness of the fixed cosmic past. The pessimist's impatient limiting of the whole arena of all relevant evidence to what is predictable in terms of the cosmic past excludes any place for resurrection or new creation. The resurrection of Christ, after all, can be approached most appropriately through a metaphysics of the future rather than by looking exclusively for "evidence" that fits a metaphysics of the dead past. Cosmic hope, accordingly, requires an epistemology that scans the horizon of the future and is willing to wait, perhaps for many generations and in the spirit of our biblical ancestors, for new events and a richer coherence to show up. It is in this context, I believe, that we can most realistically ground our hopes for resurrection and new creation. In contrast to cosmic pessimism, cosmic hope fosters an epistemological patience and, hence, a refreshing realism that refuse to put premature limits on the possible. In the world anticipated by cosmic hope, death—which to the materialist is "the intelligible par excellence"—can have no intelligible place at all. It is home instead to "the resurrection and the life" (Jn. 11:25).

Apart from God's preservative remembrance of the whole series of events that make up the cosmic story, the world would amount to nothing in the end. And no matter how hard cosmic pessimists try to salvage some kind of personal meaning in the face of what they assume will be a final personal perishing, if they are consistent they will have to admit that their own brief experience of conscious existence amounts to little in the end as well. Yet, if the world's absolute future is also infinite compassion, both the cosmic story and our individual narratives can be redeemed. Catholics are not departing from the tradition of hope for bodily resurrection when they expect their subjective identities to be somehow saved everlastingly *along with* the cosmic drama by the Spirit of God in communion with the risen Christ. As the New Testament teaches, it is only through faith and not sight that we can gain at present any sense of this destiny. Faith generates hope, however, and hope is not an escape from reality but the only access we have to the always dawning sphere of what is really real. Cosmic hope rejects cosmic pessimism because the latter makes a morbid settlement with the realm of death by cultivating a metaphysics that absolutizes the fixed and lifeless past. And cosmic hope also renounces the dualistic religious optimism that unfortunately also concedes too much to the ontology of death by separating the soul's destiny from that of the physical universe. Cosmic hope looks instead toward the transformation of the whole of creation and a fulfillment of all time—when "death will be no more" (Rev. 21:4).

Mind: From Afterthought to Axis

Evolutionary biology has considerably altered our sense of life, and it now promises to enhance our understanding of human existence and behavior as well. For some Darwinians, especially those who espouse a materialist worldview, Darwin's science is so impressive in its explanatory power that it now replaces theology as the deepest available way to explain all manifestations of life—including human intelligence. By focusing on the human mind in this chapter, however, I argue that a Catholic theological perspective on the universe—one rooted in a metaphysics of hope—can have an illuminating and noncompetitive role to play alongside of evolutionary biology (and other scientific perspectives) in contemporary attempts to understand our capacity for thinking and knowing.

First, though, is it self-evident that evolutionary science can shed much light at all on the core features of human intelligence? Darwin himself was not sure that it could. "With me the horrid doubt always arises," he wrote to one of his friends, "whether the convictions of man's mind, which has been developed from the mind of the lower animals, are of any value or at all trustworthy. Would any one trust in the convictions of a monkey's mind, if there are any convictions in such a mind?"[1] Darwin never followed up on his "horrid doubt," nor, for that matter, have most other scientists and philosophers. Recently, however, the esteemed New York University philosopher Thomas Nagel, an avowed atheist, has expressed doubt that evolutionary naturalism, precisely because it assumes a *materialist* worldview, can make much sense of mind or the evolutionary story of mind's gradual emergence. In his controversial book *Mind and Cosmos*, Nagel, known to have been a fervent materialist throughout his academic career, expresses his growing conviction that evolutionary naturalism—which claims that mind can be accounted for ultimately in terms of mindless natural selection—only clouds our understanding of life and mind.[2] The typically materialist spin that Darwinians give to the story of life on earth is not science, Nagel says, but rather a questionable nonscientific interpretation of nature. Instead of shedding any real light on life and mind, materialism reduces life to lifeless elements and denies, in effect, that when life and mind came along in cosmic history, anything truly new or remarkable was going on.

The unreasonableness of materialism becomes manifest, especially, in its failure to make sense of the most impressive chapter that has ever occurred in natural history, namely, the universe's recent awakening into consciousness with the coming of humans. I agree with Nagel that making sense of the drama of cosmic awakening demands nothing less than a whole new understanding of the natural world. What is needed is a vision of the universe that stitches the phenomenon of mind tightly and intelligibly into the physical universe while leaving the materialist baggage behind. I believe that a metaphysics of the future can provide this needed coherence. Materialism, by contrast, is conditioned to looking back toward the elemental cosmic past in search of a complete understanding of present phenomena. It is content to remark that mind came from mindlessness and that unto mindlessness it will eventually return. Nagel responds rightly, however, that such simplistic physicalism sheds precious little light on the splendid properties of human intelligence. Moreover, materialism is logically self-sabotaging, as the above citation of Darwin implies. For if our complex minds are reducible to mindless material elements, why would we take seriously any claims issued by those minds, including the minds of evolutionary naturalists?

Nagel's earlier writings about mind had already evoked much controversy, but his latest book is especially irritating to his former materialist allies. The book's subtitle is already enough to cause a stir: *Why the Materialist Neo-Darwinian Conception of Nature Is Almost Certainly False*. For my purposes here, the appearance of Nagel's book is an occasion to reflect not only on the place of mind in the unfinished cosmic journey, but also on the need for a whole new worldview to make sense of evolution. Nagel, it should be noted, has no problem with the standard scientific narrative of mind's evolution. Rather, he is concerned about whether the materialist metaphysics in which that narrative is still usually packaged can make the story of mind's emergence intelligible. He argues that it cannot, but he provides no alternative. Here I want to ask whether a metaphysics of the future can bring coherence to the story of mind's emergence.

During the nineteenth and twentieth centuries, materialism—the belief that lifeless and mindless "matter" is the ultimate origin and destiny of all being—became the main metaphysical setting for the life sciences. Nagel, however, now considers the alloying of science with materialism to be an intellectual dead end. Although evolutionary *science* is illuminating, *evolutionary naturalism*—the fusion of materialist belief with evolutionary biology—is a marriage misbegotten. Evolutionary naturalism's dimming of life becomes especially conspicuous in its failure to account for the splendid properties of mind.

Our minds, science has now demonstrated, are sewn seamlessly into the fundamental physical features of the Big Bang universe. Whatever else this may mean, it now appears that the cosmic journey is at the very least a mind-making venture. Materialists, of course, disagree. Mindless matter is for them the ground and final destiny of all being, and so the actual arrival and temporary flourishing of mind in natural history can be nothing more than a fluke. Mind's relatively recent arrival has done nothing to disturb the fundamental mindlessness, and hence pointlessness, of the universe. For the new Nagel, however, in view of the narrative togetherness of mind and cosmos, overlooking the extraordinary properties of mind while trying to understand the universe seems unreasonable. Acknowledging the inseparability of mind and nature, however, leaves Nagel trapped between two problems. The first is how to avoid materialism if life and mind arose historically, without any supernatural leaps, from mindless cosmic stuff. The second is how to avoid theology if the universe turns out to be a mind-making, and hence purposive, enterprise. Nagel does little to resolve this dilemma.

Underlying his first problem is the suspicion that evolutionary naturalism makes the universe look so dumb from the outset that Darwin himself justifiably wondered why we should ever trust the minds that have emerged from such a lowly progenitor. So Nagel is now asking his fellow materialists—think, for example, of Richard Dawkins, Daniel Dennett, or Steven Pinker—to look carefully at Darwin's reservations and critically examine their own cognitional pluck. I mention these evolutionary naturalists since they have no shortage of confidence in the stellar integrity of their own mental functioning. Yet it needs to be asked how each can justify his exceptional cognitional self-confidence if at the same time he is convinced that his mind is reducible to mindless physical stuff that has been shuffled around through time by inherently aimless algorithms and processed by impersonal natural selection and the ever-shifting winds of cultural conditioning.

The current materialist understanding of evolution is almost certainly false, Nagel claims, but the problem he faces is that the majority of contemporary scientists and philosophers are, like the three I have just mentioned, unwilling or unable to separate biology from a materialist worldview. A smothering materialism has chaperoned Darwin's science since the first publication of the *Origin of Species* (1859). In his diary Darwin revealed his own leaning toward materialism as the only available philosophical framework he could think of to house his new science. Both Karl Marx and Ernst Haeckel cited Darwin in support of their respective versions of materialism. And in the Darwinian world today materialist naturalism has become nearly the norm.

The esteemed British philosopher Simon Blackburn, for example, summarizes neatly and revealingly the kind of opposition Nagel is up against. The problem with Nagel's new book, Blackburn writes,

> is that only a tiny proportion of its informed readers will find it anything other than profoundly wrong-headed. For, as the title suggests, Nagel's central idea is that there are things that science, as it is presently conceived, cannot possibly explain. The current conception is that, given a purely physical beginning, everything else—chemistry, biology, life, mind, consciousness, intelligence, values, understandings, even science—follows on by natural processes. Particles beget atoms beget molecules beget enzymes beget proteins beget life begets *Homo sapiens* who begets the Royal Society and the rules of tennis. We do not understand every step in this process, naturally, but we can be reasonably confident of its overall shape and confident, too, that any remaining gaps that can be closed will be closed only by more understanding of the same broad kind that we already have.[3]

I am not sure that only a "tiny" number of readers will respect Nagel's efforts, but Blackburn is certainly not alone in viewing the new Nagel as an enemy of science. For example, Jerry Coyne, an evolutionist at the University of Chicago, advised Michael Chorost that contributing an essay on Nagel to the *Chronicle of Higher Education* would be comparable to writing "an article on astrology." Steven Pinker, Chorost reports, refers to Nagel's book as "the shoddy reasoning of a once-great thinker," while Daniel Dennett says the work "isn't worth anything—it's cute and it's clever and it's not worth a damn."[4] Blackburn and the other critics share the assumption that the entire history of nature, including the evolution of life and mind, is nothing more than elemental physical simplicity parading presently in the guise of complexity. Nagel, however, finds nothing illuminating about this kind of reductionism, since if cognitive complexity were reducible to mindless simplicity, there would be no reason to respect propositions issued by any mind, including those of Blackburn and the others.

If Nagel's first problem is how to tell the story of mind's gradual emergence without succumbing to Blackburn's brand of evolutionary naturalism, his second problem is how to endow evolution with even the thinnest vein of finality or purpose without implicitly importing theology into his philosophy of nature. This would be a desperate move that even Nagel, like his hardier materialist opponents, is not ready to entertain. Nagel now suspects, nevertheless, that the cosmic story has to be purposive or, as philosophers say, teleological (goal-oriented). Maybe, he speculates, the production of mind is what the cosmic story is really all about. Yet, this suggestion sounds so unscientific that it is not destined to get very far in the current intellectual setting. Throughout the past four centuries, science has sought to avoid conflation with theology by leaving the question of purpose out of its distinctive method of investigating the world. For Nagel, though, an honest examination of the close fit between mind and nature may mean that it is time to bring teleology back, that is, if we want to make the universe intelligible. He now considers the emergence of mind to be such a momentous revelation of what nature really is that he is on the verge of calling for a whole new worldview to fit the fact of mind more tightly to the story of the universe. Yet, he stops short of doing so.

Although Nagel's vocal critics disguise their disgust with his rebellion by complaining that he has turned into an enemy of science, they are really complaining about his apostasy from the culture of scientific materialism. Nagel's rejection of materialism, they say, only makes room for miracles, divine intervention, and intelligent design to account for the improbable emergence of mind in evolution. Anyone who reads *Mind and Cosmos* carefully, however, will realize that the atheist Nagel has nothing against science and that he has no theological agenda. And yet, I believe it should be of special interest to Catholic theologians that Nagel has no supernaturalist intentions. For it is significant enough that this renowned contemporary thinker, now risking his own academic popularity, is instructing his fellow philosophers of mind that evolutionary naturalism is a self-contradictory worldview regardless of its theological implications. What could be more irrational, after all, than trying to fit mind into a universe from which any real place for mind has already been removed?

An evolutionary naturalist would respond, in the manner of Richard Dawkins, that Nagel lacks an adequately nuanced sense of natural history and of what deep time can accomplish on its own. Innumerable minute organic modifications processed by impersonal natural selection are enough to account for intelligence if time is sufficient. Given enough time, mindlessness can turn into mind. To Nagel, however, such a proposal smacks of alchemy. To be sure, evolution takes a lot of time and requires countless accidents and natural selection. However, Darwin's formula for life's development cannot tell us how the golden properties of human intelligence can be created from the dross of primordial cosmic mindlessness simply by adding the elixir of deep time. Granted, telling the evolutionary story of mind's emergence is instructive and, from a scientific perspective, absolutely essential. But the story needs to be read at many different levels, and materialism, by reducing mind to mindlessness, is hardly equipped to shed much light on the drama. Evolutionary biology can specify the genetic alphabet and the grammatical rules operative in the story of life, but it lacks the tools to tell us what is really going on when a dark and silent universe dramatically awakens into the daylight of consciousness.

Condemnations of Nagel by his materialist critics have been heated, and understandably so. His opponents realize that Nagel's observations, if correct, would rip apart their worldview from bottom to top. Devotees of materialist naturalism are firm believers, dead sure of the insuperable truthfulness of their creed. Yet, while professing to be empirical, they fail to notice the anticipatory performance of their own minds and what this can tell us about the cosmos that gave birth to thought. Surely it says something significant about *the universe* that it harbors organisms who not only sleep, eat, and make love, but who also ask questions, long for meaning, seek truth, and aspire to goodness—and who cannot live, therefore, without anticipation. In the context of our unfinished universe, perhaps the human mind is not a cosmic afterthought or an unintelligible gloss on an otherwise mindless universe. Perhaps the mind epitomizes and brings out into the open an anticipatory undercurrent that accompanies the entire cosmic journey. Ultimately, I propose, only a metaphysics of the future can provide an appropriate intellectual setting for understanding both mind and the universe.

The significance of Bernard Lonergan

Even prior to the middle of the last century, Teilhard was already calling for a "new physics" that makes "thought" no less part of the universe than any other natural phenomenon. Accordingly, he was convinced that we must revise and expand our understanding of nature to make a proper home for our minds. This was one of the main arguments of *The Human Phenomenon*. The emergence of mind in evolution is not a supernatural rupturing of an essentially mindless physical continuum but the *eruption* of a seam of anticipation that had always been simmering beneath the surface. Long before Nagel became an important philosopher, Teilhard was already insisting that the phenomenon of "thought" has emerged from deep within the entrails of matter. Yet, materialists of his own day and ours alike fail to "see" that the arrival of mind might be an important key to what the cosmos is all about.

Nagel might also find support for his critique of evolutionary naturalism in the writings of the Jesuit philosopher Bernard Lonergan. No recent thinker, in my opinion, has carried out the project of fitting mind into its universe with more intellectual power than has Lonergan. In his magisterial *Insight* (1957) and elsewhere, this distinguished Catholic intellectual demonstrates that if our worldview cannot make a proper home for what goes on in our minds—in every act of attending, understanding, knowing, and deciding—we need to look for another worldview.[5] Materialism will not do, especially since its program of reducing mind to mindlessness implicitly subverts the confidence that each knower needs in order to undertake the arduous search for true understanding. Nor, I must add, will the otherworldly optimism of the analogical vision help either, since it gives a misleading picture of our minds by uprooting them from their dramatic cosmic matrix. Instead, what we need now, as an explanatory framework for understanding the relationship of mind to the universe, is an anticipatory metaphysics, one that views human intelligence not as a cosmic afterthought, but as the expression of an axis of anticipation coextensive with the whole drama of nature. Mind, in other words, is a blossoming of the cosmos rather than the aimless outcome of an essentially mindless material commotion.

A metaphysics of the future, as I have been arguing, locates the universe in a theological framework that envisages God as the world's ultimate destiny and final goal. Nagel would be disappointed, of course, that our quest for a universe wide enough to be an intelligible setting for the human mind must enlist—for the sake of its overall coherence—the assistance of theology. As a lifelong atheist, Nagel feels no inclination to talk about God at all. He has even remarked that he personally prefers a godless universe. He admits that he knows little about theology, even though lately he has shown more interest in it than previously. He should be reassured, though, that respectable theology never aspires to compete with science. Good theology wants science to push natural explanations, including those of evolutionary biology and the cognitive sciences, as far as they can possibly take us in our exploration of natural phenomena. If there is a place for theology in the human quest for understanding and truth, it is not that of plugging gaps in scientific inquiry or providing information that empirical method can gather by itself. Rather, theology enters the discussion of mind and cosmos most unobtrusively and disarmingly by addressing the imposing question that Nagel raises but from which he keeps backing off: Why is the universe intelligible at all?

A Catholic theology of creation, as implied in the works of Bernard Lonergan, has a reasonable response to that question, one that supports the scientific quest for intelligibility and truth without competing or conflicting with it in any way. By grounding the entire universe in the creative wisdom of God—that is, of unrestricted being and intelligence—theology provides an indispensable justification of the whole scientific enterprise. It grounds the trust our minds need as we reach out in anticipation of the world's intelligibility. Evolutionary naturalism, on the other hand, is an intellectual dead end, as Nagel rightly demonstrates. Its implicitly materialist metaphysics, if taken with full seriousness, subverts the intellectual confidence required to undertake scientific inquiry at all.

The evolutionary naturalist claims that the natural history leading to the appearance of the human mind is a mindless series of events, and that if the series is long enough, it can account all by itself for the emergence and splendor of mind. The Duke University philosopher Owen Flanagan, for example, has no doubt that human intelligence, even though it is a marvelous evolutionary outcome, does not require intelligence—by which he means divine intelligence—as an explanatory factor at any point in its emergence. "Evolution," he announces, "demonstrates how intelligence arose from totally insensate origins."[6] The materialist philosopher Daniel Dennett echoes Flanagan's claim: "The designs in nature are nothing short of brilliant, but the process of design that generates them is utterly lacking in intelligence of its own."[7] Many other contemporary evolutionists agree.[8]

Again, I want to make it clear that I am fully appreciative of the narrative value of evolutionary explanations. However, since our acts of understanding and knowing require that we place implicit trust in our cognitional capacities, is a purely evolutionary account of mind enough to ground this indispensable trust? Is a purely Darwinian account of intelligence sufficient to ground our cognitional confidence—as Darwin himself wondered?[9] Evolutionary naturalists claim to be lovers of truth, and they spontaneously trust their minds in the very act of claiming that minds, including their own, are reducible to mindlessness. But how then can their materialist accounts justify the trust they are now placing in their own minds? They declare that human intelligence can be accounted for ultimately in terms of mindless material stuff and processes, but why then should they trust the minds—made of the same mindless stuff—that make this claim?

Once again, there can be no doubt that evolutionary naturalists do trust their minds. Indeed, it is hard to find more spirited expressions of cognitional self-confidence than in the declarations of evolutionists such as Dawkins, Dennett, and Flanagan that mind is reducible to, and completely explainable in terms of, mindless matter and deep time. Yet, none of them seems prepared to wonder, along with Darwin and Nagel, why a materialist worldview does not logically sabotage the trust they have in their own minds' capacity to reach correct understanding.

Lonergan, on the other hand, urges us to look for close coherence between what our minds claim to be true about the world and what is required for our minds to work at all. Reflecting on Sigmund Freud's materialist account of cognition, he writes: "If enthusiasm for the achievement of Freud were to lead me to affirm that all thought and affirmation is just a byproduct of the libido . . . this very assertion of mine would have to be mere assertion from a suspect source."[10] Now let us adapt Lonergan's remarks to our critique of the Darwinian materialist's accounts of cognition: "If enthusiasm for the achievement of [Darwin] were to lead me to affirm that all thought and affirmation is just a byproduct of [blind natural selection] then . . . this very assertion of mine would be suspect."

Implications for cosmology and theology

Evolutionary naturalists fail to notice the lack of correspondence between their minds' performance and their materialist worldview because at heart they do not really believe their own minds are part of nature. A tacit dualism left over from the religious tradition of otherworldly optimism implicitly exiles their own intellectual performance from the mindless universe they are trying to understand. The cosmic story cannot be told rightly if it leaves out any mention of the recent emergence in evolution of minds that trust their capacity to understand and know. Yet, evolutionary naturalists fail to take seriously and consistently the inseparability of mind and its cosmic matrix.

Leaving their own mental functioning off their map of nature at the outset, therefore, evolutionary naturalists can hardly claim to have understood either mind or the universe.[11] Assuming nature to be fundamentally unintelligent, and intelligence merely epiphenomenal, evolutionary naturalists cannot avoid giving the impression that the emergence of critical intelligence in life's evolution is a mere fluke (or perhaps a by-product of a fluke) of nature and hence undeserving of the enormous trust they place in it. Falling back into a tacit dualism, they implicitly segregate the splendor of their own minds from what they take to be the pointless and mindless world that produced them. In the very act of exalting their minds, therefore, they rob them of any real value (or even existence).

Some philosophers of mind suspect that we will never possess the conceptual tools to bridge the gap between physicalist accounts of mind, on the one hand, and the first person discourse of intelligent subjects, on the other. For example, the philosopher John R. Searle admits that "conscious states have a subjective mode of existence in the sense that they exist only when they are experienced by a human or animal subject." At the same time, however, Searle can find no justification in his purely materialist understanding of nature for trusting his own intelligence.[12]

Is there a coherent way, therefore, of locating critical intelligence *within* the evolution of the universe while at the same time justifying the trust we spontaneously place in the performance of our minds? If so, I am convinced that nothing less than a revolution in metaphysics and cosmology is mandatory. This readjustment requires an epochal shift from the archaeological and analogical worldviews toward an anticipatory one. Whatever insights we may have gained from the first two perspectives throughout the centuries must now be set in the context of an unfinished universe. Even though analytical science has had an essential role to play in tracing the astrophysical, chemical, and biological steps that have led to the emergence of mind, this narration alone neither explains the appearance of critical intelligence sufficiently nor justifies the confidence we need to place in our minds if they are to function as reliable sources of understanding and truth.

Contrary to materialist naturalism, therefore, we may understand our intellectual longing as an extension and intensification of the anticipatory leaning of the universe itself. Contemporary astrophysics, cosmology, and biology have demonstrated that our critical intelligence has its historical roots deep down in the physical and chemical subsoil of cosmic history. Today it is more appropriate than ever theologically, therefore, to read the whole cosmic story—including the possible existence of a multiverse—as narrative anticipation, as a drama whose meaning is to make the whole of creation ready for its climactic encounter with a transcendent destiny.

After critical intelligence burst out recently in cosmic history, it began gradually to become aware, by way of religious sensitivity, of an incomprehensible horizon of being, meaning, truth, beauty, and futurity—God, in other words—in whose inviting ambience the universe has always silently dwelled and moved. Apart from this infinite horizon, our own critical intelligence could never have become actual in this or any other universe. And apart from our being already in the grasp of this horizon, as Lonergan's work confirms, we would at present have no permanently reliable reason to trust our minds.

Morality: From Perfectionism to Process

Nothing is more enlivening than the pursuit of perfection. Nothing is more deadening than the cult of perfectionism. The moral life, as Catholics have understood it, is the pursuit of perfection, but the analogical worldview adopted by the Church in antiquity has sometimes played host to a moral perfectionism motivated by the avoidance of shame rather than the longing for new life. The sense of an unfinished, anticipatory universe, I believe, makes room for a more biblical and more enlivening moral vision.

Traditional Catholic thought identified perfection with changelessness, thus associating supreme goodness with immutability. For centuries, as we have seen, the fixed arrangement of the heavens reflected—imperfectly— the unchanging perfection of God. Taking unchangingness to be a mark of perfection long ago, Catholic moral thinking has never completely abandoned the assumption that mutability is an emblem of inferiority. The idea that God descends and suffers—and in so doing undergoes internal change—therefore, has made Catholic philosophers and theologians uncomfortable. In spite of the powerful inaugural Christian idea of divine *kenosis* (God's self-emptying), Catholic moral thought and preaching still, at least unconsciously, cultivate an ideal of perfection as changelessness, an association that lessens the importance of the developmental universe to which science has lately drawn our attention—and that can even weaken our sense of divine love. The analogical vision is not ready-made, either metaphysically or cosmologically, for an unfinished universe, nor has it ever been able to represent fully the meaning of the Cross and the drama of divine self-emptying love.

A metaphysics of the eternal present, by identifying perfection with changelessness, also tacitly sanctions a religious longing to flee prematurely from temporal existence into a bodiless spiritual world apart from nature. I have been arguing that the way to correct this temptation is to think of God in a more biblical way as the world's future and of the incarnation as the coming of that future into the world. For Christians, the resurrection of Christ is the decisive arrival and opening up of that future. By adhering for many centuries to the analogical vision and simultaneously to an otherworldly religious optimism, however, Catholic thought has failed to appropriate fully the idea of God as the world's goal and future. This neglect has led to our protecting moral theology from taking into sufficient account the developmental aspect not only of the universe, but also of our personal lives.

The unfinished universe of contemporary scientific understanding provides a refreshing new backdrop for the renewal of moral theology. It roots ethical motivation in a wayfaring hope that renounces perfectionism because it expects a future of new creation up ahead. It mitigates the temptation to make premature pilgrimages into eternity, for it acknowledges that our lives are part of a long cosmic journey that will not come to fulfillment within the span of an individual's, community's, or even a species' lifetime. The world has never yet been perfected. Things have never been rounded off or brought to completion. Theologically speaking, this means that creation still has a future, and moral life a fresh significance. Since the world is not yet what it ideally could be, we cannot realistically expect it, here and now, to be fully intelligible, beautiful, or good. And yet there is always room for hope. Full intelligibility, beauty, and goodness belong to the realm of the not-yet. Perfectionism, unfortunately, expects the universe to be maximally good, beautiful, and intelligible here and now, and so it commands nature to be "intelligently designed." The underside of such impatience is both hatred of ourselves for falling short of moral perfection, and disgust with the universe for failing to meet our present perfectionistic demands.

Perfectionism also underlies much contemporary hatred of religion. As I have previously pointed out, puritanical perfectionism is as prevalent in contemporary militant atheism as it ever was in traditional morality and religion. The New Atheism of recent years, for example, is a full-blown expression of impatient resentment. Its moralistic hatred of God and religion feeds on a tacit demand that the world, if God exists, should be perfectly designed and our religions should reflect this perfection infallibly. However, an unfinished universe, to repeat our theme, means that the future is still open. The openness of the universe and human life to the future can make a difference in how we think about God, morality, worship, and the meaning of our lives. We can start by acknowledging that our religions, images of God, theologies, and moral codes are themselves unfinished and that we should not expect too much from them here and now either. For if the world is unfinished, faith and moral existence have a future too. As part of an emergent universe, they have room for maturation. We may be able to learn something from evolution and the cosmic process, therefore, about how to pitch our moral lives.

What is going on?

The philosopher Immanuel Kant thought that each of us needs to keep asking three big questions: What can I know? What ought I to do? What may I hope for? But in the age of science, I think we may add another: What is going on? To act responsibly, it is not enough to know only what is going on in human life but also what is going on in the universe that gave birth to us.

Understanding the universe is by no means irrelevant to the question of what constitutes right action, but Catholic moralists have typically thought about virtue without considering the cosmic context of our lives. The cosmos still functions for much Catholic moral thinking predominantly as a stage for the historically unfolding human drama rather than as a source of ethical insight and inspiration.

According to scientific naturalists, meanwhile, the cosmos is plainly pointless. Even though it may be mystically enchanting for a few, most scientists and philosophers view the whole of nature as completely aimless. If so, it can hardly be a guide to human conduct for secularists either. Scientific skeptics today almost universally take for granted that nothing of lasting significance is working itself out in the universe, and this assumption serves only to separate their sense of human obligation from the impersonal cosmos they see languishing senselessly in the background. With its eyes fixed on a universe still coming into being, however, Catholic moral theology, I want to suggest, may now tie the question of what we should be doing with our lives more closely than ever to what has been going on in the universe at large. A scientifically informed conviction that our lives and labors are woven into a still-unfinished cosmic process can give new zest to moral aspiration.[1] Realizing that the universe is still coming into being, that it has never yet reached a stage of completion, and that it still has room for more being, goodness, and beauty—this awareness can have the interesting consequence of delivering us from both the numbing effects of moral indifference and the crushing discouragement that accompanies moral perfectionism.

The fundamental basis of moral aspiration, I suggest with Teilhard, is that each of us is thrust from birth into a dramatic cosmic stream of becoming.[2] Once we fully realize that the universe is still unfinished, our moral life has a new meaning.

> Why act—and how to act? . . . So long as our conceptions of the universe remained static, the basis of duty remained extremely obscure. To account for this mysterious law which weighs fundamentally on our liberty, men had recourse to all sorts of explanations, from that of an

explicit command issued from outside to that of an irrational but categorical instinct. In a spiritually evolutionary scheme of the universe . . . the answer is quite simple. For the human unit the *initial* basis of obligation is the fact of being born and developing *as a function of a cosmic stream*. We must act, and in a certain way, because our individual destinies are dependent on a universal destiny. Duty, in its origins, is nothing but the reflection of the universe in the atom.[3]

The world has been a process not only of becoming but also of becoming *more* throughout its long history. And becoming more means becoming more complex, more alive, more conscious, and more liberated from blind determinism. Our sense of what we should be doing with our lives must have something to do with this great cosmic labor of liberation. Moral life means participating in and promoting a far-from-finished cosmic process, delivering life, mind, and the human spirit from the tendency to fall back toward the mindless atomic multiplicity of the remote cosmic past, and turning our focus instead toward the convergence of all things on a future unity centered in God. What we may hope for and what we must do, to put it in Kantian terms, are not so uncertain after all, once we look closely at the struggle toward fuller being during the general drift of cosmic history.

It is doubtful, moreover, that moral aspiration can be kept alive for long apart from a vision of reality that makes human action seem permanently worthwhile. Moral motivation requires that we trust, first, that our lives are worth living at all and, second, that they can make a permanent difference.[4] Neither cosmic pessimism nor otherworldly optimism can assure us that they can. We cannot expect to mobilize our moral instincts for any sustained period of time as long as life seems simply a matter of "killing time," obeying categorical imperatives, seeking a reward in the hereafter, or even improving ourselves. To live a good life in the fullest sense, I believe we must first become convinced that our moral efforts can have lasting repercussions in bringing about something *more*. Ideally, this would imply that our lives have a bearing not only on the universe but also on the inner life of God. The religious intuition that nature, even in all its transience, is taken up into God and registered there permanently gives an importance to human action that otherworldly optimism diminishes and a materialist vision explicitly denies.

The current intellectual assumption that the universe is pointless may provoke at best a tragic heroism in the face of absurdity, but it is doubtful that such a stance can be the foundation of a lasting sense of human obligation. Only a "passion *for being finally and permanently more*," Teilhard rightly reflects, can sustain an enduring commitment to goodness.[5] Moral aspiration will eventually weaken and die altogether if it is not based on a great hope, shared with others, that our efforts can have a permanent bearing on the ongoing creation of the universe and on the life of God. A sustained conviction that all cosmic events, including all human actions, are destined for absolute nothingness in the end is a dubious foundation for moral existence. Teilhard puts it this way:

> Multiply to your heart's content the extent and duration of progress. Promise the earth a hundred million more years of continued growth. If, at the end of that period, it is evident that the whole of consciousness must revert to zero, *without its secret essence being garnered anywhere at all*, then, I insist, we shall lay down our arms—and mankind will be on strike. The prospect of a *total death* (and that is a word to which we should devote much thought if we are to gauge its destructive effect on our souls) will, I warn you, when it has become part of our consciousness, immediately dry up in us the springs from which our efforts are drawn.[6]

Taking up Kant's second question (what must we do?), therefore, entails our first looking for a reasonable answer to his third (what may we hope for?). Cosmic pessimists, however, deny that there is any lasting reason to hope at all, and they seem certain that humans can learn nothing about what we must do by looking at what is going on in the universe. Highlighting the uncaring way in which natural selection brings about biological diversity, evolutionary naturalists have condemned the universe for sponsoring such a heartless mode of creation. Starting with Darwin and his bullish advocate T. H. Huxley, they have claimed that we can learn nothing from nature about how to conduct our lives, especially if we look closely at how evolution works. Stephen Jay Gould, one of Teilhard's most hostile critics, has insisted that the "cold bath" of Darwinism should have convinced us once and for all that nature can teach us nothing positive about how human beings should behave. "Darwin," he writes, "liberated us from asking too much of nature, thus leaving us free to comprehend whatever fearful fascination may reside 'out there,' in full confidence that our quest for decency and meaning cannot be threatened thereby, and can emerge only from our own moral consciousness."[7]

In view of the horrors of recent human history, Gould's assertion that the creation of values is purely and exclusively up to us seems naïve at best. What interests me here, though, is the assumption by most evolutionary materialists that a divinely created universe, if it is to be a source of ethical inspiration, should have been perfectly designed from start to finish. Their impatient resentment of the world's present imperfection leads theologically skeptical evolutionists to scorn any suggestion that nature can be a source of ethical norms. Darwinian materialists, of whom there are many, want to sterilize human ethics of contamination by the "naturalistic fallacy," the belief that we can learn what we must *do* directly from our understanding what *is*, especially from our scientific understanding of nature. Consequently, they fail to consider the possible ethical implications of what science has shown to be the dramatic texture of the whole universe. Taken in isolation from the rest of the cosmic process, one may agree, the impersonal process of natural selection is hardly an adequate model for human behavior. However, after Einstein, LeMaitre, and Hubble, the story of life's evolution needs to be situated within the much larger narrative of a universe still emerging. If one has the breadth of vision to take in the larger cosmic sweep of events, the Darwinian episodes may not be as ethically disturbing as Gould and other evolutionists have made them out to be.

The narrow perspective on the universe and ethical life taken by evolutionary naturalism, as we have already seen, is in part the product of the *analytical illusion*.[8] Scientific materialists try to understand the universe by breaking down every physical entity, including life and mind, into elemental components that, according to the materialist worldview, have been blindly gathered by aimless physical laws and processes into more complex aggregates during the course of time. The materialist and atomist metaphysics of the past, however, fails to *see* what is going on in the larger movement of the universe, and it deliberately leaves human subjectivity out of its vision of nature. Our anticipatory perspective, on the other hand, views human consciousness not as an exception to, but as an intensification of, what has always been going on in the universe. Throughout its history, the cosmos, amidst many setbacks, has gradually become *more*. The recent arrival of human beings endowed with minds and moral aspiration is a heightening of being, an intensification of the enduringly anticipatory quality of nature, not a clean break from it.

Nature as a whole, therefore, has never been indifferent to the emergence of value—even long before humans came along. A vein of anticipation, interiority, and subjective experience has become increasingly more intense in the course of cosmic history. Every living subject experiences more or less vividly its own "insideness" as a kind of striving for more being and value. Yet, scientific naturalism is constrained by its commitment to an exclusively quantitative method of investigation to omit subjectivity, the most precious of evolutionary outcomes, from its map of the world. While scientific *method* may legitimately leave out the subjective aspect of nature as it focuses exclusively on what can be measured, a richly empirical portrait of nature cannot justifiably do so. It must attend to *all* the data available for a correct understanding. Unfortunately, an almost willful inattention leads both cosmic pessimists and otherworldly optimists to ignore the clearly directional movement of matter toward increasing complexity and deeper interiority over time, a trend that eventually gave rise to life, consciousness, and moral aspiration in the larger context of cosmic history. A wider empiricism will observe that the universe's gradual increase in complexity brings along with it a dramatic intensification of subjectivity—and anticipation. Both religious dualism and evolutionary naturalism, however, persistently overlook, or regard as incidental, this most treasurable chapter in the cosmic drama.

Again, at their own levels of reading the cosmos, the scientific disciplines of physics, chemistry, and biology may justifiably try to account for the emergence of complexity without focally attending to the fact of subjectivity and the deeper anticipatory drama of natural history. Each of the various sciences is permitted a methodologically self-limiting view of natural processes. Still, what is needed as a complement to the objectifying approach of science—and not in opposition to it—is attention to the undeniable fact that in cosmic history, outward complexity has been accompanied by the emergence of increasingly animated inner awareness and, eventually, anticipatory self-awareness. This augmentation of subjectivity, and especially the recent arrival of our own reflective self-consciousness, is clearly part of the natural world process. And yet, after Darwin, scientists and philosophers of nature have seldom taken subjectivity seriously as a key to understanding the cosmos.

Catholic thought, on the other hand, has fortunately always held that being, value, and consciousness are correlative notions, so that the more consciousness intensifies, the more being and value increase. The materialist habit of consigning consciousness to the vaporous sphere of epiphenomena is both illogical (a consequence of the analytical illusion) and unempirical (a refusal to attend to *all* the available data). Scientific naturalism almost willfully turns its focus away from the most obvious and real phenomenon of all, the fact of our own subjective consciousness. Instead of approaching consciousness as a reality to be understood in depth, modern materialist metaphysics has separated the domain of mental experience from the presumed mindlessness of nature. Then, in one of the most questionable chapters in the history of thought, it has awarded the status of "reality" to lifeless and mindless material stuff alone.

This severance of mind from the cosmos has been morally disastrous, and Christian ethical reflection, including Catholic moral thought, has not yet completely disowned the modern dualism that severs humanity from nature. This is partly because moralists have not yet acquired a clear sense of the *dramatic* character of the universe to which the history of life and our personal biographies are linked. Instead of being understood as the outcome of a momentous cosmic drama, personal subjectivity has seemed either to drop into the world from out of nowhere or to reside in an immaterial world apart from nature. For several centuries, scientific naturalists have been treating human consciousness as though it is not really part of the natural world, and moral theology has tacitly shared that assumption. Today a number of scientists and philosophers, in a desperate attempt to make the cosmos appear completely objectifiable, even deny that subjectivity or consciousness has any real existence at all. While this pretense may be methodologically useful in the practice of the natural sciences, the metaphysical expurgation of the dimension of subjectivity and our own felt aliveness from the physical universe can only impede the growth of a truly accurate understanding of the real world. To fit ourselves into a mindless universe, scientific naturalism, as Thomas Nagel rightly notes, has first divested it of mind altogether.[9] This alienation of mind from nature has made it easier than ever for "enlightened" thinkers to assume that an ontological state of deadness is both the origin and final end of everything going on in the universe.[10] This moribund metaphysics cannot furnish any good reasons why we should attribute lasting importance to anything we do. It can tell us nothing about why we should trust our minds or why we should be morally responsible at all.

Catholic moralists have not been sufficiently critical of the ontology of death and cosmic pessimism that still form the intellectual backdrop of so much contemporary moral reflection. The current intellectual atmosphere is one in which moralists are still trying to decide "what we must do" by first separating personal subjects from the cosmic drama that gave rise to our anticipatory minds and moral aspirations. Even where ethical reflection still retains a religious flavor, as in official Catholic moral teaching, there remain overtones of the ageless metaphysical dualism that estranges humans from their cosmic matrix and hence renders considerations of what is going on in the universe irrelevant to moral decision. The persistent separation of mind (or soul) from physical reality forbids us to think of ourselves as fully part of a still-emerging, and hence unfinished, universe. As a result, moral aspiration often seems both rootless and undirected.

Nevertheless, by recognizing the continuity of emergent human consciousness or subjectivity (our "insideness") with the entire cosmic drama, Catholic moral theology may now come to realize that understanding what is going on in the cosmos can be both spiritually and ethically significant. Once the sharp line between the history of matter and the emergence of spirit and "souls" dissolves, both the intellectual and the theological distancing of mind from matter appear contrived. So any attempt to decide what we must do without looking at what is going on in the universe seems especially shortsighted.

Beyond perfectionism

The renewal of moral theology, however, also requires that we distinguish carefully between the pursuit of perfection, on the one hand, and a cult of perfectionism on the other. The ideal of perfection, as I noted at the beginning of this chapter, inspires the noblest of human pursuits. Perfectionism, however, can be the cause of unimaginable evils. Apart from the quest for perfection, we remain mired in mediocrity. Perfectionism, however, is unrealistically impatient. And in our shame at our own imperfection and that of the world to which we are ecologically and dramatically bound, we may lapse into unprecedented depths of immorality.[11] Moralists invite us to seek ethical perfection, but when we try impatiently to implement this ideal in our own lives, we may fall into despair, self-hatred, or condescension toward others who have not lived up to our unrealistically lofty moral ideals. Religions entice us with grand visions of human and cosmic destiny and moral purity, but impetuous attempts to implement these visions in the present can lead to self-deception, scapegoating, oppression, and even murder.

Is the solution, therefore, to get rid of religion and all ideas of God, as the New Atheists insist? Although such a prospect is enticing to an increasing number of intellectuals today, the flight from religion or theism into radical secularism is no guarantee of escape from the perniciousness of perfectionism. Perfectionism is as dominant in militant atheism, scientific naturalism, and runaway consumerism (the religion of the market) as it ever was in traditional religions. The question of how to live in genuine freedom from the impatient demands of unrealistic idealism remains as alive after the "death of God" as before. There is still as much need as ever, therefore, to pursue goodness, truth, and beauty without succumbing to the tyranny of perfectionism. This is a task not only for religious people, but also for those who have rebelled against religion.

The moral life—as Jesus was aware and biblical literature more generally confirms—comes fully to life only in an atmosphere of openness, hope, freedom, and forgiveness. Today, I believe, a radical shift in cosmology and metaphysics could do much to liberate Catholic ethical reflection from the lingering effects of centuries of impatient otherworldly pietism, clericalism, and moralistic perfectionism. Once the horizon of religious expectation shifts toward concern for the cosmic future, our ethical idealism may give priority to the thriving of all creation rather than the mere perfecting of our own souls. We may find, after all, that by attending to this wider concern— uniting our thirst for the kingdom of God to our sense of the world's ongoing creation—our moral aspirations may gain fresh focus and motivation.

What this shift requires from us practically is not necessarily a radical change in our day-to-day activities or in family and community obligations. It does not mean that we no longer have tedious chores and boring routines. Nor does it mean that Catholic moral life for the first time will be energized by a sense of belonging to the kingdom of God and contributing to the building up of the body of Christ. What it does mean is that both the kingdom of God and the body of Christ may be seen henceforth as physically and organically interwoven with an incomplete universe, a creative process that still has a future and hence one that makes room for an expansive new hope. The temporally deep and spatially enormous cosmos now being unveiled by science is an opportunity to add a new layer of meaning onto our most ordinary acts of love.

I mean by this that care for life and one another, and the practice of justice in an unfinished universe, will include keeping an eye on what may be now taking shape up ahead in the universe's own immense odyssey. At every point in the cosmic journey so far, unseen possibilities have been lurking on the horizon. Pick any period in past cosmic history—for instance, the plasmatic epoch right after the Big Bang when the universe was still a homogenous sea of radiation. An observer of the universe at that time, unless equipped with superhuman prescience, would hardly have expected that anything more interesting than this barely rippled state of matter-energy would ever occur. And yet it did. We have learned from science that it took some waiting, but even during the world's earliest and most monotonous stages of growth, the seeds of something significantly new were already beginning to sprout. After the beginning, due to the gradual emergence of a series of initially improbable recurrent physical cycles, there came atoms and later molecules; and after large molecules appeared, the probability of living cells emerged, then organisms, humans, societies, and economies. At present, a noosphere is beginning to take shape on earth, a layer of "fuller being" whose actualization can give new meaning to our deliberate acts of cooperation and care.

Even though Catholics, like other Christians, pray for the coming of God's kingdom, their expectations have usually taken the form of otherworldly optimism rather than cosmic hope. They have scarcely entertained the thought that the coming of God might include further organic transformation of the cosmos, the planet, life, and consciousness. In the light of *Gaudium et spes*, however, Catholic moral theologians may now consider how the imperative to practice justice and love may have evolutionary and cosmological outcomes that magnify in a whole new way the significance of even our most ordinary obligations. The new sense of an unfinished universe allows us to realize not only that doing justice and loving one another demonstrate our respect for the value of other persons, but also that living a fully Christian moral life contributes to the building of the earth, to the ongoing creation of the universe, and even to the fleshing out of the incarnate identity of God.

Ecology: From Preservation to Preparation

Our species is ruining the natural world. Humans are destroying forests; causing our soil to erode; poisoning the air; polluting rivers, lakes, and oceans; eliminating sources of fresh water; and overpopulating the planet. We have created a dangerous greenhouse atmosphere, reduced the protective ozone layer, and destroyed irreplaceable organic species. Common sense demands that we change our ways, but apparently we need much more than that to arouse a passionate sense of ethical responsibility for the earth's well-being. We need a vision, one that can move all of humanity toward a permanent commitment to ecological responsibility.

Can contemporary Catholic theological reflection discover in tradition and Scripture sufficient motivation for an effective sense of ecological responsibility?[1] In view of the reckless accusations by scientific naturalists that Christianity supports environmental neglect, I believe it is essential that Catholic theology clarifies the implications, positive or negative, of our faith tradition for contemporary ecological concern. It must do so in dialogue with both scientific naturalism's pessimistic view of the universe and the otherworldly optimism habitual to most Christians. Following the pattern of preceding chapters, I call these latter two alternatives, respectively, the archaeological and analogical visions of nature. After a brief description of their approaches to ecological issues immediately below, I will compare and contrast them with the anticipatory vision of the cosmos and its ecological implications.

The archaeological approach

Scientific naturalists claim that belief in God, along with Christian hope for everlasting life in the "next world," diminishes the sense of obligation to care for this world. Otherworldly piety, they claim—and not without reason—fosters a negative attitude toward nature. Hence, they argue, the only fruitful setting for environmental concern must be a consistent naturalism, the belief that nothing exists beyond the empirically accessible physical universe. Only if we humans accept once and for all that no God exists and no providential divine governance supervises the universe will we start taking full responsibility for the preservation of life on earth.[2] Looking back over the long story of life's emergence and evolution, scientific naturalism's archaeological vision values terrestrial life all the more because of the precarious, hit-or-miss itinerary of life's arrival. Life was never intended to be here, they assume, so we can only be astounded—and appreciative— that it came about at all. Life's improbability makes it all the more precious. Belief that a divine creator intended life to exist, on the other hand, adds nothing to its importance. Furthermore, religious optimism's expectation of life after death only condones human disregard for the integrity of nature here and now. Ecological sensitivity requires a frank admission that nature is our final home and not a mere station on the human journey. If we fail to appreciate nature as our only home, we will lack strong enough motivation to care for it. So only a pure naturalism, a worldview based on the belief that "this world" is all there is, could support a serious ecological ethic. The thought that the universe is godless, that life is improbable and extremely rare, and that everything living is destined eventually to perish in some final, far-off cosmic deep freeze or conflagration makes life all the more treasurable here and now.

At least, this is a common assumption among many serious environmentalists. Catholic faith, by contrast, according to its secular critics, is not good for the natural world's welfare. Catholicism is so otherworldly that it promotes a sense of cosmic homelessness. It sets our souls adrift in nature temporarily as we wait to depart for eternity, thus curbing any enthusiasm we might have for the long-term survival of terrestrial life. Otherworldly optimism, supported by a sense of the eternal present, has for centuries promoted a spirituality that, to one degree or another, makes us long to withdraw from the physical world altogether.[3]

Secular environmentalists, I believe, make an important point, one that Catholic thought has yet to address carefully enough. I hasten to add, however, that it is not supernaturalist piety alone that makes people feel as though they do not really belong to the cosmos. Scientific naturalism, at least in its typically materialist commitments, also exiles human beings from nature. No doubt, naturalists love nature, and many are exemplars of conservation. However, the love they profess to have for nature can claim no coherent intellectual justification as long as it is based on a purely materialist understanding of the world. Materialism, after all, implies that nature is reducible to an essentially lifeless and mindless state of being and that life has no distinctive claim to being real. Beneath all its apparent beauty and tragedy, according to materialist naturalism, life is *really* lifeless physical simplicity.

So if life is nothing more at bottom than lifeless physical stuff, we need to ask how such a picture of nature can justify our protecting life from ending up in the lifelessness that materialism takes to be the natural ground of all being.[4] In any case, the immediate causes of ecological distress include an industrialization supported by greed-based economic assumptions that a materialist worldview is powerless to resist. Catholics, like other Christians, are not innocent, but the Church's consistent opposition to materialism is, at least in principle, a restraining influence, and its cultivation of the virtues of moderation and humility can, in principle, help curb the modern will to use up the natural world.[5]

At the end of its archaeological journey into the cosmic past, scientific naturalism discovers only lifeless and valueless elemental stuff. It then proceeds metaphysically to rest the entirety of being, including living and thinking beings, on this empire of lifelessness. The analytical *method* of inquiry as such is entirely appropriate, as I have repeatedly pointed out, but what is questionable—this time in the context of ecological concern—is the naturalistic metaphysics of the past that makes deadness ontologically more *real* than life. In contrast to a metaphysics that gives primacy to the future, it assumes that a chronologically early phase of the cosmic process is ontologically primary. A materialist metaphysics views matter alone as ontologically real, so it cannot avoid reducing life and human consciousness, which emerge later in the cosmic story, to a lifeless mass of physical elements moving meaninglessly through space and time.[6] Logically speaking, therefore, such a worldview cannot support a robust ecological ethic of life any more than it can permit the human mind or spirit to feel fully at home in nature. Scientific naturalism, in spite of its best intentions, is no less inclined than otherworldly optimism to accept the ancient dualistic belief that we are "lost in the cosmos."

Recently, a few scientific naturalists have begun to acknowledge not only the intellectual weakness but also the moral heartlessness of materialist metaphysics.[7] They are increasingly aware that strict materialism interprets life and mind only as flukes of nature that do not really belong here. The new "soft naturalists" now agree that materialism cannot function as a serious intellectual framework for either ecological responsibility or the philosophy of nature. Their modified scientific naturalism is a significant development, and their striving for a less mechanistic understanding of nature is commendable. Yet, their tempered materialism is still weighed down by the modern archaeological assumption that the foundation of all being can be found only by going back to the cosmic and evolutionary past. The new naturalism is rightly fascinated by the phenomenon of "emergence" in which, over the course of natural history, unprecedented kinds of being such as living cells and human brains have arrived on the scene in surprising ways. Nevertheless, it still assumes that human inquiry can eventually understand emergent phenomena only by tracing their genesis back in time to an originally lifeless cosmic epoch.

Soft scientific naturalism is rightly impressed by the improbable emergent leaps that have occurred in natural history, but it is not yet ready to entertain an anticipatory metaphysics in which the ultimate explanation of emergence is the arrival of the future. Terry Deacon, for example, allows that emergent phenomena are somehow brought about by a "constitutive absence," a "particular and precise missing something" that gives direction and definition to emergent new being. His intuition seems consonant with what I have been referring to as the metaphysical primacy of the "not-yet." Nevertheless, given the contemporary physicalist intellectual climate, Deacon is not ready to abandon the metaphysics of the past that still nurtures his and most other contemporary attempts to understand the physical universe.[8]

The analogical approach

To most Catholic thinkers, a religiously respectable alternative to materialism, and a workable intellectual framework for ecological responsibility, is a metaphysics of the eternal present. According to this venerable understanding of being, all natural entities receive their inherent value by virtue of participating in the eternal mystery of God. Each level of nature's hierarchy mediates the divine mystery in proportion to its degree of proximity to eternity. I have been referring to this religious approach as the analogical or sacramental vision. A sacrament is anything through which the sacred manifests itself. Accordingly, the beauty and vitality of the natural world can give us an indispensable impression of the timeless reality, vitality, and resourcefulness of God. Sacraments are religiously important because they lift us out of total immersion in time and put us in the presence of the eternal. Bright sunshine, roaring storms, oceanic depths, fresh air, clean flowing water, the durability of rocks, the flourishing of flowering plants, the majesty of trees, forests, and deserts, the fertility of soil, and sexuality, not to mention the transcendent luminosity of the heavens—all of these function religiously to remind us of the timeless infinity in which the temporal world participates.

By acknowledging nature's inherent transparency to the divine, Catholic sacramentalism can serve, therefore, to keep us from turning our world into nothing more than raw material for our own narrowly human projects.

Nature's sacramentality, one would think, can protect it from diminishment by our objectifying intellectual control and economic acquisitiveness. If the natural world is at heart a sacramental disclosure of God and thus participates in its maker's majesty, then it merits our continuing care. The secularist accusation that Catholic faith necessarily detracts from the value of nature, therefore, is without foundation. Furthermore, sacramentalism is more prepared than cosmic pessimism to face realistically the perishability of nature, including the final demise of the entire universe. The sacramental vision is quite aware that no finite reality, including the entire physical universe, is immune to the threat of nonbeing. However, unlike cosmic pessimism, it grounds the value of nature not in its precariousness or in its dramatic texture but in its vertical *participation* in the eternal goodness of God. What gives life value, therefore, is not its perishability but the intensity of its sharing here and now, for a brief moment, in the eternal life of God.

Catholic sacramentalism's sense that all finite being participates in an eternal goodness exposes by contrast the hollowness of cosmic pessimism's claim to ecological solicitude. By rooting life in lifelessness, cosmic pessimism offers no solid metaphysical reasons for our truly treasuring it. Sacramentalism on the other hand turns out to be a vision of reality that requires our treading softly on the earth. It respects nature without absolutizing it. Following St Augustine (among others), sacramentalism realistically acknowledges that each human person is restless for the infinite. Only communion with the inexhaustible source of all being can ultimately satisfy our deepest longings. Opening our hearts to the divine, therefore, requires a detachment from finite beings, including the evanescent beauties of nature.

Our detachment, though, is not a repudiation of creation but the other side of our gratitude for it. To the sacramentalist, gratitude is the most characteristically religious of all the virtues. And it is the foundational ecological virtue because it lets us enjoy finite beings without divinizing and hence expecting too much of them. It views creation as a gift pointing to the overflowing generosity of an infinite giver. Giving thanks thus curbs our possessive impulse to use up God's creation as though we were its owners. Since so much ecological destruction is rooted in the naive economic assumption that earth's resourcefulness is unlimited, gratitude is more appropriate today than ever. In contrast to the modern disregard for the earth's limitations, Catholicism's sacramental vision fosters realistic restraint, urging us to accept our finitude and chastening our will to misuse the world on which we all depend for our existence.

Since a Catholic sacramental vision sees nature as transparent to an infinite resourcefulness, it implies that nature itself is not ultimate. When modern thought abandoned the idea of an infinite God, however, it did not extinguish the infinity of human desire. Our unquenchable thirst for "more and more," a restlessness that arises anew after each fresh acquisition, remains with each of us as an anthropological constant. Wiping away the horizon of transcendence, as a secular age demands, leaves only the finite natural world to soak up and satisfy our limitless longing. After the death of God, the restless human search for satisfaction has nowhere else to turn but to the natural world—since allegedly there is nothing beyond it. Our finite planet is left to satisfy the abysmal emptiness of our hearts, a void that only the infinite can fill. Since sacramentalism affirms both the infinity of our longing and the reality of an infinite divine mystery, it can potentially liberate nature from the impossible burden of being a substitute for God and from feeding the bottomless appetite that is the human soul. Sacramentalism's posture of thanksgiving allows us to experience the finite natural world as the expression of an infinite graciousness while setting it free from the stressful obligation of having to be "all there is."

Finally, a sacramental ecological vision is not entirely unbiblical, for it can cite passages such as: "God looked at everything he had made, and he found it very good" (Gen. 1:31). The Bible, moreover, assigns to humans the task of "caring for" the garden in which divine goodness has placed us (Gen. 2:15). In addition to gratitude, genuine stewardship requires a sense of the need to practice the life-protecting virtues of humility, moderation, detachment, and compassion.

The anticipatory approach

To be sure, the sacramental outlook of traditional Catholic spirituality has much to recommend it as the basis of an ecological theology. By bringing out the relevance of the doctrines of creation and incarnation, sacramentalism has to be an indispensable component of any specifically Catholic ecological theology. And yet, an exclusively sacramental outlook fails to capture both the biblical sense of the world's promise and the theological significance of an unfinished universe. Hence, I propose not that Catholic theology abandon its sacramental theology of nature but that the sacramental outlook be layered over with the anticipatory metaphysics I have been associating with cosmic hope. Today, after Darwin and Einstein, an entire evolving universe is still groaning to reveal the divine in a much more dramatic way than previous theological ages could ever have imagined. For ecological theology not to notice and profit from this magnificent expansion of our sense of nature would be an opportunity lost in our contemporary struggle to form an ecological ethics that conforms to both scientific understanding and Catholic tradition.

While science has been magnifying our understanding of space and time, biblical scholarship over the last century and a half has been rediscovering eschatology—concern for the "coming of God" and the world's future fulfillment—as the core of early Christian faith. Even before the birth of Christianity, the promise of future fulfillment was already the central message of the Hebrew Scriptures, and it was basic to Jesus's proclamation of the kingdom of God before it became the New Testament's main message as well. Biblically speaking, however, the future does not refer to human survival in the "next world" but to the ongoing transformation and fulfillment of this one, starting right now. Early Christian faith in resurrection, and hope for the kingdom of God, are not expressions of otherworldly optimism or a reason to avoid urgent moral choices here and now. So also today, our expectation of new creation requires an immediate response to the earth's current ecological predicament. Thus, an integral Catholic ecological vision, one attuned to biblical hope and informed by evolutionary science, rejoices that the same divine promise that brought Israel and the Church into being has for billions of years been drawing a whole universe toward an unimaginable future. Informed by cosmic hope, an ecological spirituality trusts that the divine field of attraction we refer to as the Holy Spirit is still at work in the entire cosmos, no less today than ever. The divine promise to Abraham applies not only to the "people of God" but also, as St Paul came to see, to the "whole of creation" (Rom. 8:22).

This futurist theological approach to ecological issues, however, may raise a serious objection. Most environmentalists insist that a prerequisite for ecological responsibility is that we think of the natural world, and indeed the entire material world, as our *home*. Otherwise, we are likely to trash it as having no real importance. So, instead of letting us feel at home in nature, doesn't a future-oriented faith—no less than otherworldly optimism—foster a sense of "cosmic homelessness," a disposition that allows us to think of ourselves as strangers only passing through the world? Doesn't a metaphysics of the future also contradict the ecological requirement that we experience ourselves as belonging fully to the natural world here and now?

From a biblical point of view, we need to admit, human existence on earth is an exodus journey, a pilgrimage, a desert wandering. Authentic Christian faith can never rest. If Jesus has "no place to lay his head," if his followers must set their eyes on Jerusalem and not look back, and if pursuit of the kingdom of God is more important than home and family, how can this anticipatory vision avoid giving the impression that caring for the natural world right now as our "home" is not a priority for faithful

Christians? Traditional otherworldly Catholicism, we have already noted, has often turned the sense of religious homelessness into an ecologically problematic cosmic homelessness. It has promoted a spirituality of detachment that works against a sense of being at home in nature. So, how can we reconcile a sense of ecological responsibility with the biblical requirement of living homelessly, a criterion of spiritual authenticity that also shows up in other religious traditions? Embracing our rootlessness and restlessness is a condition of liberation not just for Jesus, but also for significant strains of Islam, Buddhism, and Hinduism. So, again, how may we reconcile the practice of religious pilgrimage and our hope for future fulfillment with the ecological imperative to plant ourselves more deeply than ever in the earth here and now? May we follow the adventurous way of religious homelessness, in other words, without turning the journey of faith into an ecologically noxious cosmic homelessness?

A sense of not belonging to nature undoubtedly promotes ecological indifference. A predilection for cosmic homelessness can twist the ideal of religious homelessness into an escapism that makes nature a victim of puritanical, perfectionist spiritual detachment. Earth, in that case, comes to be seen as a place to get away from in order to find salvation. The natural world then serves the function of being only a "school" in which the soul undergoes a discipline that renders it worthy of inheriting eternal life apart from nature. How then can we love God without turning our backs on the natural world? And how can we come to cherish the natural world without surrendering our restless longing for transcendence?

These are questions that a Catholic ecological theology must address. Unfortunately, the religious formation of Catholics has led us to harbor a suspicion that human persons do not really belong to nature, and so we may interpret our religious restlessness as an excuse to keep our distance from the earth out of which we sprang and on whose richness we still depend. We may even fall back on the excuse that a sense of belonging to nature is a pagan or pantheistic perversion of monotheistic faith. So we refuse to let the roots of our lives and our struggles penetrate deeply into the cosmic soil.

Unfortunately, modern Catholic theology has done too little to prevent the divorce of persons from nature. For the past few centuries, it has typically surrendered intellectual concern for the natural world to scientific secularists and reserved for itself the role of caring for the interior life of people. Meanwhile, it has left questions about nature and the cosmic future out of the field of theological interest. After Vatican II, this lack of interest has no theological justification, but Catholic thought and instruction still show less concern about the welfare of the nonhuman natural world than is theologically warranted.

Back to our question, then: How can we hold together the ideal of religious homelessness with a sense of being fully at home in nature? We may do so, I suggest, by connecting our religious life more closely than ever to an anticipatory vision of nature. In the context of an unfinished universe and a metaphysics of the future, religious homelessness does not have to be translated into an ecologically problematic cosmic homelessness. Indeed, science's new cosmic story can serve to support the sense of being on a spiritual journey without requiring that we uproot ourselves from nature. We can practice a religious homelessness while simultaneously feeling at home in the cosmos.

How so? Over the last two centuries science has demonstrated that the natural world itself is a restless adventure. Biology, geology, astrophysics, and cosmology, as this book has noted from the start, have overthrown the ancient assumption that the universe is eternal and unchanging. No previous age had known, at least with the assuredness we now possess, that the natural world is on a pilgrimage of its own. Our religions, including Catholic Christianity, emerged long before science demonstrated that nature is itself a historical process and not something fixed or final. The cosmos, we now realize, is not a stationary set of things frozen in the same plodding status from all eternity. The universe itself is an unfinished adventure open to what is perpetually new. Teilhard has done more than any other Christian thinker to show how we may honestly appreciate that we are fully a part of the earth and the cosmos while also feeling the excitement of being on a momentous religious journey. Ours is a journey, after all, that we undertake along *with* the universe, not apart from it. Although, like others in his day, Teilhard was not explicitly sensitive to ecological concerns, he developed a deeply incarnational and hopeful spirituality that, by reinterpreting Christian faith in the context of cosmic and biological evolution, can frame our current efforts to construct an ecological theology.

We can now justifiably feel both religiously homeless *and* ecologically at home in nature—simultaneously—since the cosmos itself has not yet reached the end of its journey. The cosmos itself is on a pilgrimage, and we along with it. We may feel like exiles because the universe is still separated from its destiny, but in the meantime we can align our lives and moral efforts with a world whose anticipatory restlessness consists of its being open to more being.

Ecological concern, therefore, now has the added meaning of keeping the universe open to new being and new life. By accepting the universe's own homelessness, in other words, we allow ourselves to be fellow travelers with it. The universe, as we now realize, has been on the move for billions of years before humans emerged in life's evolution. According to contemporary cosmology, the universe has a finite past and has now embarked on an irreversible journey through time, a process that may go on for many more millions of years. The natural world is both prologue and partner to our own religious journey, so we do not have to forsake it if we feel called to embrace our own restlessness. Our intellectual, moral, and spiritual uneasiness is a blossoming of the universe's own ageless adventuring, not an invitation to leave the natural world behind as we make our way toward God. Nature does not oppose but supports our longing for the infinite. A sincere quest for God is continuous with our anticipatory universe, not an escape from it, and the life of faith is a prolongation of the universe's own leaning toward the open future where new possibilities still await it. In view of both Abrahamic faith and science's sense of an unfinished universe we may come to realize that throughout its long journey, the cosmos has always been, and will continue to be, inseparable from the promise of more being.

So I conclude from all that I have set forth in this book that the natural world is to be valued not only because it is sacramentally transparent to God, but also because in all its perishability, it bears from age to age the promise of a final, glorious future flowering. It follows that our current trashing of nature is not only a violation of nature's sacramentality, but also a suppression of the promise that underlies our universe's own restlessness. If so, our complicity in ecological desolation is not only disobedience to the divine command to be faithful stewards of creation, and not only a profanation of nature's sacramentality, but above all, an expression of hopelessness. So if gratitude is the fundamental ecological virtue for the sacramental vision, for the anticipatory vision of nature the fundamental ecological virtue is hope.[9]

An anticipatory vision of nature—in keeping with our metaphysics of the future—requires, therefore, that we revise the meaning of the divine imperative to exercise faithful stewardship toward the rest of creation. If nature is not only sacrament, but also promise, stewardship is no longer reducible to acts of conservation. Caring for what nature has already given us is essential, of course, and we need to celebrate the long drama of evolutionary creativity upon which we continue to depend for our existence. Earth's biosphere, in other words, merits our best efforts at preservation. However, stewardship now means not only preservation but also *preparation*. From the perspective of an anticipatory theology, we care for the natural world because it is pregnant with the promise of incalculable future outcomes that transcend our best predictions and deepest desires. An anticipatory theology does not give us a clear vision of the cosmic future, but it can inspire confidence that every present contains in a hidden way the promise of future fulfillment.

Humanity: From Term to Transition

What then is humanity? If the universe is unfinished, so also is the human species. Cosmic hope, the worldview I have adopted in this book as the framework for Catholic theology after Darwin and Einstein, is not content to understand the human phenomenon solely by retracing the evolutionary pathways that brought us onto the terrestrial scene. Nor is it satisfied with the deterministic bias of evolutionary naturalists who seek to explain life, mind, morality, and religion exclusively in terms of their adaptive functions in the remote evolutionary past. Sciences such as evolutionary biology, genetics, biochemistry, paleontology, and archaeology can partially illuminate the story of our emergence, but since these fields of research are usually tied to an implicit metaphysics of the past, they fall short of telling us just what humanity is in the context of an unfinished universe.

Catholic thought cannot be indifferent to what the sciences contribute to the question of human identity, but if it is both scientifically awake and stirred by an Abrahamic faith, it will also wonder what we shall become in the future. Both theology and science see only in part. Theologically, our present understanding of God can only be a sketch while scientific understanding is also uncertain in any present moment of what is to come. What we can be sure of in the meantime is that we are a forward-looking species whose vitality, intellectual passion, and moral seriousness require our acknowledging the fundamentally anticipatory orientation of our existence. Stripped of anticipation, our biological, intellectual, ethical, and spiritual lives would sink toward morbidity. For this reason I have been arguing that both the religious cult of eternal presence and the ontology of death implicit in scientific and evolutionary naturalism's focus on the cosmic past are inimical to the full unfettering of the human spirit.

In contrast to cosmic pessimism and dualistic religious optimism, cosmic hope embraces both the emergent universe of scientific discovery and the forward thrust of human being-in-the-world. Complicating the question of human identity, however, is the fact that increasingly sophisticated technical expertise is on the brink of reshaping the human world and its environment more dramatically than ever. Current scientific developments and expectations in the fields of genetics, robotics, nanotechnology, information science, artificial intelligence, evolutionary biology, and neuroscience are raising unprecedented ethical and theological questions about the direction in which we—and life on earth along with us—may be heading.[1] So if the definition of phenomena in an unfinished universe depends less on knowledge of origins than on a sense of future trajectories, this raises unprecedented moral questions. How far may those who have control of the emerging new technologies go in transforming human beings, and indeed the whole of terrestrial life, in the future? How far may they go in altering what Catholics have for centuries understood to be God's creation in general and the sanctity of human personhood in particular?

New scientific ideas and techniques are opening up the prospect of radically tailoring what it means to be human, not only socially and culturally but also physically and cognitively—a process now referred to as *transhumanism*. Will new technologies eventually lead to the point where no clearly defined human nature, at least as known by earlier generations, exists any longer? In evolutionary terms, will a time come when a sharply delineated "human species" can be supplanted by something quite different? After Darwin, the notion of *any* clearly distinct "species" has already become suspect, especially to those who understand evolution primarily in terms of populations of genes migrating from one generation to the next. New discoveries related to the human genome have now made it possible, in principle, to reconfigure radically our inherited bodily forms and behavioral repertoires, perhaps eventually transforming both into patterns now unpredictable. Sensitive artists, dramatists, philosophers, ethicists, and theologians are envisaging a wide spectrum of possible implications of current scientific research and emergent new technologies. Some projected outcomes are trivial, others monstrous, but in either case, a continually more nuanced scientific understanding of the subatomic world, the manipulability of genes, the plasticity of brains, the rules of evolutionary change, and a host of other scientific insights and discoveries now provide both the opportunity and the temptation to revamp *everything* in our world, including ourselves.

But should we allow this to happen, and, if so, are there reasonable limits? To ignore these questions would be irresponsible theologically since the future of human existence and, for theists, God's creation itself are at stake. Here I want to ask what possible contributions Catholic theology might make to the building of a worldview appropriate to any future application of the emerging new technologies. Since Catholics make up a large percentage of the world's population, it is important to ask whether our own visions of the world and God can accommodate or perhaps instruct the purveyors of transhumanism in a significant way. My question, more precisely, is whether Catholic theology, once it systematically appropriates the anticipatory biblical motifs of promise and hope, can provide a fruitful spiritual and moral framework within which to consider the implications of transhumanism.

I must begin by emphasizing, along with other environmentally concerned people today, that preoccupation solely with technology's implications for *humanity's* future is both theologically narrow and ecologically insensitive. As a result of developments in science, educated people now realize that the human drama on earth is one of many living tracks in a much more complex set of life's itineraries. Consequently, questions about the human future cannot be isolated from a wider concern about life, broadly speaking, as well as about the universe and its own destiny. A circumspect theological treatment of the possible outcomes of transhumanist projects, therefore, needs to keep in view the whole story of life and the uncertain future of a still-unfinished universe. Moreover, for all we know, the enormous amount of time that has transpired since the Big Bang may turn out in the long run to have been only the dawn of our universe's coming into being. So a properly elongated cosmic perspective means that theology must ask what specific role humans have in the process of bringing the *universe* into the sphere of fulfillment as promised by biblical tradition and its hope for new creation.

Early Christians awaited the coming of God, but they thought it would take place imminently, that is, in the near future. Catholic theology subsequently has usually been so otherworldly that the physical universe has seemed to be superfluous in the final scheme of divine creation. However, theology in the context of an unfinished universe may take from the New Testament its passionate concern to make *this world* ready for the coming of God while acknowledging that the same world is still in the throes of giving birth to more being.[2] What Christianity is about, when viewed in terms of New Testament preoccupations, is not the forsaking of the earth and the universe, but preparing our habitat to receive God more fully. Because we are now aware that we are tied into the evolution of life and cosmic emergence in ways previously unknown to religious thought, we must also realize that human transformation involves the liberation of matter and the whole of life and not just the human sector. Now that science has demonstrated our physical and genetic continuity with the whole cosmic story, transhumanist projects must be subjected to a critical investigation of what they mean not just for us, but also for the universe.

Three options

In the distant cosmic future, will human history turn out to be anything more than an ephemeral crossing-over to now unpredictable episodes in an enormously inventive cosmic drama whose final outcome is currently in doubt? To scientifically educated people, human history is not the whole show, and the story of the universe itself may turn out to be one in which the human period on earth will eventually have been relegated to the status of a transitional chapter. Is it time, then, to entertain transhumanist dreams? Let us look—all too briefly—at how our three distinct visions of nature might respond to the question.

1. *The archaeological approach.* True to its metaphysics of the past, scientific naturalism assumes that the universe will end badly since there is no eternal principle of creativity and redemption sustaining the course of physical events. Hope for any meaningful cosmic outcome is unreasonable according to the dominant contemporary ideology of cosmic pessimism. Generally speaking, scientific naturalism, as we have seen repeatedly in previous chapters, understands present and future realities to be the outcome of a deterministic series of causes set in motion somehow during the distant cosmic past. Scientific naturalism claims that lifeless matter and impersonal laws of nature are the ultimate source and explanation of everything. No divine intentionality and no eternal ethical mandates constrain human action in the world or provide guidelines for the future. Evolution has locked humans into adaptive behavioral routines that we dignify with the label "morality," and the impersonal laws of physics have predestined everything to ultimate futility. Once human culture emerged in the cosmic process, the illusion of freedom came along with it and ironically gave us the sense that we can control our destiny at least to some extent. To motivate our conduct, however, we have only pragmatic social concerns informed perhaps by a sense of what works biologically to preserve the human gene pool.

There is nothing in this worldview to keep technologically adventurous experts from radically transforming human existence in accordance with their own desires. Lacking all hope for a positive final outcome to the cosmic process, some naturalists are excited nevertheless by the prospect that we humans can postpone indefinitely a final cosmic calamity through information technology.[3] New developments in cognitive science and digital computing may open up ways to enhance human consciousness virtually in spite of the irreversible loss of physical energy in the cosmos overall. Medical technology may retard the aging process, and robotics may give us new mobility and exploratory capacity. From the perspective of science, however, nothing can prevent the universe from eventually dying of energy collapse.

Logically consistent scientific naturalists, therefore, have to be cosmic pessimists as well. And even though cosmic pessimists allow for periodic spasms of optimism as the world moves along, most of them are realistic enough to acknowledge the possibility that our technologies may eventually turn destructively against us. Cosmic pessimism, since it is based on a metaphysics of the past that reduces the world to lifeless and mindless matter, must view with sobriety even the most enthusiastic plans for a radical technological enhancement or transformation of humanity. Lacking any long-term hope for the cosmos, and expecting nothingness to be the ultimate end of all physical movement and human striving, scientific naturalism's archaeological vision cannot provide fully convincing reasons for our escaping ethical nihilism even here and now. It is hard then to feel positively about its future willingness to practice constraint in the carrying out of transhumanist projects.

2. *The analogical option.* A traditional Catholic alternative to cosmic pessimism is based on a metaphysics of the eternal present. It opposes transhumanist scenarios by denouncing any dramatic changes to nature generally and to human nature in particular. Our having the means to transform humanity genetically or technologically, it claims, is not enough to justify our doing so. Transhumanism is a violation of the archetypally fixed forms of human and other species abiding timelessly in the mind of the creator. Furthermore, even at a mundane level of evaluation, the risks of technological adventurism are always, at best, ambiguous. The safer path, therefore, is to preserve the cosmological, biological, and anthropological status quo.

The analogical vision values "creation" for the simple reason that nature, in spite of being soured by sin, is sacramentally revelatory of God. This traditional Catholic way of looking at the world has assumed that finite nature's transparency to the infinite requires a relatively fixed, hierarchical understanding of the world. Accordingly, major adjustments to natural and human existence would imperil not only nature, but also our whole sense of God and creation. If we lose nature, says the Catholic environmentalist Thomas Berry, we lose God.[4] Sacramentalists these days are especially sensitive to the environmental disasters that have accompanied the Industrial Revolution, nuclear technology, the deployment of complex and expensive modern weaponry, energy-wasting transportation, and countless other modern inventions. Sacramentalists do not condemn science as such since it helps us understand God's creation, and it has made useful technologies possible. But sacramentalists are exceptionally aware that science has come with enormous environmental costs. Scientific knowledge, at least as it has been applied in modern times, has had positive outcomes, but it has been accompanied by horrific by-products including the ruination of immense swaths of our planet's ecosystems. And today space technology is spreading a new trail of debris across the heavens that for centuries symbolized the perfection of God.

The pure sacramentalist, therefore, wonders whether the gains of scientific technology can ever outweigh the evils that the same technology enables. Aren't transhumanists naïve to suppose that unfettered human technology can avoid a catastrophic disfiguring of life and persons? At the present time in human and cosmic history, is it pragmatically prudent or morally responsible to undertake dramatic changes to God's creation? Ethically speaking, a sacramental sensibility requires conservation rather than transformation of nature. And religiously speaking, a radical alteration of life and humanity would make nature less transparent to transcendent mystery than ever before.

3. *The anticipatory option.* This response to transhumanist proposals is rooted in cosmic hope and based on a metaphysics of the future. Its open-ended and dramatic view of nature features above all the virtue of patience. Acknowledging a dramatic universe's need to wait until things ripen, cosmic hope is wary of the hyper-enthusiastic recklessness and perfectionism of secular transhumanist proposals. However, it is equally concerned that the analogical/sacramental vision may, in its own way, also be out of touch with the *dramatic* character of natural process. Doesn't the sacramental alternative, attractive as it may be to many Catholics today, especially in view of the current global environmental predicament, unnecessarily ignore the periodicity and larger cycles of cosmic transformation? Sooner or later, if we take the long view, doesn't every present have to give way to a new future? Is the sacramental option, even in all its innocence, open to the full liberation of life? Is it sufficiently open to nature's promise of new creation?

Furthermore, isn't the transforming of our natural surroundings and of ourselves along with them, consistent with being fully human? After all, even most nonhuman species have to alter their own environments to make them habitable. Spiders weave webs, and beavers build dams. Environmental niches are not always already "out there" ready-made, waiting to be filled in or adapted to, but are in some degree products of their inhabitants' creativity. And, in turn, our environments dialectically transform their living inhabitants. If it is natural for animals to alter their natural settings, shouldn't it be all the more so for ourselves? Are we so unlike other kinds of life that we should keep our instruments off the physical universe altogether?

Humans, quite naturally, survive and thrive only because of their capacity to change their environments artificially. And since we are part of nature too, are we exempt from self-transformation along with our environments?

Who then is to say where a transhumanist extension of our creative instincts must start or stop? If openness to the future can lead to a reckless, runaway progressivism, isn't there also the risk of a stagnating perfectionism motivated by the analogical vision's idealizing of timeless essences? Is it possible that sacramentalism, with its metaphysics of the eternal now, stifles our sense of nature's habitual anticipation of more being?

An anticipatory theological vision cannot ignore these questions. It has to assume that the cosmos is a work in progress and that humanity's vocation is one of extending the creativity of cosmic process into an indeterminate future. Wouldn't it be a violation of human nature and dignity, as well as an irresponsible abandonment of our vocation before God, to suppress our creative capacities in the way a pure sacramentalism seems to demand? An anticipatory Catholic theology would deny that the relatively new technologies of late modernity are unambiguously evil. Rather, they are essential to bringing "more being" into the evolving drama of life in an unfinished universe.[5] Certainly, trade-offs occur whenever technology tries out new inventions, but, in a way, isn't that life? Biological history carries risks of loss and temporary environmental disruptions with every new emergent chapter, but does this mean that experiments and risks should be avoided altogether? If nature had not previously allowed for experiments, blind alleys, and dead ends in its evolution, matter could never have reached the point of complexity that allowed for the eventual emergence of sentience, consciousness, and reflective thought. Isn't it possible that the universe has other dramatically innovative chapters in reserve? If so, is it altogether forbidden theologically to support transhumanist ideals?

A proposal

I am raising these questions only in a spirit of extreme caution and hopeful patience. I am not advising any precipitous, unreflective transhumanist experiments. I am one with Teilhard when he writes:

> Not all directions are good for our advance: one alone leads upward, that which through increasing organization leads to greater synthesis and unity. Here we part company with the wholehearted individualists, the egoists who seek to grow by excluding or diminishing their fellows, individually, nationally or racially. Life moves towards unification. Our hope can only be realized if it finds its expression in greater cohesion and greater human solidarity.[6]

Any advance has to involve an intensification rather than a diminishment of intercommunion and differentiation. At the present point in cosmic evolution, momentous changes must from the start promote life's integrity and human solidarity. Still, an absolutist stand against any transformations of the biological and anthropological status quo seems excessive in view of what we now understand about the universe. Why should we not assume that the unfinished universe, today as in the past, is still open to new creation? Shouldn't the natural creative impulses of human beings be allowed to express themselves, even with respect to our own bodily forms, for the sake of fulfilling our cosmic vocation? Isn't it conceivable that the Spirit of God and God's vision of new creation may sponsor a gradual transformation of our own behavioral and cognitive characteristics in a way that promotes deeper integration, unity, freedom, and difference?

The anticipatory vision I have been developing allows, in principle, for a biblically inspired shift from an exclusively sacramental affirmation of the inherent value of life and human dignity to a vision that integrates more deliberately the biblical themes of promise and liberation (including, especially, the theme of prophetic justice). According to this third approach, it may be not only humanly possible, but also ethically obligatory, to examine whether our species is necessarily a final or culminating chapter in the cosmic drama. Contemplating transhumanist possibilities, even if they are never implemented, would, at the very least, be theologically interesting and maybe even illuminating. Speculating about transhumanist possibilities may also have the added advantage of preparing people of faith for an eventual encounter with extraterrestrial intelligent beings if they exist.

Having said this, however, I want to propose a very circumspect adventurism as far as transhumanism is concerned. My suggestion, in fact, carries a stricter set of constraints than those proposed by either the archaeological or the analogical visions. In an unfinished universe, fidelity to the biblical theme of promise combined with full openness to evolutionary biology, cosmology, and other sciences requires a patient and prayerful exercise of human creativity. To be more specific, there are at least three inviolable rules of life, embedded in every evolutionary milestone, that any proposals for the enhancement of God's creation, including human organisms, must keep in mind as a condition for appropriate future creation.

A. The first constraint is concern for the intensification of *vitality*. Life must increase rather than decrease. If life fails to become more, it stagnates and dies. To understand what true vitality means, however, we need first to ask how living beings differ from nonliving beings. One mark that distinguishes them is their capacity to succeed or fail. The philosopher Michael Polanyi thinks that the defining feature of life can be grasped only by our learning the "logic of achievement." This means paying attention to the fact that organisms do not just exist, they also strive. Striving to achieve some goal is what sets living beings apart ontologically from lifeless and mindless kinds of being. And because living beings have the capacity to strive, they also have the capacity to succeed or fail.[7]

Organisms are bent on achievement, and intuitively we all realize this. We experience living beings as distinctly alive because we *personally* identify with their capacity for endeavor and hence with the possibility of their either achieving or failing to achieve a goal (or goals). Inanimate physical and chemical processes differ decisively from those we consider to be alive. Physical and chemical processes do not strive, struggle, try, achieve, or fail. Rather, they just adhere to unswerving routines blindly and unfeelingly. By contrast, precisely because living beings are capable of striving (even if only to stay alive), their mode of existence is irreducible to their subsidiary physical and chemical processes. A living being strives, whether it is a parasite searching for nourishment, a bird seeking its prey, or a human being reading books in quest of the meaning of life. Even the simplest instances of metabolism exercise a minimal kind of effort by building membranes that protect their internal self-structuring from being swamped by their chemical and physical environments.[8] Evolutionists implicitly recognize the "conative" (or striving) character of life whenever they talk about the "struggle to exist" in a world limited by natural selection. They would not rightly use such terms as striving or struggling if they were referring only to inanimate objects or processes.

Going beyond Polanyi, however, I believe the capacity to strive can be fully acknowledged and elaborated only from within the context of a metaphysics of the future. A metaphysics of the past with its materialist ontology of death cannot even *see*, let alone understand, life. I have already observed, for example, that materialism cannot allow for any final resurrection since it fails to acknowledge even the first arrival of life in cosmic history. Even as materialists personally strive (ironically) to reduce life to its physical and chemical makeup, they are blind to the conative—and broadly *anticipatory*—quality of their own existence. Evolutionary naturalists, who think of natural selection as a blindly mechanical process that can account fully for the behavioral characteristics of all living beings, overlook the logic of achievement that makes life distinctive and that underlies their own intellectual efforts.

A purely analogical or sacramental vision also fails to take into account, or fully illuminate, the futurity of life. Within the framework of a metaphysics of the eternal present, the value of life consists of its (always imperfect) participation in the fullness of divine life. A sacramental vision may connect

life to transcendent goodness and beauty, but not necessarily to the futurity
of being. It too easily overlooks the *anticipation of more being* that gives life
its distinctive definition. Nor is sacramentalism able to capture the dramatic
fact that, with the coming of life, the universe was delivered decisively from
imprisonment by its past.

It is the uniquely anticipatory aspect of life that transhumanist projects
must at all costs strive to sustain. Even though in a broad sense the entire
cosmos is anticipatory as I have been arguing, there is clearly a duality of ways
of being in the universe. Living beings, especially by virtue of their exceptional,
and increasingly subjective and centered capacity for anticipation, stand out
sharply from their inanimate chemical background. As far as transhumanism
is concerned, therefore, the important theological question is whether the
capacity to strive, that is, to act in accordance with the logic of achievement,
will continue to be an essential aspect of future transformations of the
universe, life, and human existence. Can the anticipatory quality of life be
transplanted into technologically engineered forms of being? And will the
urge to strive, which is an essential attribute of vitality (as well as of moral
and religious existence), avoid being completely devoured by the metaphysics
of the past that conditions so much human thought and culture today?

Transhumanist projects are themselves instances of human striving in
accordance with the logic of achievement, but the danger now is that these
projects will formally reduce life and intelligence to inanimate mechanical or
computational processes where the quality of anticipation no longer survives.
The often unspoken objective of much contemporary biology and cognitive
science, since they are still usually guided by materialist assumptions, is to
expel vitality from the sphere of being altogether. To the extent that technology
and cognitive sciences mechanize or virtualize life and intelligence, the
more serious becomes the question of whether vitality can survive such a
transformation. The more transhumanists seek to replace striving beings with
entities that fail to function in accordance with the logic of achievement—
and this includes the whole sphere of artificial intelligence—the more urgent
becomes our concern about the survival of life into the indefinite future. As
of now, it is hard to imagine how even the most complex and sophisticated
future technologies will protect rather than destroy the attribute of centered,
anticipatory striving that is essential to living beings as we know them now.

Polanyi rightly insists that it is "personal knowledge" rather than the
impersonal methods of science that allows human beings to mark off for
special study a distinct domain of vitality in the natural world.[9] The fact
that academicians have set departments of biology administratively apart
from those of physics and chemistry is witness to a tacit acknowledgment
that living beings are distinct from nonliving beings since they share with

personal beings the trait of striving. Only because we humans, as personal organisms, are anticipatory beings (e.g., in our *longing* to understand, our *desiring* to know, and our *struggle* to find out what is good) are we able to recognize the trait of striving and anticipation that endows a whole distinct class of nonhuman beings with the gift of vitality.

Most transhumanists, from everything I can tell, are scientific naturalists who follow a creed that ignores the logic of achievement essential to all instances of life, including their own striving to transform life and human nature. They are indifferent to the question of how to protect the centered striving and anticipation that defines human vitality. Since humans share with other living beings the trait of striving and, along with it, the possibility of tragic defeat, will a transhumanist world still leave room for beings that possess the capacity for failure and a sense of tragedy? If the transhumanist world ends up leaving behind the capacity to strive, exchanging it for technologically engineered projects operating only in accordance with mechanically or chemically deterministic processes, will that be an advance toward more being? Or, rather, would it not amount to a great terrestrial and cosmic catastrophe?

B. The second condition for embarking on transhumanist adventures, already implicit in the first, is that they must sustain or intensify *subjectivity*. Reflection on the fact of striving leads us to acknowledge in each living being at least a minimum of centeredness or interiority, that is, subjectivity. An undeniable trend in the universe's evolution so far has been that of bringing about a gradual increase in sentience, perceptivity, consciousness, and—at least in human beings—self-awareness, moral aspiration, freedom, the longing for love, and other manifestations of an interior life. All vital striving must have a subjective center in which the experience of trying, succeeding, or failing is registered. Otherwise, living beings would be indistinguishable from physical processes that do not strive or feel in any sense.

The striving of each living being is centered in the ontological domain of subjectivity, an immediately palpable but unobjectifiable reality. A subjective center, by definition, eludes the objectifying grasp or control of modern science and engineering. At present, however, transhumanist idealizations of future forms of intelligence are conceived narrowly in terms of the modern picture of a cosmos devoid of subjects. Transhumanist visions are presently weighed down by the assumption that nature is inherently mindless and impersonal, that it is devoid of the immeasurable dimension of subjectivity that constitutes the core of human personhood. Consequently, as long as expectations of a transformed humanity and universe lack any concern to protect and enhance subjectivity, they point to a considerably diminished, rather than an enhanced, cosmic future.

C. A third criterion for embarking on transhumanist projects is that they must sustain or increase the world's capacity for *creativity*. Implied in our first two criteria, creativity in an unfinished universe means the capacity for bringing about fuller being. Theologically speaking, creativity means the world's participation in the divine task of bringing something *new* into existence. It means not only preservation (which indeed is absolutely essential), but also preparation of the world for new creation up ahead. It is the function of a biblically based transhumanist ethic not only to conserve life systems on our planet, but also to take measures that will foster opportunities for the enhancement of vitality, subjectivity, freedom, diversity, and relationality in the future up ahead. As long as transhumanist projects contribute to this creative enhancement, they would seem to be justifiable in terms of a Catholic theology of nature.

Failure to align our lives faithfully and docilely with the values that have already been established in the emergence of the universe could lead to horrifying consequences. From a Christian point of view, such neglect would be equivalent to spurning the coming of God. If our creativity were to conform only to what human beings desire at any particular moment or phase in past history, the consequences could be fearsome since human desiring is always subject to perversion by impatience and perfectionism. Christian faith instructs us that patient hope and courageous waiting must always accompany human aspirations and creative adventures.

Both contemporary science and biblical hope view the universe as open to dramatic transformation. Transhumanism reminds us that we may anticipate still more dramatic outcomes in the future. Cosmological, geological, and biological accounts of cosmic events teach us that nature has always had a dramatic character. And, now that we understand the natural world as an ongoing creative process, we may see it as having a much wider meaning than that of simply being a stage for human ambitions. Neither the archaeological nor the analogical visions are fully able to acknowledge the degree to which the world rests on the future. For our purposes here, on the other hand, cosmic hope (as distinct from cosmic pessimism and otherworldly optimism) provides an appropriate setting for theology to forge a fruitful alliance with scientists and futurists. An anticipatory cosmic vision allows Catholic theologians to ponder whether nature, having given rise to increasing vitality, subjectivity, and creativity in the past, may still have room for future enhancement.

Four billion years ago, in the sudden arrival of life and biogenetic processes on earth, the universe underwent an "information" explosion.[10] More recently, with the emergence of complex brains and minds on our planet (and perhaps analogous outcomes elsewhere in the universe), the cosmos began to undergo a "thought" explosion. And much more recently, with the emergence of social organisms, life began to undergo a "cultural" explosion, one that, at least on earth, has included the invention of language, economics, politics, education, artistic expression, religious hope, and scientific inquiry. Currently, with the appearance of transhumanist possibilities, human beings are at last witnessing what may turn out to be a distinctively new explosion in the unfolding of our far-from-finished universe. I believe that theology must approach the specter of transhumanism with the reverence of the sacramental vision, but at the same time, with an anticipatory instinct to enhance rather than diminish the vitality, subjectivity, and creativity to which our universe has already labored so long to give birth.

The theological scheme that motivates my proposal is one in which nature itself is seen not only as sacrament, but also as promise. Our unfinished universe is not yet fully revelatory of the divine. It awaits future creativity and development. In light of the theological recovery of eschatology in the twentieth century, I am especially partial to a theology of hope according to which all Christian theology in the future is bathed in the extravagant flood of covenantal promises that the Bible associates with a creative and renewing God. But the divine invitation to move into an open future of new possibilities applies to the fourteen-billion-year-old cosmic process and not just the human future. Once again, then, I want to affirm that the idea of the "promise of nature" provides an essential point of departure for a scientifically informed Catholic theology of nature that can guide us into the transhumanist epoch.[11]

14

Meaning: From Order to Information

The central issue in conversations between theologians and scientists is whether the cosmic drama carries a meaning or purpose. Meaning has to do with value, and to have a purpose means to be directed toward the realization of a value or set of values. When reflecting on the meaning of our own lives, for example, we ask what values are guiding us. Commitment to something self-evidently good ties together the moments of our lives and gives significance to our personal stories. To ask whether the cosmos is meaningful or purposeful, then, is to ask whether it too is a series of events that moves, overall, toward the realizing of a value or set of values. Is something of lasting importance working itself out in the universe? Is the cosmos moving toward fuller being, goodness, or beauty? If so, it has a meaning or purpose.

But does it? Traditional Catholic theology pictured the universe as clearly purposeful. The cosmos was thought of as a ladder of hierarchically distinct levels that receive their meaning from participating in, and being drawn toward, the infinite transcendent goodness and beauty of the creator God who orders everything from on high. Natural theology sought support for Catholicism's trust in cosmic meaning by highlighting natural phenomena that seemed to be "designed," that is, intentionally ordered toward a goal. We have seen, however, that most Darwinians deny that adaptive design requires any ordering principle at all. Even during his voyage on HMS Beagle, Darwin began to doubt that a divine intentionality patterns the natural world in a direct way. What he found was not design pointing toward an ordering deity, but imperfect, experimental adaptations that made the universe seem undirected and unaffected by any principle of meaning and guidance. Evolutionists today, citing the abundance of "design-flaws" in nature, usually assume that nature carries no meaning or purpose at all. Whatever meanings nature may seem to have are nothing more than the illusory constructs of human beings who find it hard to live without such "fictions." The materialist neo-Darwinian philosopher Daniel Dennett, for example, claims that in view of evolution the only message we can read off the universe is that "it has no message."[1]

In this final chapter, however, I want to argue, first, that the notion of information, already briefly introduced in Chapter 8, carries implications that the bare notions of order and design lack and, second, that understanding how information works may help Catholic theology ponder the question of cosmic meaning in the setting of what we now know to be a dramatic and still-unfinished cosmos.

In a prescientific world, religious believers took for granted that a transcendent principle of meaning orders all things. The intuition that "mind" or "wisdom" patterns the universe came to expression, for example, in ancient Greek philosophy, the Wisdom literature of the Hebrew Scriptures, philosophical Daoism, Stoicism, and classical Catholic metaphysics. Aquinas, Descartes, Leibniz, Kant, Hegel, and most other philosophers until quite recently have assumed that the universe is intentionally ordered in one way or another.

Today, however, the life process scarcely seems to be an embodiment of benign divine intentionality. Contrary to the picture of cosmic order taken for granted by traditional Catholic thought, evolution involves endless experimentation with many different "forms," most of which are eventually discarded and replaced by a relative few that by accident turn out to be more suited than others to the demands of natural selection. The impersonal evolutionary proliferation of experimental organisms, only a few of which are permitted to survive and reproduce, seems to reflect no divine planning whatsoever. Instead, contingency rules. The spontaneity of life's origin, the randomness of genetic variation, and the undirected course of natural history give to the story of life an unpredictability that seems inconsistent with any superintending divine influence.[2]

This picture of nature differs sharply from Catholic tradition's strong history of natural theology, a discipline that looks to the natural world for confirming evidence of divine governance. The analogical/sacramental vision of classical Catholic metaphysics has given strong support to natural theology, but I have argued that our new awareness of an unfinished universe demands that the analogical vision of classical metaphysics be overlaid by a biblical sense of the metaphysical priority of the future. This means that the marvelous instances of natural design that theologians formerly took to be analogies of timeless perfection may better be thought of as *anticipations*—installments of a future yet to be actualized. That they would be anticipations rather than finalized actualizations seems consistent with a cosmos that exists basically as an ongoing drama rather than a factory of designs.

The universe, therefore, functions as revelatory not so much by providing analogies as by parading momentary anticipations of God. Whether we call them analogies or anticipations, however, Catholic theology willingly acknowledges the figurative nature of religious discourse about the anticipated God. Theology relies on prescientific modes of mythic and symbolic discourse that can never be translated into terms of modern scientific thought. Trying to be scientifically specific about how God is present to the universe—for example, by speculating that divine intentionality may be at work in the realm of quantum events hidden from direct scientific observation—implicitly makes God part of, rather than infinitely distinct from, natural processes. And God, as theologian Paul Tillich rightly emphasizes, cannot be one cause among others without ceasing to be God.[3]

Symbolic rather than literal reference, Tillich rightly argues, is indispensable in all attempts to understand God's relationship to the world. Nevertheless, the fact that religious faith has to use symbolic language is not something for which theology ever has to apologize, as though clear and distinct discourse would be superior to mythic, symbolic, metaphorical, or analogical expression. Symbols are essential to protect the divine from profanation, and faith from losing its depth. Theology should never aspire to exchange symbolic or paradoxical reference to God for the kind of clarity sought by science. Faith, after all, is more a matter of being grasped than of grasping. Indeed, the further theology drifts from the naive discourse of its original inspiration, the more it loses its power to transform.[4] This is why theology need never be troubled by the current vulgar scientistic mockery of people of faith for having to use symbolic or metaphorical language.

Still, if the language of symbol, metaphor, and analogy is essential to religious awareness, some symbols, analogies, and metaphors are more theologically appropriate than others. I have been arguing, for example, that the idea of design is misleading in referring to how God relates to living phenomena, especially in view of evolutionary accounts of life. The universe and life are more analogous to drama than design, and the regularities of nature are more like grammatical rules than deterministic laws.

Language is powerful, and a shift in our metaphors and analogies can sometimes transform our whole sense of reality and meaning. For this very reason I want to argue here that *information*, an idea that has become increasingly common lately in scientific and philosophical discourse, has both anticipatory and dramatic overtones that make it superior to the idea of design or order in theology's search for analogies expressive of what is going on in the universe. Our unfinished universe, I want to argue, is not so much designed by an ordering deity as it is an *information system* that may be carrying a dramatic revelatory meaning. To understand this proposal, however, we need to keep in mind, first, this book's central argument that the drama of life and mind is inseparable from a universe that is still coming into being and, second, that a still-unfinished universe cannot presently be completely intelligible to us.

Information and meaning

What then is information? In the broadest sense, "information" can be defined as whatever gives form, order, pattern, or identity to something, whether an electron, a crystal, the human mind, a civilization, or an economic system. In this broad sense, information is similar to what Aristotle means by formal cause. As used in communications theory, however, information means the reduction of uncertainty.[5] According to this contemporary usage, the more uncertainty is reduced in any communication, the more information it may be said to carry. It is especially in this sense that I want to explore the suggestiveness of the idea of information for Catholic theology today. Can a universe that sponsors evolution, even though failing to fit comfortably the analogy of order or design, perhaps be viewed intelligibly as "informational," and hence as open to being influenced by a transcendent principle of meaning?

If the universe is to be the carrier of dramatic meaning, it may be thought of as analogous to an information system.[6] An information system is a structure that gathers, stores, and carries information from a source to a recipient. In order to function, however, it has to have boundaries or channels that keep the content that is being communicated from fading off into indefiniteness.[7] Every information system, according to communications theory, is limited. It can handle only a finite amount of data. Hence, care must be taken to encode a message in such a way as to fit within the boundaries of what the medium allows. According to communications theory, the danger always exists that the message will be lost in static and other kinds of interference. So to prevent such obstacles to communication, the message must be encoded in a way that allows it to be received over and above the scrambling effects of noise. This is why an information process must typically have an aspect of "redundancy."[8] Accordingly, a message may need to be repeated, or reformulated in multiple ways, to ensure its being received accurately. (The sentence I have just written is an example of redundancy.) Redundancy lessens the economy and speed of a communication, but it compensates for the sluggishness of information flow by rendering the transmission of meaning more reliable than may otherwise be the case. Of course, by overdoing redundancy, a message can be reduced to what is merely probable. In that case, since it barely reduces uncertainty, it is only minimally informative. Excessive redundancy makes information lose its informative edge, but without at least some degree of redundancy, noise may wipe out the message.

For a message to be informative, therefore, it must contain a degree of improbability or unexpected novelty. The *amount* of information in a message is in proportion to its improbability. If the recipient expects all the messages from a given source to be the same, then any one of them, upon delivery, will carry very little information since there is no uncertainty to be reduced. The more probable a message is, in other words, the less informative it will be. By contrast, the more informative a message is, the more improbable it will seem to the recipient.

Consequently, if the universe is anything like an information system, then the most revelatory message it may be communicating will be accompanied by the least redundancy. Such a message would amount to something like what cosmologists call a singularity, and as such it would be inaccessible to conventional science. Scientific method, after all, is most at home in the realm of what is predictable and probable. Indeed, it tries to reduce what may seem initially improbable to what should have been expected. This is why scientific naturalists are most comfortable intellectually with a metaphysics of the past, according to which every present outcome is nothing more than a product of a predictable series of routine events. By contrast, any truly informative message the cosmic drama may be conveying would be unavailable to comprehension by a metaphysics of the past. Perhaps, though, it would fit comfortably into a metaphysics of the future.

Conventional science, in any case, cannot deal with the uniqueness of improbabilities insofar as it denies that there is any real certainty to be reduced. It strives to reduce improbability to what is merely probable. Any religiously revelatory message being communicated via the cosmos, therefore, would lie completely beyond the horizon of scientific inquiry and detection. Any dramatic meaning the universe may have would elude altogether the objectifying grasp of scientific method.

Noise, redundancy, and revelation

Theology in the context of an unfinished universe, therefore, looks for meaning not in instances of order alone but also in the novelty that keeps our universe open to the future. The communication of information has to avoid the two extremes of noise and redundancy if it is to be truly informative. Both excessive noise and surplus redundancy interfere with the flow of information. "Noise" means the indefiniteness, randomness—and hence pointlessness—into which a message can lapse. By analogy, the narrative of life seems constantly threatened by the unsystematic noise of accidents in the flow of genes from one generation to the next or by the contingencies in natural history that propel the life story onto indeterminate trajectories.[9] This is why it may seem to be carrying "no message," as Dennett puts it.

Ever since Darwin, the existence of accidents in evolution has raised questions about the credibility of theological claims that life is the direct work of a governing divine providence. Now, however, the accidents in evolution can become intelligible once we understand them in terms of information. In a dramatic understanding of the cosmos, what strike us as "accidents" are simply events that have not yet been brought into a *narrative coherence* that may emerge only later on. If the universe is an information system carrying an unpredictable message, occurrences within that system at any present moment would swing ambiguously between the extremes of noise on the one side and redundancy on the other. Contingency or chance, especially in life's evolution, however, would not rule out the possibility that the universe is carrying messages whose intelligibility can be anticipated only by hope. Cosmic meaning, then, would not show up in any scientific models of the physical world, nor could it be located by tracking a series of efficient and material causes into the cosmic past.

If the cosmic process, then, is mediating a religiously relevant content, it must also avoid being smothered by the redundancy embedded in the predictable habits of nature that I have been referring to as grammatical rules. Scientists are accustomed to calling these invariant principles *laws* of nature, viewing them collectively as a pantheon of fateful forces that provide the ultimate explanation of whatever happens in the natural world. However, informationally speaking, these regulations may not be brute causes of anything, but instead grammatical boundaries that facilitate the flow and delivery of cosmic meaning.

Modern scientific naturalism, adhering to a metaphysics of the past, has generally assumed that nature is a closed continuum of physically inviolable causes and effects, and hence completely impermeable to any possible transcendent principle of meaning. For example, Albert Einstein's well-publicized rejection of belief in a personal, responsive God follows from his assumption that everything in nature is fully determined by impersonal physical laws.[10] However, if we suppose that the cosmos is analogous to an information system, such an extreme claim is unreasonable. There is room for both inviolable grammatical regulations *and* the emergence of new meaning over the course of cosmic time. The cosmos, viewed informationally, is irreducible to either chance or necessity. Instead, it is comparable to an information system through which meaning can pass between the extremes of noise and redundancy.

Any communication of meaning has to follow grammatical rules, but the rules may be understood as enabling conditions rather than imprisoning restraints. To employ another analogy, the sentences I am writing on this page obey invariant grammatical rules, but these rules do not force me to adhere to only one predetermined sequence of letters and words. The content of this paragraph demands my scrupulous adherence to grammatical rules, but what exactly I have to say here by way of content is not fixed in advance by these rules. As I write, I am choosing letters from an alphabet and words from a lexicon. To function as potential bits of information, however, the letters of the alphabet reside in an imaginary "mixing-pot," and the words reside in the cumulative lexicon of my native tongue. But the rules of grammar, strict though they are, still allow me to place the letters and words in an endless array of indeterminate informational sequences.

Any communication of meaning through the use of letters of a code has to have a randomizing—or noisy—quality that allows the letters, figuratively speaking, to disassemble if they are to be reassembled in a pattern that permits the communication of meaning. Suppose, on the contrary, that the alphabet I am using were fixed inflexibly into only one determinate sequence, so that *b* always had to be attached irremovably to *a; c* to *b; d* to *c; e to d*, and so on. Such a rigidly formatted sequence of letters would be ordered, but this stiff, predetermined chain of letters would have very low information content. In fact, an inflexibly ordered sequence of letters would make the communication of written information impossible. The letters have to be separable, mixable, and randomizable if they are to be informationally useful.

Analogously, too much order or design in the life story would prevent the flow of information and with it any truly dramatic meaning. If the cosmos were perfectly "designed," a setup that scientific naturalists require as a condition for believing in the reality of God, it would be frozen from the start into a solid state resistant to the mixing that is essential to the communication of meaning. Design, therefore, is an informational and theological dead end. Any rigidly ordered prearrangement of cosmic stuff would impede both the emergence and transmission of information. Too high an initial degree of order in the universe would be antithetical to its having any dramatic significance at all.

Again, the analogy of the universe to an information system locates cosmic meaning somewhere between the two extremes of noise and redundancy. This way of situating the cosmic drama responds to both the atheism of evolutionary naturalists, on the one hand, and the rejection of evolution by ID devotees, on the other. Both sides claim that a Darwinian world is incompatible with their perfectionist idealization of divinely established order. Much religious antipathy to evolution these days is rooted in the assumption that a world that is tolerant of accidents or contingencies is too noisy to fit the idea of divine wisdom.[11] And evolutionary naturalism implicitly embraces the same assumption. In its obsession with "design," evolutionary naturalism insists that any reasonable affirmation of cosmic meaning would require that living organisms exhibit perfect engineering at every present moment.[12]

By contrast, even though Catholic Christianity has a strong tradition of natural theology, it has not always embraced the idea that God is simply a "designer." Nor has it always insisted that divine action is reducible to "design." Even before Darwin's *Origin* appeared, Cardinal John Henry Newman, for example, had insisted that theology has little use for William Paley's brand of natural theology with its narrow focus on design. Design-oriented theology, he insisted, could "not tell us one word about Christianity proper. . . ." Paley's "physical" theology—which was formative of Darwin's theological mind-set before he sailed off on HMS Beagle—"tends, if it occupies the mind, to dispose it against Christianity."[13]

Looking at the cosmic drama informationally, then, is not limited to looking for ordered perfection in the natural world. The fact that nature and life play host to accidents and spontaneities need not be taken as a sign of the universe's "pitiless indifference." An informational perspective, in fact, cannot do without contingency, for otherwise the universe would not be open to a new future where faith must look for narrative coherence. Without nature's present capacity for moments of deconstruction, no evolutionary drama could be inscribed in it. Without a constant leaning toward a state of noise, the universe would be too inelastic to be the carrier of rich meaning, nor could it "rest on the future." For this reason, theology should have no problem embracing the Second Law of Thermodynamics according to which the universe has a constant and irreversible tendency toward disorder. The idea of an entropic universe is completely consistent with the notion of information as well as with the idea that the universe is a drama rather than a design. Accordingly, the fact of random, undirected occurrences in life's evolution, or, for that matter, in the wider cosmic process, is not a decisive obstacle to belief that the universe carries a transcendent meaning. And the Einsteinian claim that nature runs by inviolable "laws" is not proof of the universe's imperviousness to purpose either, since from a dramatic point of view nature's strict regulations can now be likened to grammatical rules.

Especially since the nineteenth century, cosmic pessimists have become accustomed to fixing their attention on either entropy or impersonal physical "laws" as though either of these tendencies entails a pointless universe.[14] They have observed correctly that any ordered system tends to lapse into disorder. However, cosmic pessimists have failed to understand that the communication of any truly meaningful *story* requires a dimension of contingency and indefiniteness that lets in enough novelty to overcome sheer redundancy. They fail to entertain the possibility that our universe, even if it is destined to eventual death by entropy, may still be the carrier of meaning precisely *because* it has a tendency to lapse into disorder.

A meaningful cosmos requires the breakdown of present order, the dismantling of temporary instances of rigid design, if it is to have a narrative informational character. Cosmic despair, however, feeds parasitically on the gratuitous absolutizing of either noise or redundancy. Its devotees refuse to consider the possibility that noise and redundancy are informational necessities rather than capricious causal agencies. One wing of cosmic pessimism exaggerates the cosmic trend toward disorder and "explains" the precarious instances of emergent order such as a cell, an eye, or a brain as nothing more than momentary reversals of the general trend of the universe toward energetic collapse.[15] Meanwhile, the other wing of cosmic pessimism is so entranced by the metaphorical understanding of physical constraints as "laws" that it considers emergent phenomena to be nothing more than inevitable outcomes of a deterministic process. Both wings of cosmic pessimism, however, are anachronistically fixated on the early modern obsession with lawfully driven mechanical order—rather than dramatic meaning—as paradigmatic for understanding the universe. Consequently, after failing to discover any indisputable evidence of flawless divine engineering in nature, they confidently declare that the universe is pointless.[16] An informational perspective, on the other hand, allows for an alternate interpretation of nature as a narrative blending of indeterminacy, reliability, and deep time.

Information and emergence

During the cosmic process, increments in information are essential to the evolution of increasingly complex forms of being, life, and consciousness. As the cosmos has transited in its evolution from matter to life, and then to consciousness, ethical sensitivity, artistic creativity, and religious longing, something new, and hence relatively improbable, has been added in each new chapter of the story. This emergent novelty is real, and not just an illusory cover-up of what is taken to be at bottom either absurd "chance" or blind "necessity." But where does the novelty—which is essential for fuller being—come from? It cannot be accounted for, as I have been arguing, simply by tracking a series of physical causes into the remote cosmic past. What is needed, I believe, is a metaphysics of the future to make sense of emergence.

To the materialist mind-set, on the other hand, nothing new can ever *really* happen in the cosmic process. There is only a reshuffling of atoms and molecules. Increasingly today, however, scientists are realizing that classical atomistic science has left something out of its world picture. In addition to order, there is also an ingredient of novelty in our emergent universe that consists, in part at least, of the quiet influx of information. Information, however, comes into the cosmos without trumpet blasts and lavish parades. In living phenomena, for example, information settles humbly and unobtrusively into the physical universe without altering the laws of thermodynamics. Just as unprecedented strings of letters and words can be introduced into my word processor without modifying the hardware or the syntax governing the computational process, so also the insinuation of novel informational patterns into the fabric of the universe can happen so unostentatiously that it goes unnoticed altogether by materialist and atomistic scientific sensibilities. It arrives on the wings of the future.

Even though it is not produced by physical force, new information can, nevertheless, *dramatically* influence the course of life and the cosmic process without disturbing any of the rules operative in the cosmos. The all-important biological flow of genes across many generations, for example, does not require the suspension or alteration of the "laws" of chemistry and physics, but if material processes are the only thing we focus on, we will fail to notice the dramatic character of life. The drama of life cannot be registered by eyes and minds accustomed only to reading nature at the level of its atomic and molecular particulars or in terms of a metaphysics of the past.

Concretely, the universe is a narrative *blend* of order and novelty, steering its way across deep time between absolute redundancy, on the one hand, and absolute noise, on the other. It should not surprise us, therefore, that any universe that carries a meaning or meanings would permit its content to meander adventurously between the two extremes of deadly design and unintelligible chaos. Hence, any meaning that our universe may be carrying would go unnoticed both by a science that looks only for what is predictable, and by a tragic "realism" that expects the final cosmic state to be the complete triumph of chance and necessity.

A different kind of reading competency, one cultivated by the virtue of hope, may be necessary if we are to discern any meaning coming to expression in the cosmic process. Even if we allow ourselves to be grasped by such a meaning, however, we will still have to wait until the story is complete before we make any final judgments about it. At present, the universe's deepest intelligibility can be only dimly discerned, if at all, only if we turn our minds—and hearts—toward the future. Adopting a posture of hope, of course, is a thoroughly religious challenge, but it is not one that contradicts science, especially if we think of the cosmos in informational terms.

Information, as we have seen, can be eclipsed by excessive chaos or deadened by too much order.[17] The notions of excessive redundancy and unnecessary noise, therefore, may provide analogies for two distinct types of evil that occur in the life-world in general and human experience in particular. The "evil of redundancy" consists of the endless repetition of routines, at any level of emergence, when the introduction of novel information would allow for the entry of fuller being and value into the cosmic process. At the human level of cosmic emergence, an example of the "evil of redundancy" is any rigid obsession with certitude or existential security that screens out the complexity of the real world. It might take the form of a resistance to novelty and adventure essential to the thriving of life and culture. On the other side, evil can take the form of unnecessary noise. The "evil of noise," when considered in the context of an informational cosmology, consists of an excessive disregard for rules of order without which the communication of meaning becomes impossible.

The presence of these two types of evil in the world does not logically contradict our trust in the reality of a meaningful cosmos cared for by a providential God. If our theology starts with the revelatory image of a self-giving God who keeps the future open, we should not be surprised that, informationally speaking, cosmic evolution and human existence would often take an "erring" and meandering course, leaning at times toward either excessive noise or too much redundancy, yet over the long haul inscribing an informative dramatic meaning between the extremes. In summary, information does not require that there be no deviations from order. For if the cosmos is an information system, at least some degree of disorder and redundancy would show up at the margins of the meaning it may be carrying. But since an informational universe remains open to a new future, there remains room for hope.

Notes

Introduction

1 Since 2000, my books on science and religion include *Science and Faith: A New Introduction* (New York: Paulist Press, 2013); *Making Sense of Evolution: Darwin, God, and The Drama of Life* (Louisville: Westminster/John Knox Press, 2010); *God and the New Atheism: A Critical Response to Dawkins, Harris, and Hitchens* (Louisville: Westminster/John Knox Press, 2008); *God After Darwin: A Theology of Evolution*, 2nd edition (Boulder, CO: Westview Press, 2000); *Christianity and Science* (Maryknoll: Orbis Press, 2007); *Is Nature Enough: Meaning and Truth in the Age of Science* (Cambridge: Cambridge University Press, 2006); *Deeper Than Darwin: the Prospect for Religion in the Age of Evolution* (Boulder, CO: Westview Press, 2003); and *Responses to 101 Questions on God and Evolution* (New York: Paulist Press, 2001).

2 Sam Harris, *Letter to a Christian Nation* (New York: Knopf, 2007), 60–61.

3 Richard Dawkins, *The God Delusion* (New York: Houghton Mifflin, 2006); Sam Harris, *The End of Faith: Religion, Terror, and the Future of Reason* (New York: W.W. Norton & Co., 2004); Christopher Hitchens, *God Is Not Great: How Religion Poisons Everything* (New York: Hachette Book Group USA, 2007).

4 Bernard Lonergan, *Method in Theology* (New York: Herder and Herder, 1972), 235–37.

5 Sam Harris, *The Moral Landscape: How Science Can Determine Human Values* (New York: The Free Press, 2010).

6 Richard Dawkins, *The God Delusion* (New York: Houghton Mifflin, 2006).

7 Other recent examples are Jerry A. Coyne, *Why Evolution Is True* (New York: Viking, 2009); Sam Harris, *The End of Faith: Religion, Terror, and the Future of Reason* (New York: W.W. Norton & Co., 2004); Christopher Hitchens, *God Is Not Great: How Religion Poisons Everything* (New York: Hachette Book Group USA, 2007); Victor J. Stenger, *God: The Failed Hypothesis: How Science Shows that God Does not Exist* (Amherst, NY: Prometheus Books, 2007); Carl Sagan, *The Demon-Haunted World: Science as a Candle in the Dark* (New York: Ballantine Books, 1997); Steven Weinberg, *Dreams of a Final Theory* (New York: Pantheon, 1992); Michael Shermer, *How We Believe: The Search for God in an Age of Science* (New York: W. H. Freeman, 2000); Owen Flanagan, *The Problem of the Soul: Two Visions of Mind and How to Reconcile Them* (New York: Basic Books, 2002).

8 http://preposterousuniverse.com/writings/dtung/.

9 For example, Lawrence Krauss, *A Universe from Nothing: Why there is Something rather than Nothing* (New York: The Free Press, 2012).

10 On the notion of limit-questions, see David Tracy, *Blessed Rage for Order* (New York: Seabury, 1975), 91–118; and Stephen Toulmin, *An Examination of the Place of Reason in Ethics* (Cambridge: Cambridge University Press, 1970), 202–21.

Chapter 1

1 Excerpts from Gerard Manley Hopkins's poems "Spring" and "God's Grandeur."

2 Pierre Teilhard de Chardin, *The Prayer of the Universe*, trans. René Hague (New York: Harper & Row, 1973), 120–21.

3 Pierre Teilhard de Chardin, *The Human Phenomenon*, trans. Sarah Appleton-Weber (Portland, Oregon: Sussex Academic Press, 1999), 162–63.

4 In contrasting Hopkins to Teilhard, I am not casting blame on the former but simply pointing out that in the light of more recent science and the biblical recovery of the themes of hope, theology today needs to add a more futurist accent to its spiritual vision of nature than that reflected in the work of Hopkins.

5 *The Catechism of the Catholic Church* (#302) states explicitly that even though "Creation has its own goodness and proper perfection . . . it did not spring forth complete from the hands of the Creator." The universe was created "in a state of journeying" *(in statu viae)* toward an ultimate perfection yet to be attained, to which God has destined it." (http://www.vatican.va/archive/ccc_css/archive/catechism/p1s2c1p4.htm). Nevertheless, Catholic theology and spirituality have yet to unfold the implications of this relatively new acknowledgment by the Church that creation remains unfinished.

6 Pierre Teilhard de Chardin, "The Meaning and Constructive Value of Suffering" in Neville Braybrooke, ed., *Teilhard de Chardin, Pilgrim of the Future* (London: Libra, 1964), 23.

7 Pierre Teilhard de Chardin, *Human Energy*, trans. J. M. Cohen (New York: Harvest Books/Harcourt Brace Jovanovich, 1962), 43–47.

8 Pierre Teilhard de Chardin, *The Heart of Matter*, trans. René Hague (New York: Harcourt Brace Jovanovich, 1978), 212.

9 For specific references to *Gaudium et spes*, see Chapter 4.

10 Jürgen Moltmann, *Theology of Hope: On the Ground and the Implications of a Christian Eschatology*, trans. James W. Leitch (New York: Harper & Row, 1967), 95–138.

Chapter 2

1 In *God After Darwin: Toward a Theology of Evolution* (Boulder, CO: Westview Press, 2000, 2007) and other works I have made some initial efforts toward rethinking Christian faith in an evolutionary way. Here I focus more explicitly on the theological implications of an unfinished universe for Catholic thought.

2 Jürgen Moltmann, *Theology of Hope: On the Ground and the Implications of a Christian Eschatology*, trans. James W. Leitch (New York: Harper & Row, 1967), 92.

3 Pierre Teilhard de Chardin, *Christianity and Evolution*, trans. René Hague (New York: Collins, 1969), 79.

4 See Chapter 4.

5 Teilhard, *Christianity and Evolution*, 79–95.

6 For examples see Walter M. Abbott, ed., *The Documents of Vatican II* (New York: Guild Press, 1966), 203–04; 218; 233.

7 This is one of the main arguments in Teilhard de Chardin's *The Human Phenomenon*, trans. Sarah Appleton-Weber (Portland, Oregon: Sussex Academic Press, 1999).

8 Pierre Teilhard de Chardin, *Activation of Energy*, trans. René Hague (New York: Harcourt Brace Jovanovic, 1970), 231–43.

9 I am not certain about the origin of the expression "metaphysics of hope." I believe it may have been used first by the German philosopher Ernst Bloch. In any case, I am adopting it as a label for the worldview that I believe best fits an unfinished universe.

10 For much of the spirit, if not always the letter, of what I am arguing for in this book I am indebted to Jürgen Moltmann's *Theology of Hope*. Nevertheless, as I will demonstrate later on, the Catholic thinker Teilhard de Chardin discovered the metaphysical meaning of futurity long before Moltmann and other twentieth-century theologians of hope.

11 Teilhard, *Christianity and Evolution*, 84–86; 131–32.

12 In Chapter 14, I discuss what this additional natural ingredient may be.

13 One of the most unrelenting contemporary examples of this materialist atomism is Daniel Dennett, *Darwin's Dangerous Idea: Evolution and the Meaning of Life* (New York: Simon & Schuster 1995).

14 Hans Jonas, *The Phenomenon of Life* (New York: Harper & Row, 1966), 9–10.

15 Pierre Teilhard de Chardin, *Human Energy, Human Energy*, trans. J. M. Cohen (New York: Harcourt Brace Jovanovich, 1962), 172–73. For a book-length critique of the materialist assumptions underlying the analytical illusion see John F. Haught, *Is Nature Enough? Meaning and Truth in the Age of Science* (Cambridge: Cambridge University Press, 2006).

16 Alex Rosenberg, *The Atheist's Guide to Reality: Enjoying Life Without Illusions* (New York: W.W. Norton & Co., 2012), 20–21.

17 I am indebted especially to Moltmann's *Theology of Hope* both for my description and critique of the metaphysics of the eternal present.

18 Teilhard, *Human Energy*, 29; *Christianity and Evolution*, 178–79.

19 Teilhard, *Human Energy*, 79.

20 See Abbott, *The Documents of Vatican II*, 203–4; 218; 233.

21 Teilhard, *The Heart of Matter*, 15–79.

22 See Alex Rosenberg, "Why I Am a Naturalist," *New York Times*, September 17, 2011.

23 Pierre Teilhard de Chardin, *Activation of Energy*, trans. René Hague (New York: Harcourt Brace Jovanovisch, 1970), 139, 239.

24 Teilhard, *Christianity and Evolution*, 240. Although the Protestant theologian Wolfhart Pannenberg is known for having developed something akin to what I am calling a metaphysics of the future, his thought has not significantly influenced my own argument in the present book. I believe that Teilhard discovered the metaphysical priority of the future long before Pannenberg, Moltmann and other theologians of hope, although he is seldom given credit for having done so.

25 Teilhard, *Christianity and Evolution*, 76–95.

Chapter 3

1 Don O'Leary, *Roman Catholicism and Modern Science: A History* (New York: Continuum, 2006), 13–19.

2 Pope John Paul II, "Address to the Pontifical Academy of Sciences," November 10, 1979 in *Origins, CNS Documentary Service* 9, 24 (November 29, 1979), 391; see also Cardinal Poupard, "Galileo: Report on Papal Commission Findings," *Origins*, 22, 22 (November 12, 1992), 375; Pope John Paul II, "Letter to the Reverend George V. Coyne, S.J., Director of the Vatican Observatory," *Origins* 18, 23 (November 17, 1988), 377.

3 St Augustine of Hippo, *De Genesi ad Litteram*.

4 For these and other examples, see my book *God and the New Atheism: A Critical Response to Dawkins, Harris, and Hitchens* (Louisville: Westminster/John Knox Press, 2008).

5 A literalist conflation of the Bible with science is also still typical of many Darwinian critics of Christianity. For a recent example see Steve Jones, *The Serpent's Promise: The Bible Interpreted Through Modern Science* (Berkeley, CA: Pegasus Books, 2014).

6 See O'Leary 2006, 213–18.

7 Bernard Lonergan, *Insight: A Study of Human Understanding*, 3rd ed. (New York: Philosophical Library, 1970), 121–39.

8 Lonergan, *Insight*, 121–39. "Design" here is to be carefully distinguished from contemporary anti-Darwinian "Intelligent Design" theory.

9 Lonergan, *Insight*, 132–34.

10 Lonergan, *Insight*, 121–39. See also Patrick H. Byrne and Frank Budenholzer, "Bernard Lonergan's Transformation of the Darwinian Worldview," in Louis Caruana, ed., *Darwin and Catholicism* (New York: Continuum, 2009), 75–91.

11 See Chapter 2 for a discussion of how the archaeological and analogical visions differ from the anticipatory vision of nature that I am adopting.

12 Karl Rahner, "Christology within an Evolutionary Worldview," *Theological Investigations*, vol. 5 (New York: Seabury, 1975), 157–92; and *Hominization: The Evolutionary Origin of Man as a Theological Problem* (Freiburg: Herder, 1965).

13 See, however, Denis Edwards, *The God of Evolution* (New York: Paulist, 1999).

14 The book was published first in English as *The Phenomenon of Man*, trans. Bernard Wall (New York: Harper & Row, 1959) and more recently as *The Human Phenomenon*, trans. Sarah Appleton-Weber (Portland, Oregon: Sussex Academic Press, 1999).

15 The preceding is only one way of many to sketch Teilhard's rich synthesis of science and spirituality. Subsequent chapters will flesh out and go beyond these Teilhardian essentials. To readers interested in pursuing Teilhard's ideas on their own, I recommend starting with a collection of Teilhard's short essays such as *The Future of Man*, trans. Norman Denny (New York: Harper & Row, 1964) or *Human Energy*, trans. J. M. Cohen (New York: Harcourt Brace Jovanovich, 1962), instead of plunging immediately into the much more difficult, though indispensable, *Phenomenon*. For those interested in an adventurous Catholic spirituality for the age of evolution, *The Divine Milieu* (New York: Harper & Row, 1965) is a good place to start. For a bold critique of the limitations of prescientific Catholic theology, I recommend Teilhard's *Christianity and Evolution*, trans. René Hague (New York: Harcourt Brace Jovanovich, 1969).

16 *Christianity and Evolution*, 76–95.

Chapter 4

1 Teilhard de Chardin, *Activation of Energy*, trans. René Hague (New York: Harcourt Brace Jovanovich), 229–44.

2 Peter W. Atkins, *The 2nd Law: Energy, Chaos, and Form* (New York: Scientific American Books, 1994), 200.

3 The notion of God as "absolute future" is that of Karl Rahner, S.J., *Theological Investigations*, vol. 6, trans. Karl Kruger and Boniface Kruger (Baltimore: Helicon, 1969), 59–68. For a parallel theological turn to the future in Protestant theology, see Wolfhart Pannenberg, *Faith and Reality*, trans. John Maxwell (Philadelphia: Westminster Press, 1977); and *Toward a Theology of Nature*, ed. Ted Peters (Louisville: Westminster/John Knox

Press, 1993); for a readable summary and development of the new futurist sense of God, see also Ted Peters, *God—The World's Future: Systematic Theology for a New Era*, 2nd ed. (Minneapolis: Fortress Press, 2000).

4   Walter M. Abbott, ed., *The Documents of Vatican II* (New York: Guild Press, 1966), 730–71. Closing statement to "Men of Thought and Science," read by Paul Emile Cardinal Leger of Montreal, assisted by Antonio Cardinal Caggiano of Buenos Aires and Norman Cardinal Gilroy of Sydney, Australia.

5   Abbott, ed., *The Documents of Vatican II*, 730–71.

6   Abbot, *Documents*, 203–04; 218; 233.

7   Pierre Teilhard de Chardin, *The Human Phenomenon*, trans. Sarah Appleton-Weber (Portland, Oregon: Sussex Academic Press, 1999); Pierre Teilhard de Chardin, *The Divine Milieu* (New York: Harper & Row, 1965).

8   Henri de Lubac, S.J., *The Eternal Feminine: A Study of the Text of Teilhard de Chardin* (London: Collins, 1971), 136, cited by David Lane, *The Phenomenon of Teilhard: Prophet for a New Age* (Macon, GA: Mercer University Press, 1996), 88.

9   Robert Faricy, S.J., *All Things in Christ: Teilhard de Chardin's Spirituality* (London: Fount Paperbacks, 1981), 52 (cited by David Lane, *The Phenomenon of Teilhard*).

10 Teilhard's Catholic orthodoxy is well defended by his fellow Jesuit Henri de Lubac in *Teilhard de Chardin: The Man and His Meaning*, trans. René Hague (New York: New American Library, 1967); and *The Religion of Teilhard de Chardin* (Garden City: Image Books, 1968). See also David Grumett, *Teilhard de Chardin: Theology, Humanity and Cosmos* (Leuven and Dudley, MA: Peeters, 2005).

11 "Warning Considering the Writings of Father Teilhard de Chardin," Sacred Congregation of the Holy Office, June 30, 1962.

12 Reported by Wayne Kraft, *The Relevance of Teilhard* (Notre Dame, IN: Fides, 1968), 29.

13 Fulton J. Sheen, *Footsteps in a Darkened Forest* (New York: Meredith, 1967), 73.

14 Teilhard, *Activation of Energy*, 239.

15 Teilhard, *The Human Phenomenon*, 122–25 and *passim*.

16 Pierre Teilhard de Chardin, *The Future of Man*, trans. Norman Denny (New York: Harper Colophon Books, 1964), 75.

17 Teilhard de Chardin, *The Human Phenomenon*, 186.

18 Chet Raymo, "Intelligent Design Happens Naturally," *The Boston Globe* (May 14, 2002).

19 Pierre Teilhard de Chardin, *Hymn of the Universe*, trans. Gerald Vann (New York: Harper Colophon, 1969), 108.

20 Teilhard, *The Human Phenomenon*, 27, 207.

21 Pierre Teilhard de Chardin, *Christianity and Evolution*, trans. René Hague (New York: Harcourt Brace & Co., 1969), 240.

22 Pierre Teilhard de Chardin, *Human Energy*, trans. J. M. Cohen (New York: Harvest Books/Harcourt Brace Jovanovich, 1962), 82–102.

23 Teilhard, *Christianity and Evolution*, 92–93.
24 Teilhard, *Christianity and Evolution*, 92–93.
25 Teilhard, *Christianity and Evolution*, 94–95.

Chapter 5

1 Jerry A. Coyne, *Why Evolution Is True* (New York: Viking, 2009), 81–85.
2 David Barash, "Does God Have Back Problems Too?" *Los Angeles Times*, June 27, 2005.
3 Proponents of Intelligent Design include (most recently) Stephen C. Meyer, *Darwin's Doubt: The Explosive Origin of Animal Life and the Case for Intelligent Design* (New York: HarperCollins, 2014); other proponents include Phillip E. Johnson, *The Wedge of Truth: Splitting the Foundations of Naturalism* (Downers Grove, IL: InterVarsity Press, 1999); Jonathan Wells, *Icons of Evolution: Science or Myth? Why Much of What We Teach About Evolution Is Wrong* (Washington, DC: Regnery, 2000); Michael J. Behe, *Darwin's Black Box: The Biochemical Challenge to Evolution* (New York: The Free Press, 1996); William A. Dembski, *Intelligent Design: The Bridge Between Science and Theology* (Downers Grove, IL: InterVarsity Press, 1999).
4 Chet Raymo, "Intelligent Design Happens Naturally," *Boston Globe*, May 14, 2002.
5 See Pierre Teilhard de Chardin, *Christianity and Evolution*, trans. René Hague (New York: Harcourt Brace & Co., 1969), 79.
6 Pierre Teilhard de Chardin, *Activation of Energy*, trans. René Hague (New York: Harcourt Brace Jovanovich, 1970), 139.
7 A good recent example, as noted in Chapter 2, is Alex Rosenberg's *The Atheist's Guide to Reality* (New York: W. W. Norton & Company, 2011).
8 See, for example, Jerry Coyne, *Why Evolution Is True*; Barash, "Does God Have Back Problems Too?"; Richard Dawkins, *The Blind Watchmaker* (New York: W. W. Norton & Co, 1986); *River Out of Eden* (New York: Basic Books, 1995); *Climbing Mount Improbable* (New York: W. W. Norton & Co., 1996); Daniel C. Dennett, *Darwin's Dangerous Idea: Evolution and the Meaning of Life* (New York: Simon & Schuster, 1995).
9 Peter W. Atkins, *The 2nd Law: Energy, Chaos, and Form* (New York: Scientific American Books, 1994), 200.
10 Pierre Teilhard de Chardin, *Hymn of the Universe*, trans. Gerald Vann (New York: Harper Colophon, 1969), 77. See also Teilhard de Chardin, *Activation of Energy*, 239.
11 In Chapter 9, I address the pessimistic objection that the eventual "death" of the universe is a decisive refutation of cosmic hope.
12 Pierre Teilhard de Chardin, *The Heart of Matter*, trans. René Hague (New York: Harcourt Brace Jovanovich, 1978), 18.

13 Pierre Teilhard de Chardin, *Writings in Time of War*, trans. René Hague (New York: Harper and Row, 1965), 14–71.

14 Teilhard de Chardin, *Heart of Matter*, 27.

15 Teilhard de Chardin, *Heart of Matter*, 15–79.

16 Teilhard de Chardin, *Activation of Energy*, 139.

17 Pierre Teilhard de Chardin, *Letters from a Traveler*, trans. René Hague et al. (New York: Harper and Row, 1962), 101.

18 For a fuller development, see my book *Making Sense of Evolution: Darwin, God, and the Drama of Life* (Louisville: Westminster John Knox Press, 2010).

19 See Thomas Berry, *The Dream of the Earth* (San Francisco: Sierra Club Books, 1988), 79.

20 See Robert Hinde, *Why Gods Persist: A Scientific Approach to Religions* (New York: Routledge, 1999); Walter Burkert, *Creation of the Sacred: Tracks of Biology in Early Religions*; Pascal Boyer, *Religion Explained: The Evolutionary Origins of Religious Thought* (New York: Basic Books, 2001).

21 Pierre Teilhard de Chardin, *The Human Phenomenon*, trans. Sarah Appleton-Weber (Portland: Sussex Academic Press, 1999), 186.

22 Pierre Teilhard de Chardin, *How I Believe*, trans. René Hague (New York: Harper & Row, 1969), 43–44.

23 Teilhard de Chardin, *How I Believe*, 35.

Chapter 6

1 His understanding of contingency in natural history is developed at book length in Stephen J. Gould, *Wonderful Life: The Burgess Shale and the Nature of History* (New York: W. W. Norton, 1989); Stephen Jay Gould and R. C. Lewontin, "The Spandrels of San Marco and the Panglossian Paradigm: A Critique of the Adaptationist Programme," *Proceedings of the Royal Society* 205, no. 1161 (1979), 581–98.

2 Richard Dawkins, *The Blind Watchmaker* (New York: W. W. Norton & Co., 1986); *River Out of Eden* (New York: Basic Books, 1995); *Climbing Mount Improbable* (New York: W. W. Norton & Co., 1986).

3 A modern classic on the reduction of nature to the interplay of chance and necessity is Jacques Monod's *Chance and Necessity* (New York: Knopf, 1970).

4 Bernard Lonergan, as I noted in Chapter 3, refers to this narrative "design" of the universe as "emergent probability," requiring a "genetic" method of understanding when it comes to understanding living processes.

5 Bernard Lonergan, *Insight: A Study of Human Understanding*, 3rd ed. (New York: Philosophical Library, 1970), 121–39.

6　See Joseph M. Hallman, *The Descent of God: Divine Suffering in History and Theology* (Minneapolis: Fortress Press, 1991).

7　Pope John Paul II, *Fides et Ratio,* Encyclical Letter (September 1998) #93: http://www.vatican.va/holy_father/john_paul_ii/encyclicals/documents/hf_jp-ii_enc_15101998_fides-et-ratio_en.html.

8　Richard Dawkins, *The God Delusion* (New York: Houghton Mifflin, 2006), 31–73.

9　Cited by Louise Young, *The Unfinished Universe* (New York: Oxford University Press, 1986), 201–02.

10　Nora Barlow, ed., *The Autobiography of Charles Darwin* (New York: Harcourt 1958), 88–89.

11　Richard Dawkins, *River Out of Eden* (New York: Basic Books, 1995), 133.

12　George Williams, "Mother Nature Is a Wicked Old Witch!" in Matthew H. Nitecki and Doris V. Nitecki (eds.), *Evolutionary Ethics* (Albany: State University of New York Press, 1995), 217–31.

13　Stephen J. Gould, "Introduction," to Carl Zimmer's *Evolution: The Triumph of An Idea From Darwin to DNA* (London: Arrow Books, 2003), xvi-xvii.

Chapter 7

1　For a theologically informed study of this evidence, see Wentzel van Huyssteen, *Alone in the World?: Human Uniqueness in Science and Theology* (Grand Rapids: Wm. B. Eerdmans Publishing Company, 2006).

2　*The Catechism of the Catholic Church* #396–421: http://www.catholicdoors.com/catechis/. See Joan Acker, H.M., "Creation and Catholicism," *America* (December 16, 2000), 6–8; and Daryl Domning, "Evolution, Evil, and Original Sin," *America* (November 12, 2001): https://www.americamagazine.org/content/article.cfm?article_id=1205. As I mentioned earlier, *The Catechism* (#302) does allow in principle for an evolutionary understanding of *cosmic* creation overall: "Creation . . . did not spring forth complete from the hands of the Creator." However, it does not consider seriously the meaning of the gradualness of human evolution.

3　See Don O'Leary, *Roman Catholicism and Modern Science* (New York: Continuum, 2006). A notable exception among Catholic bishops is the late Polish philosopher Józef Życiński, author of *God and Evolution: Fundamental Questions of Christian Evolutionism*, trans. Kenneth W. Kemp and Zuzanna Maslanka (Washington, DC: Catholic University of America Press, 2006).

4　The "Science and Human Values" committee of the American Conference of Catholic Bishops sponsored several discussions of evolution, involving scientists and theologians (1984–2003). This committee, however, no longer exists. The Vatican itself has occasionally sponsored conferences that deal with biological evolution. The proceedings of the best of these meetings is to be found in Robert John Russell, William R. Stoeger, SJ, and Francisco J. Ayala (eds.), *Evolutionary and Molecular Biology: Scientific Perspectives on Divine Action* (Vatican City State: Vatican Observatory Publications, 1998, published by University of Notre Dame Press, South Bend, IN). In general, however, the Church has done little, in my opinion, to promote the thoroughgoing reformation of Catholic thought that science now requires.

5 Pope Benedict XVI, Encyclical Letter *Spe Salvi* #5 (November 30, 2007): http://www.vatican.va/holy_father/benedict_xvi/encyclicals/documents/ hf_ben-xvi_enc_20071130_spe-salvi_en.html.

6 Philip Kitcher, *Living With Darwin: Evolution, Design, and the Future of Faith* (New York: Oxford University Press), 124.

7 John Paul II, "Message to the Pontifical Academy of Sciences" (1996): http://www.catholicculture.org/culture/library/view.cfm?id=80. Other important statements on science by Pope John Paul II include "Address to the Pontifical Academy of Sciences," November 10, 1979; *Origins, CNS Documentary Service* 9, 24 (November 29, 1979), 391; see also Cardinal Poupard, "Galileo: Report on Papal Commission Findings," *Origins* 22 (November 12, 1992), 375; Pope John Paul II, "Letter to the Reverend George V. Coyne, S.J., Director of the Vatican Observatory," *Origins* 18, 23 (November 17, 1988), 377.

8 "Communion and Stewardship: Human Persons Created in the Image of God," International Theological Commission (July 2004) #69: http://www. bringyou.to/apologetics/p80.htm.

9 Kitcher, 73.

10 Kitcher, 73–116. Kitcher, like Richard Dawkins and other evolutionary materialists, apparently thinks that divine providence means intelligent design. This is just one more example of an evolutionary naturalist playing the role of the theologian by privileging creationist and ID notions of deity as the only ones worth debating.

11 See Chapter 2 above.

12 Pierre Teilhard de Chardin, *Christianity and Evolution*, trans. René Hague (New York: Harcourt Brace & Co., 1969), 81.

13 See, for example, Eileen Flynn and Gloria Thomas, *Living Faith: An Introduction to Theology*, 2nd ed. (New York: Rowman and Littlefield, 1989), 246–56.

14 On "divinization" and its meaning for Christians East and West, see Stephen Finlan and Vladimir Kharlamov (eds.), *Theiosis, Deification in Christian Theology* (Eugene, OR: Pickwick Publications, 2006).

15 Pierre Teilhard de Chardin, *How I Believe*, trans. René Hague (New York: Harper & Row, 1969), 42.

16 Paul Ricoeur, *The Conflict of Interpretations: Essays in Hermeneutics*, ed. Don Ihde (Evanston, IL: Northwestern University Press, 1974), 354–77. In an expiatory understanding of suffering, "punishment only serves to preserve an already established order." Paul Ricoeur, *History and*

Truth, trans. Charles Kelbley (Evanston: Northwestern University Press, 1965), 125.

17 Teilhard, *Christianity and Evolution*, 83–84.

18 Here I am echoing themes suggested by Teilhard, especially in *Christianity and Evolution*.

19 Even in the Adamic myth, however, the figure of the serpent represents the intuition that evil is more than a human product. Ricoeur, *The Conflict of Interpretations*, 294–95.

20 See Teilhard, *Christianity and Evolution*, 81.

21 The distinction between a theoretical core and auxiliary hypotheses is developed by the philosopher Imre Lakatos (1922–74). *The Methodology of Scientific Research Programmes*, vol. I (Cambridge: Cambridge University Press, November 28, 1980). I am not trying to make an argument for Imre's particular philosophy of science, but merely using his ideas somewhat freely here to make a theological point.

22 John 9:2-4 (New Revised Standard Version).

23 Gerd Theissen, *The Open Door*, trans. John Bowden (Minneapolis: Fortress Press, 1991), 161–67.

24 See Hebrews 12:5ff.

25 John Hick, *Evil and the God of Love* (New York: Harper & Row, 1978).

26 Kitcher, 126–27.

27 Ricoeur, *Conflict*, 354–77.

Chapter 8

1 Arthur Lovejoy, *The Great Chain of Being: A Study of the History of an Idea* (Cambridge, MA: Harvard University Press, 1936), 244.

2 Steven Pinker, "The Stupidity of Dignity," *The New Republic*, http: //pinker.wjh.harvard.edu/articles/media/The%20Stupidity%20of%20 Dignity.htm (2008).

3 Holmes Rolston, III, *Three Big Bangs: Matter-Energy, Life, Mind* (New York: Columbia University Press, 2010).

4 Francis H. C. Crick, *Of Molecules and Men* (Seattle: University of Washington Press 1966), 10; and J. D. Watson, *The Molecular Biology of the Gene* (New York: W.A. Benjamin, 1965), 67.

5 Michael Polanyi, "Life's Irreducible Structure," in Marjorie Grene (ed.), *Knowing and Being* (London: Routledge and Kegan Paul, 1969), 225–39.

6 Polanyi, *Knowing and Being*, 225–39.

7 Polanyi, *Knowing and Being*, 225–39.

8 Polanyi, *Knowing and Being*, 225–39.

9 Unfortunately, advocates of ID are also conditioned by the modern metaphysics of the past to trace the origin of information *back in time* to events that took place earlier, rather than to think of it in terms of the

arrival of the future. As a recent example, see Stephen Meyer, *Darwin's Doubt: The Explosive Origin of Animal Life and the Case for Intelligent Design* (New York: Harper one, 2013), vi.

10 Again, I can think of no better recent example of this atomism than that of the Duke University philosopher Alex Rosenberg's *The Atheist's Guide to Reality: Enjoying Life Without Illusions* (New York: W.W. Norton & Co., 2012).

11 Martin Rees, *Just Six Numbers: The Deep Forces that Shape the Universe* (New York: Basic Books, 2000); and Martin Rees, *Our Cosmic Habitat* (Princeton: Princeton University Press, 2001).

12 For example, Max Tegmark, *Our Mathematical Universe: My Quest for the Ultimate Nature of Reality* (New York: Alfred A. Knopf, 2014); and Alan Lightman, *The Accidental Universe: The World You Thought You Knew* (New York: Pantheon Books, 2014).

Chapter 9

1 Algernon Charles Swinburne, "The Garden of Persephone."

2 See, for example, Albert Camus, *The Myth of Sisyphus, and Other Essays*, trans. Justin O'Brien (New York: Knopf, 1955).

3 For example, Steven Weinberg, *Dreams of a Final Theory* (New York: Pantheon Books, 1992), 256.

4 Paul Tillich, *Systematic Theology*, vol. III (Chicago: University of Chicago Press, 1963), 19; Hans Jonas, *The Phenomenon of Life* (New York: Harper & Row, 1966), 9.

5 Alfred North Whitehead, *Science and the Modern World* (New York: The Free Press, 1925), 51, 58.

6 Alfred North Whitehead, *Science and the Modern World* (New York: The Free Press, 1967), 191–92.

7 An articulate representative of such skeptics is the former Catholic and now devotee of evolutionary naturalism Chet Raymo. See his *Skeptics and True Believers: The Exhilarating Connection Between Science and Religion* (New York: Walker and Company, 1998).

8 See, for example, the essays in Pierre Teilhard de Chardin, *The Future of Man*, trans. Norman Denny (New York: Harper & Row, 1964).

9 For example, Owen Flanagan, *The Problem of the Soul: Two Visions of Mind and How to Reconcile Them* (New York: Basic Books, 2002), 167–68.

10 See Tomas Hacik, *Patience with God: The Story of Zacchaeus Continuing in Us*, trans. Gerald Turner (New York: Random House, 2009).

11 Flanagan, 319.

12 Here I am indebted in part to aspects of the "process" philosophical perspective as laid out especially by Alfred North Whitehead, *Process and Reality*, corrected ed., eds. David Ray Griffin and Donald W. Sherburne

(New York: The Free Press, 1968), 29, 34–51, 60, 81–82, 86–104, 340–51; and Alfred North Whitehead, "Immortality," in Paul A. Schillp (ed.), *The Philosophy of Alfred North Whitehead* (Evanston and Chicago: Northwestern University Press, 1941), 682–700. See also Charles Hartshorne, *The Logic of Perfection* (Lasalle, IL: Open Court Publishing Co., 1962), 24–62, 250. Although Catholic theology does not accept every aspect of process theology, I believe it can easily assimilate Whitehead's understanding of the world as made up of events that, even while perishing, remain present and objectively immortal in subsequent happenings in cosmic process, and that remain forever immediately vivid in the conscious and compassionate experience of God. Unlike Whitehead, however, Catholic theology rightly makes room for subjective immortality as well.

13 Charles Hartshorne, *The Logic of Perfection*, 24–62, 250. Even though I will perish, as will everything else in cosmic process, the *fact* that I have existed at all, even if only for a brief time, will never perish.

Chapter 10

1 Letter to W. Graham, July 3, 1881, *The Life and Letters of Charles Darwin*, ed. Francis Darwin (New York: Basic Books, 1959), 285.

2 Thomas Nagel, *Mind and Cosmos: Why the Materialist Neo-Darwinian Conception of Nature Is Almost Certainly False* (New York: Oxford University Press, 2012).

3 Simon Blackburn, "Thomas Nagel: a Philosopher Who Confesses to Finding Things Bewildering," *The New Statesman* (November 8, 2012): http://www.newstatesman.com/culture/culture/2012/11/thomas-nagel-philosopher-who-confesses-finding-things-bewildering.

4 Citations from Michael Chorost, "Where Thomas Nagel Went Wrong," *Chronicle of Higher Education* (May 13, 2013): http://chronicle.com/article/Where-Thomas-Nagel-Went-Wrong/139129/.

5 Bernard Lonergan, *Insight: A Study of Human Understanding*, 3rd ed. (New York: Philosophical Library, 1970).

6 Owen Flanagan, *The Problem of the Soul: Two Visions of Mind and How to Reconcile Them* (New York: Basic Books, 2002), 11.

7 Daniel Dennett, *Breaking the Spell: Religion as a Natural Phenomenon* (New York: Viking, 2006), 87.

8 For example, Steven Pinker, *The Blank Slate: The Modern Denial of Human Nature* (New York: Penguin Books, 2002).

9 Lonergan does not focus on this component of "trust" in the way I am doing here, but his awareness of its role in our cognitional performance is implicit in his citing the need for "self-affirmation" as a condition for making correct judgments. See *Insight*, 328–32.

10 Lonergan, *Insight*, 329.
11 Colin McGinn resignedly admits as much in *The Mysterious Flame: Conscious Minds in a Material World* (New York: Basic Books, 1999).
12 John R. Searle, *Mind: A Brief Introduction* (Oxford: Oxford University Press, 2004), 135–36.

Chapter 11

1 Pierre Teilhard de Chardin, *Activation of Energy*, trans. René Hague (New York: Harcourt Brace Jovanovich, 1970), 229–44.
2 Teilhard de Chardin, *Activation of* Energy, 229–44.
3 Pierre Teilhard de Chardin, *Human Energy*, trans. J. M. Cohen (New York: Harcourt Brace Jovanovich, 1962), 29 (emphasis original).
4 John E. Smith, *Reason and God* (New Haven: Yale University Press 1961), 200–02; Schubert Ogden, *The Reality of God and Other Essays* (New York: Harper & Row, 1977), 32ff.
5 Pierrre Teilhard de Chardin, *How I Believe*, trans. René Hague (New York: Harper & Row, 1969), 42.
6 Teilhard de Chardin, *How I Believe*, 43–44 (emphasis original).
7 Stephen J. Gould, "Introduction," to Carl Zimmer, *Evolution: The Triumph of An Idea From Darwin to DNA* (London: Arrow Books, 2003), xvi-xvii.
8 Teilhard, *Activation of Energy*, 139.
9 See Chapter 10, above.
10 Hans Jonas, *The Phenomenon of Life* (New York: Harper & Row, 1966), 9–10.
11 See Eric Neumann, *Depth Psychology and a New Ethic*, trans. Eugene Rolfe (New York: Harper Torchbooks, 1973), 101–35: "The time has now come for the principle of perfection to be sacrificed on the altar of wholeness" (134).

Chapter 12

1 Some landmark writings expressing Catholic concern for the well-being of nature include Pope John Paul II, "Peace with God the Creator, Peace with All of Creation" (World Day of Peace Message, January 1, 1990); The American Conference of Catholic Bishops, "Renewing the Earth" (1991); Drew Christiansen, S.J. and Walter Grazer (eds.), *And God Saw That It Was Good* (Washington, DC: United States Catholic Conference, 1996); and the Northwest American Bishops' Pastoral letter, "The Columbia River Watershed: Caring for Creation and the Common Good" (February 2001).

2 John Passmore, *Man's Responsibility for Nature* (New York: Scribner, 1974), 184; see also Lynn White, "The Historical Roots of our Ecological Crisis," *Science* 155 (1967), 1203–07.

3 See note 2 above.

4 See Barry Commoner, "In Defense of Biology," in Ronald Munson (ed.), *Man and Nature* (New York: Dell Publishing Co., 1971), 44.

5 See Herman E. Daly and John B. Cobb, Jr., *For the Common Good* (Boston: Beacon Press, 1989), 25–110. For a fuller development of this point, see my book *The Promise of Nature* (Mahwah: Paulist Press, 1993), 11–38.

6 Again, a good example of this worldview is Alex Rosenberg's *The Atheist's Guide to Reality: Enjoying Life Without Illusions* (New York: W.W. Norton & Co., 2012).

7 For example, Stuart A. Kaufmann, *At Home in the Universe* (New York: Oxford University Press, 1995).

8 Terry Deacon, *Incomplete Nature: How Mind Emerged from Matter* (New York: W.W. Norton, 2012), 548.

9 American Conference of Catholic Bishop's Pastoral "Renewing the Earth" (1991) also identifies hope as the fundamental ecological virtue.

Chapter 13

1 Joel Garreau, *Radical Evolution: The Promise and Peril of Enhancing Our Minds, Our Bodies—and What It Means to Be Human* (New York: Doubleday, 2005).

2 See, for example, N. T. Wright, *Surprised By Hope* (San Francisco: HarperOne, 2008).

3 See, for example, Frank Tipler, *The Physics of Immortality* (New York: Doubleday, 1994; and Freeman Dyson, *Infinite in All Directions* (New York: HarperCollins, 1988).

4 This is a constant theme in the writings of Thomas Berry. See especially his *Dream of the Earth* (San Francisco: Sierra Club Books, 1988); see also my critique of Berry in *The Promise of Nature* (Mahwah and New York: Paulist Press, 1993), 104–06.

5 Pierre Teilhard de Chardin, *Activation of Energy*, trans. René Hague (New York: Harcourt Brace Jovanovich, Inc., 1970), 231–43; and *How I Believe*, trans. René Hague (New York: Harper & Row, 1969), 42.

6 Teilhard de Chardin, *The Future of Man*, trans. Norman Denny (New York: Harper & Row, 1964), 75.

7 Michael Polanyi, *The Tacit Dimension* (Garden City, New York: Doubleday Anchor Books, 1967); "Life's Irreducible Structure," in Marjorie Grene (ed.), *Knowing and Being* (Chicago: University of Chicago Press 1969), 225–39.

8 Hans Jonas, *The Phenomenon of Life* (New York: Harper & Row, 1966), 75–76.
9 Michael Polanyi, *Personal Knowledge* (New York: Harper Torchbooks, 1964).
10 Holmes Rolston, III, *Three Big Bangs: Matter-Energy, Life, Mind* (New York: Columbia University Press, 2010), 41–88.
11 See John F. Haught, *The Promise of Nature* (Mahwah: Paulist Press, 1993).

Chapter 14

1 Daniel Dennett, as interviewed in John Brockman, *The Third Culture* (New York: Touchstone, 1995), 187.
2 Richard Dawkins, *The Blind Watchmaker* (New York: W. W. Norton & Co., 1986).
3 Paul Tillich, *Systematic Theology*, 3 vols. (Chicago: University of Chicago Press, 1967), vol. I, 238.
4 On faith as a matter of "being grasped," see Paul Tillich, *Dynamics of Faith* (New York: Harper Torchbooks, 1958), 76–85.
5 Jeremy Campbell, *Grammatical Man: Information, Entropy, Language and Life* (New York: Touchstone, 1982), 255.
6 Here, of course, the "universe" includes humans and their own creations.
7 John Bowker, *Is Anybody Out There?* (Westminster, MD: Christian Classics, Inc., 1988), 9–18; 112–43.
8 Charles Seife, *Decoding the Universe: How the New Science of Information Is Explaining Everything in the Cosmos, from Our Brains to Black Holes* (New York: Viking, 2006), 5–20.
9 Examples of the role of contingency in shaping the story of life on earth can be found abundantly in the many writings of the late Harvard paleontologist Stephen Jay Gould. See, for example, his book *Wonderful Life: The Burgess Shale and the Nature of History* (New York: W. W. Norton, 1989).
10 Albert Einstein, *Ideas and Opinions* (New York: Bonanza Books, 1954), 11.
11 I believe that Cardinal Schoenborn's critique of neo-Darwinian biology in his New York Times op-ed piece, discussed in Chapter 3 above, followed essentially the same set of assumptions.
12 In his most recent bestseller *The God Delusion* (New York: Houghton Mifflin, 2006), *Dawkins* defines God as "*a superhuman, supernatural intelligence who deliberately designed and created the universe and everything in it, including us*" (31). My objection here is not to Dawkins's atheism, but to his theology.
13 John Henry Newman, *The Idea of a University* (Garden City: Image Books, 1959), 411. Newman also stated that he believes in design because of God, not in God because of design. See the discussion of Newman by

Alister McGrath, "A Blast from the Past? The Boyle Lectures and Natural Theology," *Science and Christian Belief* 17 (April 2005), 29f.

14 "All that science reveals to us," says Cornell historian of science William Provine, "is chance and necessity. . . . Modern science directly implies that the world is organized strictly in accordance with mechanistic principles. There are no purposive principles whatsoever in nature. There are no gods and no designing forces that are rationally detectable. The frequently made assertion that modern biology and the assumptions of the Judeo-Christian tradition are fully compatible is false." William Provine, "Evolution and the Foundation of Ethics," in Steven L. Goldman (ed.), *Science, Technology, and Social Progress* (Bethlehem, PA: Lehigh University Press, 1989), 261.

15 For example, Jacques Monod, *Chance and Necessity*, trans. Austryn Wainhouse (New York: Vintage Books, 1972).

16 Monod's thought, in *Chance and Necessity*, oscillates back and forth between one type of cosmic pessimism and the other.

17 Here I have been influenced in a general way by Whiteheadian process theology. See, for example, John B. Cobb, Jr. and David Griffin, *Process Theology: An Introductory Exposition* (Philadelphia: Westminster Press, 1976).

Bibliography

Abbott, Walter M., ed. *The Documents of Vatican II*. New York: Guild Press, 1966.

Acker, Joan, H. M. "Creation and Catholicism." *America*, December 16, 2000, 6–8.

American Conference of Catholic Bishops. "Renewing the Earth" (Pastoral Letter on the Environment), 1991.

Atkins, Peter W. *The 2nd Law: Energy, Chaos, and Form*. New York: Scientific American Books, 1994.

Atran, Scott. *In Gods We Trust: The Evolutionary Landscape of Religion*. New York: Oxford University Press, 2002.

Barbour, Ian G. "Five Ways to Read Teilhard." *The Teilhard Review* 3 (1968): 3–20.

Barlow, Nora, ed. *The Autobiography of Charles Darwin*. New York: Harcourt, 1958.

Barrow, John, and Frank Tipler. *The Anthropic Cosmological Principle*. Oxford: Clarendon Press, 1986.

Behe, Michael J. *Darwin's Black Box: The Biochemical Challenge to Evolution*. New York: The Free Press, 1996.

Bergson, Henri. *Creative Evolution*. Translated by Arthur Mitchell. Lanham, MD: University Press of America, 1983.

Berry, Thomas. *The Dream of the Earth*. San Francisco: Sierra Club Books, 1988.

Blackburn, Simon. "Thomas Nagel: a Philosopher Who Confesses to Finding Things Bewildering." *The New Statesman*, November 8, 2012, http://www.newstatesman.com/culture/culture/2012/11/thomas-nagel-philosopher-who-confesses-finding-things-bewildering.

Bowker, John. *Is Anybody Out There?* Westminster, MD: Christian Classics, Inc, 1988.

Boyer, Pascal. *Religion Explained: The Evolutionary Origins of Religious Thought*. New York: Basic Books, 2001.

Braybrooke, Neville, ed. *Teilhard de Chardin, Pilgrim of the Future*. London: Libra, 1964.

Brockman, John. *The Third Culture*. New York: Touchstone, 1995.

Burkert, Walter. *Creation of the Sacred: Tracks of Biology in Early Religions*. Cambridge, MA: Harvard University Press, 1996.

Burtt, E. A. *The Metaphysical Foundations of Modern Science*. Garden City, New York: Doubleday Anchor Books, 1954.

Byrne, Patrick H., and Frank Budenholzer. "Bernard Lonergan's Transformation of the Darwinian Worldview." In *Darwin and Catholicism*, edited by Louis Caruana, 75–91. New York: Continuum, 2009.

Campbell, Jeremy. *Grammatical Man: Information, Entropy, Language and Life*. New York: Touchstone, 1982.

Camus, Albert. *The Myth of Sisyphus, and Other Essays*. Translated by Justin O'Brien. New York: Knopf, 1955.

Chorost, Michael. "Where Thomas Nagel Went Wrong." *Chronicle of Higher Education*, May 13, 2013, http://chronicle.com/article/Where-Thomas-Nagel-Went-Wrong/139129/.

Christiansen, Drew SJ, and Walter Grazer, eds. *And God Saw That It Was Good*. Washington, DC: United States Catholic Conference, 1996.

Cobb, John B. Jr., and David Griffin. *Process Theology: An Introductory Exposition*. Philadelphia: The Westminster Press, 1976.

Commoner, Barry. "In Defense of Biology." In *Man and Nature*, edited by Ronald Munson, 44. New York: Dell Publishing Co., 1971.

Coyne, Jerry A. *Why Evolution Is True*. New York: Viking, 2009.

Crick, Francis H. C. *Of Molecules and Men*. Seattle: University of Washington Press, 1966.

Daly, Herman E., and John B. Cobb, Jr. *For the Common Good*. Boston: Beacon Press, 1989.

Darwin, Charles. "Letter to W. Graham, July 3rd, 1881." In *The Life and Letters of Charles Darwin*, edited by Francis Darwin. New York: Basic Books, 1959[1881].

Dawkins, Richard. *The Blind Watchmaker*. New York: W. W. Norton & Co., 1986.

Dawkins, Richard. *River Out of Eden*. New York: Basic Books, 1995.

Dawkins, Richard. *Climbing Mount Improbable*. New York: W. W. Norton & Co., 1996.

Dawkins, Richard. *The God Delusion*. New York: Houghton Mifflin, 2006.

de Lubac, Henri, SJ. *Teilhard De Chardin: The Man and His Meaning*. Translated by René Hague. New York: New American Library, 1967.

de Lubac, Henri, SJ. *The Religion of Teilhard de Chardin*. Translated by René Hague. Garden City: Image Books, 1968.

de Lubac, Henri, SJ. *The Eternal Feminine: A Study of the Text of Teilhard de Chardin*. London: Collins, 1971.

Deacon, Terry. *Incomplete Nature: How Mind Emerged from Matter*. New York: W.W. Norton, 2012.

Dembski, William A., ed. *Mere Creation: Science, Faith and Intelligent Design*. Downers Grove, IL: InterVarsity Press, 1998.

Dembski, William A. *Intelligent Design: The Bridge Between Science and Theology*. Downers Grove, IL: InterVarsity Press, 1999.

Dennett, Daniel C. *Darwin's Dangerous Idea: Evolution and the Meaning of Life*. New York: Simon & Schuster, 1995.

Dennett, Daniel C. *Breaking the Spell: Religion as a Natural Phenomenon*. New York: Viking, 2006.

Domning, Daryl. "Evolution, Evil, and Original Sin." *America*, November 12, 2001.

Dyson, Freeman. *Infinite in All Directions*. New York: HarperCollins, 1988.

Edwards, Denis. *The God of Evolution*. New York: Paulist Press, 1999.

Einstein, Albert. *Ideas and Opinions*. New York: Modern Library, 1994.

Faricy, Robert, SJ. *All Things in Christ: Teilhard de Chardin's Spirituality*. London: Fount Paperbacks, 1981, 52.

Ferris, Timothy. *Coming of Age in the Milky Way*. New York: Harper Perennial, 2003.

Finlan, Stephen, and Vladimir Kharlamov, eds. *Theiosis, Deification in Christian Theology*. Eugene, OR: Pickwick Publications, 2006.

Flanagan, Owen. *The Problem of the Soul: Two Visions of Mind and How to Reconcile Them*. New York: Basic Books, 2002.

Flynn, Eileen, and Gloria Thomas. *Living Faith: An Introduction to Theology*, 2nd ed. New York: Rowman and Littlefield, 1989.

Garreau, Joel. *Radical Evolution: The Promise and Peril of Enhancing Our Minds, Our Bodies—and What It Means to Be Human*. New York: Doubleday, 2005.

Gould, Stephen Jay. *Ever Since Darwin*. New York: W. W. Norton, 1977.

Gould, Stephen Jay. *Wonderful Life: The Burgess Shale and the Nature of History*. New York: W. W. Norton, 1989.

Gould, Stephen Jay. "Introduction" to Carl Zimmer. *Evolution: The Triumph of An Idea From Darwin to DNA*. London: Arrow Books, 2003, xvi–xvii.

Gould, Stephen Jay, and R. C. Lewontin. "The Spandrels of San Marco and the Panglossian Paradigm: A Critique of the Adaptationist Programme." *Proceedings of the Royal Society* 205, no. 1161 (1979): 581–98.

Grumett, David. *Teilhard de Chardin: Theology, Humanity and Cosmos*. Leuven and Dudley, MA: Peeters, 2005.

Hacik, Tomas. *Patience with God: The Story of Zacchaeus Continuing in Us*. Translated by Gerald Turner. New York: Random House, 2009.

Hallman, Joseph. *The Descent of God: Divine Suffering in History and Theology*. Minneapolis: Fortress Press, 1991.

Harris, Sam. *The End of Faith: Religion, Terror, and the Future of Reason*. New York: W.W. Norton & Co., 2004.

Harris, Sam. *Letter to a Christian Nation*. New York: Knopf, 2007.

Harris, Sam. *The Moral Landscape: How Science Can Determine Human Values*. New York: The Free Press, 2010.

Hartshorne, Charles. *The Logic of Perfection*. Lasalle, IL: Open Court Publishing Co., 1962.

Haught, John F. *Religion and Self-Acceptance*. New York: Paulist Press, 1976.

Haught, John F. *What Is God? How to Think about the Divine*. Mahwah and New York: Paulist Press, 1986.

Haught, John F. *Mystery and Promise: A Theology of Revelation*. Collegeville: Liturgical Press, 1993.

Haught, John F. *The Promise of Nature*. Mahwah and New York: Paulist Press, 1993.

Haught, John F. *Science and Religion: From Conflict to Conversation*. Mahwah and New York: Paulist Press, 1995.

Haught, John F. *Deeper Than Darwin: The Prospect for Religion in the Age of Evolution*. Boulder, CO: Westview Press, 2003.

Haught, John F. *Is Nature Enough? Meaning and Truth in the Age of Science*. Cambridge: Cambridge University Press, 2006.

Haught, John F. *Christianity and Science*. Maryknoll: Orbis Press, 2007.

Haught, John F. *God After Darwin: A Theology of Evolution*, 2nd ed. Boulder, CO: Westview Press, 2008.

Haught, John F. *God and the New Atheism: A Critical Response to Dawkins, Harris, and Hitchens*. Louisville: Westminster/John Knox Press, 2008.

Haught, John F. *Making Sense of Evolution: Darwin, God, and The Drama of Life*. Louisville: Westminster/John Knox Press, 2010.

Haught, John F. *Science and Faith: A New Introduction*. New York: Paulist Press, 2013.

Hawking, Stephen W. *A Brief History of Time*. New York: Bantam Books, 1988.

Hick, John. *Evil and the God of Love*, rev. ed. New York: Harper & Row, 1978.

Hinde, Robert. *Why Gods Persist: A Scientific Approach to Religions*. New York: Routledge, 1999.

Hitchens, Christopher. *God Is Not Great: How Religion Poisons Everything*. New York: Hachette Book Group USA, 2007.

Hopkins, Gerard Manley. "Spring" and "God's Grandeur." http://www. poemhunter.com/gerard-manley-hopkins/poems/.

International Theological Commission. "Communion and Stewardship: Human Persons Created in the Image of God," July 2004, #69: http://www.bringyou. to/apologetics/p80.htm.

Johnson, Phillip E. *The Wedge of Truth: Splitting the Foundations of Naturalism*. Downers Grove, IL: InterVarsity Press, 1999.

Jonas, Hans. *The Phenomenon of Life*. New York: Harper & Row, 1966.

Jones, Steve. *The Serpent's Promise: The Bible Interpreted Through Modern Science*. Berkeley, CA: Pegasus Books, 2014.

Kaufmann, Stuart A. *At Home in the Universe*. New York: Oxford University Press, 1995.

King, Thomas. *Teilhard's Mass: Approaches to "The Mass on the World."* New York: Paulist Press, 2005.

Kitcher, Philip. *Living With Darwin: Evolution, Design, and the Future of Faith*. New York: Oxford University, 2007.

Kraft, Wayne. *The Relevance of Teilhard*. Notre Dame, IN: Fides, 1968.

Krauss, Lawrence. *A Universe from Nothing: Why there is Something rather than Nothing* New York: The Free Press, 2012.

Lakatos, Imre. *The Methodology of Scientific Research Programmes: Volume I*. Cambridge: Cambridge University Press, 1980.

Lane, David. *The Phenomenon of Teilhard: Prophet for a New Age*. Macon, GA: Mercer University Press, 1996.

Lightman, Alan. *The Accidental Universe: The World You Thought You Knew*. New York: Pantheon Books, 2014.

Lonergan, Bernard. "Cognitional Structure." In *Collection*, edited by F. E. Crowe, SJ , 221–39. New York: Herder and Herder, 1967.

Lonergan, Bernard. *Insight: A Study of Human Understanding*, 3rd ed. New York: Philosophical Library, 1970.

Lonergan, Bernard. *Method in Theology*. New York: Herder and Herder, 1972.

Lovejoy, Arthur O. *The Great Chain of Being: A Study of the History of an Idea.* Cambridge, MA: Harvard University Press, 1936.

Lovejoy, Arthur O. *The Great Chain of Being: A Study of the History of an Idea.* New York: Harper & Row, 1965.

Macquarrie, John. *The Humility of God.* Philadelphia: The Westminster Press, 1978.

McGinn, Colin. *The Mysterious Flame: Conscious Minds in a Material World.* New York: Basic Books, 1999.

McGrath, Alister. "A Blast from the Past? The Boyle Lectures and Natural Theology." *Science and Christian Belief* 17 (2005): 25–34.

Meyer, Stephen C. *Darwin's Doubt: The Explosive Origin of Animal Life and the Case for Intelligent Design.* New York: HarperCollins, 2014.

Moltmann, Jürgen. *Theology of Hope: On the Ground and the Implications of a Christian Eschatology.* Translated by James W. Leitch. New York: Harper & Row, 1967.

Monod, Jacques. *Chance and Necessity: An Essay on the Natural Philosophy of Modern Biology.* Translated by Austryn Wainhouse. New York: Vintage Books, 1972.

Nagel, Thomas. *Mind and Cosmos: Why the Materialist Neo-Darwinian Conception of Nature Is Almost Certainly False.* New York: Oxford University Press, 2012.

Neumann, Eric. *Depth Psychology and a New Ethic.* Translated by Eugene Rolfe. New York: Harper & Row, 1973.

Newman, John Henry. *The Idea of a University.* Garden City: Image Books, 1959.

Niebuhr, H. Richard. *The Responsible Self: An Essay in Christian Moral Philosophy.* Westminster: John Knox Press, 1999.

Northwest American Bishops' Pastoral letter. "The Columbia River Watershed: Caring for Creation and the Common Good", 2001, http://www. columbiariver.org.

O'Leary, Don. *Roman Catholicism and Modern Science: A History.* New York: Continuum, 2006.

Ogden, Schubert. *The Reality of God and Other Essays.* New York: Harper & Row, 1977.

Paley, William. *Natural Theology.* Oxford: Oxford University Press, 2006[1816].

Pannenberg, Wolfhart. *Faith and Reality.* Translated by John Maxwell. Philadelphia: Westminster Press, 1977.

Pannenberg, Wolfhart. *Toward a Theology of Nature.* Edited by Ted Peters. Louisville: Westminster/John Knox Press, 1993.

Papineau, David. *Philosophical Naturalism.* Cambridge, MA: Blackwell, 1993.

Passmore, John. *Man's Responsibility for Nature.* New York: Scribner, 1974.

Peters, Ted. *God—The World's Future: Systematic Theology for a New Era*, 2nd ed. Minneapolis: Fortress Press, 2000.

Phipps, William E. *Darwin's Religious Odyssey.* Harrisburg, Pennsylvania: Trinity Press International, 2002.

Pinker, Steven. *The Blank Slate: The Modern Denial of Human Nature.* New York: Penguin Books, 2002.

Pinker, Steven. "The Stupidity of Dignity," 2008, http://pinker.wjh.harvard.edu/articles/media/The%20Stupidity%20of%20Dignity.htm.

Polanyi, Michael. *Personal Knowledge.* New York: Harper Torchbooks, 1964.

Polanyi, Michael. *The Tacit Dimension.* Garden City, New York: Doubleday Anchor Books, 1967.

Polanyi, Michael. *Knowing and Being.* Edited by Marjorie Grene. Chicago: University of Chicago Press, 1969.

Pope Benedict XVI. Encyclical Letter *Spe Salvi,* 2007, http://www.vatican.va/holy_father/benedict_xvi/encyclicals/documents/hf_ben-xvi_enc_20071130_spe-salvi_en.html.

Pope John Paul II. "Address to the Pontifical Academy of Sciences." *Origins, CNS Documentary Service* 9, no. 24 (November 29, 1979): 391.

Pope John Paul II. "Letter to the Reverend George V. Coyne, S.J., Director of the Vatican Observatory." *Origins* 18, no. 23 (November 17, 1988): 377.

Pope John Paul II. "Peace with God the Creator, Peace with All of Creation." *World Day of Peace Message,* January 1, 1990.

Pope John Paul II. "Message to the Pontifical Academy of Sciences," 1996, http://www.catholicculture.org/culture/library/view.cfm?id=80.

Pope John Paul II. Encyclical Letter *Fides et Ratio* (September 1998), #93, http://www.vatican.va/holy_father/john_paul_ii/encyclicals/documents/hf_jp-ii_enc_15101998_fides-et-ratio_en.html.

Poupard, Cardinal Paul Joseph John. "Galileo: Report on Papal Commission Findings." *Origins* 22 (November 12, 1992): 375.

Provine, William. "Evolution and the Foundation of Ethics." In *Science, Technology, and Social Progress,* edited by Steven L. Goldman. Bethlehem, PA: Lehigh University Press, 1989.

Rahner, Karl, SJ. *Hominization: The Evolutionary Origin of Man as a Theological Problem.* Translated by W. T. O'Hara. Freiburg: Herder, 1965.

Rahner, Karl, SJ. *Theological Investigations,* vol. 6. Translated by Karl Kruger and Boniface Kruger. Baltimore: Helicon, 1969.

Rahner, Karl, SJ. *Theological Investigations* V. Translated by Karl-H. Kruger. Baltimore: Helicon, 1966.

Raymo, Chet. *Skeptics and True Believers: The Exhilarating Connection Between Science and Religion.* New York: Walker and Company, 1998.

Raymo, Chet. "Intelligent Design Happens Naturally." *The Boston Globe,* May 14, 2002.

Rees, Martin. *Just Six Numbers: The Deep Forces that Shape the Universe.* New York: Basic Books, 2000.

Rees, Martin. *Our Cosmic Habitat.* Princeton: Princeton University Press, 2001.

Richard, Lucien J. *A Kenotic Christology.* Lanham, MD: University Press of America, 1982.

Ricoeur, Paul. *History and Truth.* Translated by Charles Kelbley. Evanston: Northwestern University Press, 1965.

Ricoeur, Paul. *The Symbolism of Evil*. Translated by Emerson Buchanan. Boston: Beacon Press, 1969.

Ricoeur, Paul. *The Conflict of Interpretations: Essays in Hermeneutics*. Edited by Don Ihde. Evanston, IL: Northwestern University Press, 1974.

Rolston, Holmes, III. *Three Big Bangs: Matter-Energy, Life, Mind*. New York: Columbia University Press. 2010.

Rosenberg, Alex. "Why I Am a Naturalist." *New York Times*, September 17, 2011.

Rosenberg, Alex. *The Atheist's Guide to Reality: Enjoying Life Without Illusions*. New York: W.W. Norton & Co., 2012.

Rue, Loyal. *By the Grace of Guile: The Role of Deception in Natural History and Human Affairs*. New York: Oxford University Press, 1994.

Ruse, Michael. *Darwin and Design: Does Evolution Have a Purpose?* Cambridge, MA: Harvard University Press, 2003.

Russell, Robert John, William R. Stoeger, SJ, and Francisco J. Ayala, eds. *Evolutionary and Molecular Biology: Scientific Perspectives on Divine Action*. Vatican City State: Vatican Observatory Publications and South Bend IN: University of Notre Dame Press, 1998.

Sagan, Carl. *The Demon-Haunted World: Science as a Candle in the Dark*. New York: Ballantine Books, 1997.

Searle, John R. *Mind: A Brief Introduction*. Oxford: Oxford University Press, 2004.

Seife, Charles. *Decoding the Universe: How the New Science of Information Is Explaining Everything in the Cosmos, from Our Brains to Black Holes*. New York: Viking, 2006.

Sheen, Fulton J. *Footsteps in a Darkened Forest*. New York: Meredith, 1967.

Shermer, Michael. *How We Believe: The Search for God in an Age of Science*. New York: W. H. Freeman, 2000.

Smith, John E. *Reason and God*. New Haven: Yale University Press, 1961.

Stenger, Victor J. *God: The Failed Hypothesis: How Science Shows that God Does Not Exist*. Amherst, NY: Prometheus Books, 2007.

Tegmark, Max. *Our Mathematical Universe: My Quest for the Ultimate Nature of Reality*. New York: Alfred A. Knopf, 2014.

Teilhard de Chardin, Pierre. *The Divine Milieu*. New York: Harper & Row, 1960.

Teilhard de Chardin, Pierre. *Human Energy*. Translated by J. M. Cohen. New York: Harvest Books/Harcourt Brace Jovanovich, 1962.

Teilhard de Chardin, Pierre. *Letters from a Traveler*. New York: Harper & Row, 1962.

Teilhard de Chardin, Pierre. "The Meaning and Constructive Value of Suffering." In *Teilhard de Chardin, Pilgrim of the Future*, edited by Neville Braybrooke. London: Libra, 1964.

Teilhard de Chardin, Pierre. *The Future of Man*. Translated by Norman Denny. New York: Harper & Row, 1964.

Teilhard de Chardin, Pierre. *The Vision of the Past*. Translated by J. M. Cohen. New York: Harper & Row, 1966.

Teilhard de Chardin, Pierre. *Writings in Time of War*. Translated by René Hague. New York: Harper & Row, 1968.

Teilhard de Chardin, Pierre. *Hymn of the Universe.* Translated by Gerald Vann. New York: Harper Colophon, 1969.

Teilhard de Chardin, Pierre. *Christianity and Evolution.* Translated by René Hague. New York: Harcourt Brace Jovanovich, 1969.

Teilhard de Chardin, Pierre. *How I Believe.* Translated by René Hague. New York: Harper & Row, 1969.

Teilhard de Chardin, Pierre. *Activation of Energy.* Translated by René Hague. New York: Harcourt Brace Jovanovich, 1970.

Teilhard de Chardin, Pierre. *The Prayer of the Universe.* Translated by René Hague. New York: Harper & Row, 1973.

Teilhard de Chardin, Pierre. *The Human Phenomenon.* Translated by Sarah Appleton-Weber. Portland, Oregon: Sussex Academic Press, 1999.

Catechism of the Catholic Church, http://www.vatican.va/archive/ccc_css/archive/catechism/p1s2c1p4.htm.

Theissen, Gerd. *The Open Door.* Translated by John Bowden. Minneapolis: Fortress Press, 1991.

Tillich, Paul. *Dynamics of Faith.* New York: Harper Torchbooks, 1958.

Tillich, Paul. *Systematic Theology,* 3 vols. Chicago: University of Chicago Press, 1952, 1957, 1963.

Tipler, Frank. *The Physics of Immortality.* New York: Doubleday, 1994.

Toulmin, Stephen. *An Examination of the Place of Reason in Ethics.* Cambridge: Cambridge University Press, 1970.

Towers, Bernard. *Concerning Teilhard, and Other Writings on Science and Religion.* London: Collins, 1969.

Tracy, David. *Blessed Rage for Order.* New York: The Seabury Press, 1975.

van Huyssteen, Wentzel. *Alone in the World?: Human Uniqueness in Science and Theology.* Grand Rapids: Eerdmans, 2006.

Watson, J. D. *The Molecular Biology of the Gene.* New York: W.A. Benjamin, 1965.

Weinberg, Steven. *Dreams of a Final Theory: The Scientist's Search for the Ultimate Laws of Nature.* New York: Pantheon, 1993.

Wells, Jonathan. *Icons of Evolution: Science or Myth? Why Much of What We Teach About Evolution Is Wrong.* Washington, DC: Regnery, 2000.

White, Lynn. "The Historical Roots of our Ecological Crisis." *Science* 155 (1967): 1203–7.

Whitehead, Alfred North. *Science and the Modern World.* New York: The Free Press, 1925.

Whitehead, Alfred North. "Immortality." In *The Philosophy of Alfred North Whitehead,* edited by Paul A. Schillp, 682–700. Evanston and Chicago: Northwestern University Press, 1941.

Whitehead, Alfred North. *Process and Reality,* corrected edition. Edited by David Ray Griffin and Donald W. Sherburne. New York: The Free Press, 1968.

Williams, George. "Mother Nature Is a Wicked Old Witch!" In *Evolutionary Ethics,* edited by Matthew H. Nitecki and Doris V. Nitecki. Albany: State University of New York Press, 1995.

Wright, N. T. *Surprised By Hope*. San Francisco: HarperOne, 2008.

Young, Louise. *The Unfinished Universe*. New York: Oxford University Press, 1986.

Zimmer, Carl. *Evolution: The Triumph of an Idea From Darwin to DNA*. London: Arrow Books, 2003.

Życiński, Józef. *God and Evolution: Fundamental Questions of Christian Evolutionism*. Translated by Kenneth W. Kemp and Zuzanna Maslanka. Washington, DC: Catholic University of America Press, 2006.

Index